WITHDRAWN

MODERNISM AND WORLD WAR II

The Second World War marked the beginning of the end of literary modernism in Britain. However, this late period of modernism and its response to the War have not yet received the scholarly attention they deserve. In the first full-length study of modernism and the Second World War, Marina MacKay offers historical readings of Virginia Woolf, Rebecca West, T. S. Eliot, Henry Green and Evelyn Waugh set against the dramatic background of national struggle and transformation. In recovering how these major authors engaged with other texts of their time – political discourses, mass and middlebrow culture – this study reveals how the Second World War brought to the surface the underlying politics of modernism's aesthetic practices. Through close analyses of the revisions made to modernist thinking after 1939, MacKay establishes the significance of this persistently neglected phase of modern literature as a watershed moment in twentieth-century literary history.

MARINA MACKAY is Assistant Professor of English at Washington University in St. Louis.

MODERNISM AND WORLD WAR II

MARINA MACKAY

CAMBRIDGE UNIVERSITY PRESS
Cambridge, New York, Melbourne, Madrid, Cape Town, Singapore, São Paulo

Cambridge University Press
The Edinburgh Building, Cambridge CB2 2RU, UK

Published in the United States of America by Cambridge University Press, New York

www.cambridge.org
Information on this title: www.cambridge.org/9780521872225

© Marina MacKay 2007

This publication is in copyright. Subject to statutory exception
and to the provisions of relevant collective licensing agreements,
no reproduction of any part may take place without
the written permission of Cambridge University Press.

First published 2007

Printed in the United Kingdom at the University Press, Cambridge

A catalogue record for this publication is available from the British Library

Library of Congress Cataloguing in Publication data

MacKay, Marina, 1975–
Modernism and World War II / Marina MacKay.
p. cm.
Includes bibliographical references and index.
ISBN-13: 978-0-521-87222-5 (hardback)
ISBN-10: 0-521-87222-7 (hardback)
1. English literature – 20th century – History and criticism.
2. Modernism (Literature) – Great Britain.
3. World War, 1939–1945 – Great Britain – Literature and the war.
4. World War, 1939–1945 – Influence.
5. War and literature – Great Britain.
6. War in literature.
I. Title.
II. Title: Modernism and World War Two.
III. Title: Modernism and World War 2.
PR478.M6M33 2006
820.9'112–dc22
2006025232

Cambridge University Press has no responsibility for the persistence or accuracy of URLs for external or third-party internet websites referred to in this publication, and does not guarantee that any content on such websites is, or will remain, accurate or appropriate.

Contents

Acknowledgements	*page vi*
Introduction: Modernism beyond the Blitz	1
1 Virginia Woolf and the pastoral patria	22
2 Rebecca West's anti-Bloomsbury group	44
3 The situational politics of *Four Quartets*	71
4 The neutrality of Henry Green	91
5 Evelyn Waugh and the ends of minority culture	118
Coda: National historiography after the post-war settlement	142
Notes	157
Bibliography	179
Index	189

Acknowledgements

Portions of Chapters 2 and 5 of this book appear in a different form in the essay 'Doing Business with Totalitaria: British Late Modernism and the Politics of Reputation', *ELH* © The Johns Hopkins University Press, 2006. The Woolf chapter is rewritten from an article in *MLQ* 66 (2005), and I thank Duke University Press for letting me revisit this work here; the kind responses of Marshall Brown, Barbara Fuchs and Mark Wollaeger to that early piece of work were – and are – warmly appreciated.

I realise how lucky I am to have this book published by Cambridge University Press, and I thank the senior editor Ray Ryan for being absolutely lovely to work with, and I am grateful to his colleague Maartje Scheltens for so attentively shepherding the manuscript to this stage. The advice I received from the anonymous readers who reported on the manuscript for Cambridge was sometimes no less than transformative, and I am immensely thankful for their incisive, generous readings.

My former supervisor Vic Sage inadvertently initiated this project when, some time post-PhD, he told me I really should read Rebecca West's *Black Lamb and Grey Falcon*, and that is the least of my debts to the person who taught me – or tried hard to teach me – to think and write properly. I would like also to thank Phyllis Lassner, Petra Rau and Lyndsey Stonebridge for generously sharing ideas with me over the last few years that I know improved the book. I am grateful, as well, to participants in my 'Modernism beyond the Blitz?' seminar at MSA 7 in Chicago, to the students in my graduate seminar of the same name at Washington University in St. Louis and also to the many wonderful undergraduates who have helped me think through this material. I was especially fortunate to have an undergraduate research assistant, Jill Baughman, in the final months of writing.

I thank my colleagues in the English department at Washington University. David Lawton started it all, and I hope he knows how much his support continues to matter to me, and Joe Loewenstein has also been a kindly mentor since the moment I got here. It is also a real pleasure to have this chance to thank Miriam Bailin, Guinn Batten, Lara Bovilsky, Dillon Johnston and Wolfram Schmidgen for collegiality that often went well beyond the call of duty.

Ceud mìle taing to Donald MacKay for his humbling confidence in this book's undeserving author. Affectionate thanks, finally, to Dan Grausam for being a brilliant interlocutor as well as a loyal booster, and for having the heart to observe Auden's wise injunction about private faces in public places.

Introduction: Modernism beyond the Blitz

> What we call the beginning is often the end
> And to make an end is to make a beginning
> The end is where we start from.
> T. S. Eliot, *Little Gidding* (1942)[1]

'Either you had no purpose', Eliot writes in his wartime *Little Gidding*, 'Or the purpose is beyond the end you figured / And is altered in fulfilment'.[2] The work of a poet concluding a career of unparalleled significance, Eliot's *Four Quartets* speculate continually about what it would mean to make a good end, where an end is an objective or a conclusion, an intended destination or just a termination – and perhaps, but not necessarily, both. So if I begin this book by saying that its subject is the end of modernism, I mean 'end' in Eliot's double sense: the end of modernism signifies both its realisation and its dissolution. Vindicated, certainly, but melancholy in its vindication, the mood of late modernism in England resembles the watershed event that it recorded: the Second World War, too, was both a win and a winding up. In the chapters that follow, I suggest that the correlation between late modernism in England and the world-changing circumstances with which it overlapped amounts to more than a historical coincidence.

It would be hard to overstate the continuing centrality of the war in contemporary English culture – this is always just 'the war', colloquially, as if there had been no other – 'remarkably resonant', as one historian summarises it, 'appearing in many different sites of memory and permeating just about every level of national, local and personal culture'.[3] The reasons why the war should have accrued this tenacious importance for the national imaginary speak directly to late modernism's characteristic preoccupations. In geopolitical terms, a conflict that had initially been deferred because of the virtual impossibility of protecting an empire sprawling across potential war fronts on the Atlantic, Pacific and

Mediterranean finally led to national bankruptcy and the termination of Britain's status as a superpower. This was Britain's final moment as the kind of global force that most English modernists, inheritors of late-Victorian liberalism, had heartily loathed, and whatever Britishness or Englishness could be made to mean for the future, imperial grandeur would play no part in it. The nation's newly minor status is the keynote of both the war's literature and its subsequent discursive construction, and so, for instance, the most powerful emotional investments have been made not in military triumphs that recall Britain's former imperial glory but in moments of national vulnerability. Such nostalgia magnets as 'the Blitz' and 'Dunkirk' commemorate nothing more than the pathos of passive defence and a horrifically outnumbered retreat. This is the war as scripted by modernism: post-imperial, anti-heroic and totally unwanted.

'Standing alone', as the 1940 cliché had it, Britain acquired a master narrative for national isolation from the continent that also goes some way towards accounting for the war's enduring cultural significance. Often evoked in the intermittently strained relations between the United Kingdom and the rest of Europe, the repercussions of Britain's wartime singularity, its period of isolation between the fall of France and the entry of the United States into the war, might be seen either as a defence of the small and particular against the undemocratically homogenising or as the bloody-minded insularity of a defunct power. The literature of the Second World War presents a return to the source, when modernists were compelled to scrutinise the political and moral claims of insular nationality at a time when allegiance was demanded as rarely before, the national culture at risk as it had not been in centuries. These cosmopolitan and European-minded intellectuals saw for the first time that their transnational interests could be imperial privilege as well as enlightened internationalism and that national identification could mean anything from pernicious parochialism to the freedom from totalitarian occupation. All of the texts discussed in this book are in their different ways national allegories, and if it is a factor of their modernism that these writers' responses to national feeling turned out to be so conflicted, it was surely a factor of their extraordinary mid-century moment that these metropolitan modernists should think nationality the most pressing issue of all. Among the writers discussed in later chapters, for example, Rebecca West finds herself holding to critical account the Anglocentric underpinnings of modernist internationalism even as she catalogues at extraordinary lengths the devastating effects of imperialist nationalism; conversely, Evelyn Waugh ends up mourning an aborted modernist cosmopolitanism in *Brideshead Revisited*, a novel that he wrote as a memorial to traditional feudal England.

Waugh's post-war persona as a diehard of pantomime proportions is a blunt reminder of how important the war's domestic as well as global transformations were ultimately to become in the second half of the century. The exigencies of total war permanently changed the role of the state in relation to its citizens as they changed Britain from a class-bound empire into a medium-sized welfare state. As early as ten months into the war even the conservative *Times* was proposing that 'The European house cannot be put in order unless we put our own house in order first', arguing that the only hope for a new international order rested on the realisation of a social arrangement no longer based 'on the preservation of privilege, whether the privilege be that of a country, of a class, or of an individual':

> If we speak of democracy we do not mean a democracy which maintains the right to vote but forgets the right to work and the right to live. If we speak of freedom, we do not mean a rugged individualism which excludes social organization and economic planning. If we speak of equality, we do not mean a political equality nullified by social and economic privilege. If we speak of economic reconstruction, we think less of maximum production (though this too will be required) than of equitable distribution.[4]

Dismantling the hollow patriotism of the Great War of 1914–1918 – the fight for Democracy, Freedom and Equality against oppressive Hunnery – by recalling the broken political promises of the decades that had followed it, this radical social formulation was a statement of closing horizons and a newly critical form of nationalism. The post-imperial state that might survive the war had to look to itself.

Both in content and in tone, the *Times* editorial's call for reform captured the political atmosphere of the moment: a total rejection of the political inertia of 1930s government, a torpor so profound that it had not only made the negative policy of appeasement seem a viable option (even to the *Times* itself, it should be said), but had made laissez faire look like lazy complacency about the conditions in which the bulk of the population still subsisted: 'Hunger, to a certain extent', one Member of Parliament had opined in the blighted 1930s, 'is a very good thing'.[5] 'Do not let me hear of the wisdom of old men', Eliot writes in *East Coker*, and goes on to castigate their 'fear of fear and frenzy, their fear of possession, / Of belonging to another, or to others, or to God'.[6] On the face of it, one would no more expect radical denunciations of a timeserving and quietist interwar establishment from the Tory Eliot than from the Tory *Times*, and yet in 1940 they came anyway.

Two years later, Sir William Beveridge's much-hyped *Social Insurance and Allied Services* would promise social security from the cradle to the grave; as a direct result, the war hero Churchill would be beaten in the general election landslide of 1945 by Clement Attlee's Labour Party because, although Beveridge's overwhelming reception had forced all parties to commit to massive reforms, their interwar record clearly made the Conservatives the party least likely to realise the greater social justice that had become a war aim long before a British victory was even plausible. Literally totalitarian conditions on the war's home front made possible a long-term shift in the balance of private and public ownership, raised taxes for redistributive purposes and gave the working classes reliable access to health care and education. To say that it revolutionised British society would likely make political historians wince: surely even the most spectacular of watershed events has a longer evolution and less clear-cut outcomes (and the long history and muddled outcomes are central to this book). Nonetheless, the war was experienced in nothing short of revolutionary terms, and the public debate surrounding these domestic transformations are crucial because they forced modernist writers belatedly to scrutinise their own social and political investments. Watching late modernism embark on this process of stocktaking offers a way to avoid the short cuts offered by the individual case – say, by Ezra Pound's fascism on one side and Hugh MacDiarmid's communism on the other. The writers in whom I am interested here occupy the same narrow spectrum as parliamentary politics: Liberals and liberals, socialists and liberal socialists, one-nation Tories and Tory radicals, they compel a more measured and historically responsible approach to the persistent critical debate surrounding the politics of modernism.

This book aligns the renovation of the public sphere in Britain with the aesthetic discourses that had anticipated its necessity and came to record it in the process of taking shape. It emphasises moments that illuminate how the war came to mean what it does to the post-imperial imagination. Some of these landmarks are historical in the textbook sense: the nerve-strung early months of waiting known as the Phoney War; the passing of the Emergency Powers (Defence) Act, which turned Britain into a totalitarian state in the spring of 1940; the Blitz that followed later in the year, when 'British' territory came closer to invasion than it had in a millennium; the publication of the Beveridge Report at the end of 1942; the Labour landslide in the spring of 1945. Utterly implicated in this more conventionally historical narrative is the sequence of less bounded imaginative happenings in which the late modernists also participated: the rebranding of stratified imperialist Britain as something that might conceivably be worth going to war over this second time; the creative mapping of the archipelago in pursuit of a part, whether ravaged metropolis or timeless rural backwater, to stand for the newly postimperial whole; the collapse of interwar polarities into unprecedented political consensus; the dawning crisis of minority culture in the era of the welfare state and the early Cold War. Late modernism gives the critical and affective content to the story of England's cultural remaking.

In historical and political terms, the story that late modernism tells is so compellingly dramatic that it is not immediately obvious why it should have gone untold in the first place. But despite tremendous recuperative work by recent surveys of this long neglected period, little of the war's literature has ever fully registered on the critical field of vision, and even now the final wartime work of canonical writers like Eliot and Woolf is read comparatively little; their late writing is largely the lonely domain of single-author specialists, as if these valedictory masterpieces have nothing important to say about modernism or mid-century culture more generally.[7] The commonplace that this was 'a war to which literature conscientiously objected'[8] was already good for a joke by 1941, when Cyril Connolly opened a famous *Horizon* editorial with 'About this time of year articles appear called "Where are our war poets?" The answer (not usually given) is "under your nose"'.[9] The criteria for what constituted proper war literature had already been established by the Great War, without regard to the sheer secondness of the Second World War and without acknowledgement of what had happened in between. The soldier poets of the Great War set the standard by which the literature of the second war was judged wanting, as if next time around there could have been a reprise of the bitterly disillusioned goodbyes-to-all-that which flooded the literary market of the 1920s. The war literature of 1914–18 was nothing if not an anti-war literature, and its authors had for once and for all trashed the militarist mystique by writing so harrowingly of its betrayals. The literature of the Second World War was always going to be different: that it does not take as its raison d'être the position that war is stupid, wasteful and ugly is certainly not because writers mistook state-sanctioned violence on the grand scale for anything other than what it is, but exactly because, after the Great War, they took this as given. The exhaustion of the Great War mode even seeps into later combatant writing, as when Keith Douglas in

1943 addressed an important Great War precursor with: 'Rosenberg I only repeat what you were saying'.[10]

Killed in action as Isaac Rosenberg had been, Douglas has always for good reason been considered the most significant British poet of 1939–45, but there's an important sense in which Cyril Connolly was right to locate the war writers 'under your nose'. What makes the cultural context of the second war so radically different from that of the first was the new primacy of the civilian experience: whereas the 'home front' was primarily a propaganda metaphor in 1918, the Second World War was halfway through before the number of dead British combatants exceeded that of dead British civilians.[11] And, as Tony Judt points out in his important new history of post-war Europe, only in Britain and Germany did military losses finally outnumber the civilian death toll; in total more than 19 million non-combatants were killed across Europe.[12] That the Second World War continues to be perceived as largely a civilian war gives it some of its enduring and resonant pathos, because even if the Great War poets comprehensively demystified the glories of warfare, admiration for the courage of passive defence – for those who cannot kill, but can be killed – flows readily enough. War's homecoming, or the new significance of the non-combatant experience, loosens the boundaries of its possible literatures, and Randall Stevenson was surely right to speculate that the absence of a major Second World War literature in Britain 'may simply be a consequence of looking for it in the wrong place'.[13] As a conflict in which the civilian experience was paramount, its literature urges a reshaping of what counts as the literature of war in order to include authors who were not combatants and texts that are not 'about' war in any straightforwardly mimetic way. It demands, in other words, the modes of reading that the non-combatant modernisms of the Great War made possible.

I say this because modernist writing produced between 1914 and 1918 stretched the concept of 'aboutness' almost to its breaking point in its approach to the war that saw its publication. Ford Madox Ford's *The Good Soldier* (1915) is tauntingly titled: no war story, *The Good Soldier* tells of a deracinated American discovering that the perfect paragon of heroic English masculinity is privately a philandering liar, and trying to reconcile this new knowledge with his own desire to be 'a good soldier' of the same kind as his hero. Meanwhile, Ford's old collaborator Joseph Conrad was also investigating treacherous ideals of male leadership and turned *The Shadow-Line* (1917), an autobiographical account of his disastrous first captaincy, into a war story when he added a prefatory dedication to his son at the Front. The war appears literally nowhere in the body of these novels, and yet one would have to unlearn the novels' dates in order to evade the timeliness of these dissections of pre-1914 England's destructive fantasies about manly virtue. Like the wartime late modernisms this book describes, such novels as those Ford and Conrad produced during the Great War are preoccupied less by the war as a self-contained event than by its social, epistemological and psychological meanings: the devastating insufficiency of normative English masculinity; the impossibility of discerning the truth about events amid a swamp of public lies; the stigmatised debility of traumatic experience in a culture of the stiff upper lip. Novels such as these speak to the war in which they were published without necessarily speaking about it at all.

Their address to the war is more than a question of modernist literature's famously oblique thematic. Almost exactly a year after the Armistice, Katherine Mansfield wrote in a well-known letter to her husband John Middleton Murry that Virginia Woolf's new novel *Night and Day* (1919) was 'a lie in the soul. The war has never been, that is what its message is':

> I don't want G. forbid mobilisation and the violation of Belgium – but the novel cant [*sic*] just leave the war out. It is really fearful to me the 'settling down' of human beings. I feel in the *profoundest* sense that nothing can ever be the same [,] that as artists we are traitors if we feel otherwise: we have to take it into account and find new expressions [,] new moulds for our new thoughts & feelings.[14]

Provoked by the refusal of Woolf's second novel to acknowledge the war explicitly (thematically), Mansfield argued that 'leaving the war in' was as much an issue of narrative idiom as of manifest content. Many experimental treatments of the Great War share Mansfield's sense that modernist form was something close to a historical obligation imposed by unprecedented recent violence. The narrator of Rebecca West's shellshock novel *The Return of the Soldier* (1918) even states outright the link between textual crisis and the war in progress when she describes her soldier's insanity as 'a triumph over the limitations of language which prevent the mass of men from making explicit statements about their spiritual relationships'.[15] The soldier of the novel's title has returned from the Front having forgotten his entire adult life, and the political implications of his 'triumph over the limitations of language' could not be starker when his madness represents his wholesale rejection of pre-war male privilege as feudal landowner, commercial imperialist and breadwinning husband. More canonical intersections of linguistic crisis, war damage and social protest could obviously be found in the predicament of Woolf's Septimus Smith and Eliot's nerve-wracked residents of *The Waste Land*, in post-war texts whose formal modernity arises from the erosions that they undertake of traditional distinctions between public and private spheres, war front and home front, between conventionally historical events and the painfully permeable psychic life. Woolf's experiments at the really subjective end of free indirect discourse in the rendering of the war-ravaged Septimus Smith (*Mrs Dalloway* is the first of her novels written in what became her characteristic style) and Eliot's spasmodic, syncopated verse in the passages of *The Waste Land* that deal with similarly broken homecomings ('What are you thinking of? What thinking? What? / . . . I think we are in rats' alley / Where the dead men lost their bones') make it inviting to connect the Great War's causes and effects to the emergence of new textual forms.[16]

After all, it was the First World War that had showed the agonising incommensurability of the old realist historiography of decisive battles, victory and defeat, with the shapeless and essentially unbounded damage that war inflicts. War had ceased to look formal, was no longer believably contained by the sporting discourse, gendered and class-bound, of winners and losers. That uniquely modern lesson about the amorphousness of the war experience surely stands behind the argument made by one seminal feminist essay on war studies, that we have to think 'beyond the exceptional, marked event, which takes place on a specifically militarized front or in public and institutionally defined arenas, to include the private domain and the landscape of the mind'.[17] Shifting beyond the artificially circumscribed public histories of the event is modernism de rigueur, or what Woolf in a different context wrote of as the need to 'do away with exact place & time' in her experimental fiction, 'this appalling narrative business of the realist . . . false, unreal, merely conventional'.[18] As a mode of historical representation modernism works indirectly and inwardly: renouncing totalising and documentary ambitions, it tries to expand the categories of what constitutes historical experience. Its abiding preoccupations with 'the private domain and the landscape of the mind' potentially explain the time-honoured identification of modernism with the Great War: modernist inwardness versus shattering public failure. You could pit the conscientiously objecting modernists ('the private domain and the landscape of the mind') against the tub-thumping jingoes (the 'public and institutionally defined') who defended a war that became synonymous with unprecedented suffering. Modernism thus becomes subversive because its formal waywardness disrupts the hierarchically imposed version of the real; by their nature dissident, modernist forms renounce the mindlessly habitual, unthinkingly collective perspectives that make war possible; modernism's fractured and estranging modes simultaneously mimic the damage of war and blow to bits the lazy mental habits of mind that produced and sustained it.

What I would like to suggest in this book is that any such semi-allegorical rendering of war and modernist politics has to be supported, or else qualified, by attention to historical particularity. In his groundbreaking *Institutions of Modernism*, Lawrence Rainey warns against causally vague and politically optimistic conflations of modernist form and progressive politics, made possible only by 'excessive faith in our capacity to specify the essence and social significance of isolated formal devices and to correlate them with complex ideological and social formations'.[19] Primarily, his book shows how the impulse to read modernism's anti-commercial difficulty as an assault on the values of the bourgeois economy is compromised by attention to the publishing and marketing structures within which modernist writers actually wrote; but the wider implication of Rainey's work is that historically more attuned analysis of modernist contexts renders problematic the impulse to rescue modernism from its long and damning association with reactionary politics by radicalising experimental form. The same applies to the link between modernism and the Great War because, although some of the experimental writing produced in and around that period lends real support to the identification of anti-conservative politics and a distinctively new aesthetic, the identification is supported immeasurably better by some texts and writers than by others, and there can be something unhistorical, even anti-historical, about a general conflation of formal and political heroism in this period as in any other. It is as well to keep in mind that some canonical 'Men of 1914' managed to sound even more hysterically militaristic than their parliamentary counterparts (and who would vote for T. E. Hulme over Lloyd George?), even as much of the experimental writing that came after 1918 traces critical connections among public violence, linguistic rupture and a broader context of social dereliction and political failure.

But what the Great War initiated, the Second World War realised. Britain's political culture finally caught up with its interwar avant-garde, and this closing gap means that there's a historical moment at which the polemical conflation of poetry and protest, literary and political dissent, ceases to ring true. Obviously late Romantic when seen in its longer lineage, the conflation also owed something to the characteristic modalities of the Great War: Paul Fussell's classic *The Great War and Modern Memory* describes how the polarising imaginative habits of 1914 ('"We" are all here on this side; "the enemy" is over there') escaped their jingo origins to land in the work of combatants who were protesting the war: men against women; soldiers against civilians. Finally, fatuous ideas of military heroism get replaced by the imaginative heroism of literary truth-telling.[20] The identification of poetry and political protest became familiar interwar tropology, and, like the other Second World War commentators who wondered where the war poets were, Cecil Day Lewis clearly thought that any legitimate war writing was an anti-war writing. He says this directly in his 1943 poem 'Where are the War Poets?'

> It is the logic of our times,
> No subject for immortal verse –
> That we who lived by honest dreams
> Defend the bad against the worse.[21]

For Day Lewis, there is no 'immortal verse' in the era of the political consensus; equating literary achievement with political opposition, he could not countenance the possibility of a literature that would take this tension between creative transcendence and political actuality as its starting point.

This is a crucial issue because all major British writers of the mid-century made the guilty compromise, knowing it to be exactly that, of supporting the Second World War, and it produced not only formidable work by established writers like Eliot and Woolf, but also the most significant writing that younger modernists such as Rebecca West, Henry Green and Evelyn Waugh were ever to produce. George Orwell had insisted right up until the end of the 1930s that fascism and capitalist democracy were 'Tweedledum and Tweedledee',[22] but in an aphorism that would do service for all these writers, E. M. Forster described Orwell's final change of heart as the belief that 'All nations are odious but some are less odious than others, and by this stony, unlovely path he reaches patriotism. To some of us, this seems the cleanest way to reach it'.[23] In stark contrast to the Great War, writers would not use their much greater liberty of expression to speak out against the Second World War: and if the imperialist causes and catastrophic effects of the Great War became easy retrospectively to denounce, the experimental writing produced in the subsequent war records more complicated conversations between literary experiment and political culture.

'Defence of England' Woolf chewed over the Churchillian rhetoric in her diary for 1940: 'Not all claptrap'.[24] Her remarks are typical of the equivocal and undeluded responses that the Second World War provoked, insofar as she could accept the legitimacy of the war without buying into discredited old nationalisms. There is little evidence that the violent binarism encouraged in the Great War, the polarities that Fussell summarises as 'adversary proceedings', survived the disillusionments of the years after the Armistice.[25] It was, to give just one example, a problem for political language and not simply a matter of political history in the narrow sense that the prevailing climate should have become so antipathetic to rabble-rousing nationalism that anti-appeasement politicians like Churchill spent the 1930s in the political wilderness for arguing that the signs from Germany were becoming too ominous to ignore, while the head of the Foreign Office got the sack for writing about Nazi Germany in a manner that was taken to resemble dangerously the Hun-hating invective of 1914. Indeed, the overblown demonising of the Kaiser's Germany in the First World War made it impossible for public figures to describe the Nazi agenda, in years when its enormities might have beggared the imagination of the First World War's infamously gothic propagandists, without being discredited as a warmonger of the Great War stripe. A friend of Lord Vansittart at the Foreign Office, Rebecca West worried mid-war about the impossibility of writing about what the Nazis were really up to, suggesting that interlocutors with every reason to despise these crimes were priding themselves on their 'superior wisdom and culture' in seeing two sides to a story that was starting to look as if it only had one: why, she wondered, was it so difficult to say that 'what the Germans have done is flatly abominable'.[26] In a hauntingly awful legacy of the Great War, hostility towards violently affective appeals was so pervasive and profound that evidence of the real atrocities being perpetrated in Nazi Germany could be dismissed by many as the reflux of sensationalist propaganda from twenty-five years earlier.

Insofar as the proselytising pro-war pamphlet might be thought of as the literary antithesis of modernism's complex eloquence, it is surely telling that even the propaganda of the Second World War made such an important feature of its introspective complexity, lingering at length on its own soul-searching difference from the conventions of its genre. In his *For Civilization* (1940), the philosopher and public intellectual Cyril Joad summarised what it meant to be a pacifist, a socialist, an anti-imperialist and newly a supporter of the war. He explained why he had once backed appeasement:

> It was not merely that war was savage and cruel; that it entailed physical agony in its grossest form for thousands of human beings; that it parted men from those who loved them and those whom they loved; that it used the bright talents of man for destruction; that it dulled and stupefied his spirit with boredom and brutalised it with violence. ... There are few of us to-day who have illusions as to the nature of war.[27]

For Civilization is emblematic of the anti-propagandistic propaganda that the Second World War produced: propaganda that worked by foregrounding, in order to renounce, the genre's characteristic deceptions. If Joad's high-stepping rhetoric inclines the reader immediately to suspect his political designs, the Labour Member of Parliament Harold Nicolson produced a more engagingly blunt example in his contribution to the mass-circulation Penguin Specials series: 'The old slogan of "Make the world safe for democracy" awakes no response whatsoever in [people's] hearts. The cry of "Down with Hitler" does not appeal to any sensible person as an objective for which it is worth sacrificing the lives of many men'.[28]

Contemporary responses to the Second World War were dominated by the scepticism that came from memories of the Great War, from its brutal devaluing of individual life and its gross abuses of anti-German propaganda. This was 'a war of which we are all ashamed', as Cyril Connolly said in 1940, 'and yet a war which has to be won'.[29] No writer of any political sensitivity could mistake how ideologically incoherent the war was from beginning to end: the distinction between bigoted Nazi expansionism and the intransigent racism of the British imperial project initially seemed a bit finely drawn, while Germany's oppressively stratified culture offered an ugly mirror image of domestic class, race and gender politics. In the later years of the war, political incredulity could only be aggravated by the pragmatic transformation of the Soviet Union from a cynical Nazi partner into our gallant Russian ally (even leaving aside the subsequent fall from grace in 1945). Despite all that, the war remained resilient to polemical dissent. Such attempts made to avoid fighting the war as British appeasement, American isolationism and French collaboration were, then as now, sources of widespread shame; in any case, it would take revisionist courage of a quixotic kind to suggest that in a showdown between the German (Nazi) and British (Tory-led coalition) governments, it did not much matter who won. The period's writers were uncomfortably mindful of the parallels, though.

The coincidence of consensus politics with a distinguished phase of late modernism has implications for modernism's successors, or maybe inheritors, because this anti-transcendent, concessionary development makes it possible to see where the subdued and deflationary ironies of post-war English writing came from (Philip Larkin gave to an early volume of his poetry the beautifully eloquent title of *The Less Deceived*). Of course there are equally significant implications for late modernism's past because the final willingness to make these concessions invites us to take modernist politics a little less at their own self-legitimising evaluation and to recognise the degree to which the modernist rhetoric of alienation tended as much towards the rhetorical as the alienated; the proximity of modernism to the centres of political power starts to become clearer as modernism reaches its closing stages. One instructive late modernist example here might be Wyndham Lewis, modernism's most belligerent English spokesperson, and the self-styled 'Enemy'. Published in 1937, his memoir *Blasting and Bombardiering* is characteristically iconoclastic in some respects, but what it more quietly discloses is a love affair between high modernism and high society going back over twenty years: 'It was at Lady Ottoline's that I met for the first time Lord Oxford, then Mr. Asquith and Prime Minister ... Mr. Asquith unquestionably displayed a marked curiosity regarding the 'Great London Vortex''; 'I have always considered Lord Beaverbrook the brightest of the Press Barons and he must have a very remarkable instinct for affairs. ... He always showed towards me an extreme courtesy'; 'Sir William Rothenstein ... made me very conceited by the generous praise he bestowed upon all he saw'; 'Nancy Cunard I had first met when she was a débutante before the War, in the house of the Countess of Drogheda off Belgrave Square'.[30] And so on. If in modernism's twilight it started to feel as if the figureheads of avant-garde and public culture in London had been assiduously cultivating one another all along, it may well be a mistake to take self-legitimising trope ('The Enemy') for useable cultural history by seeing modernist writers in romantically antagonistic terms to the political world – plainly not as stultifying and philistine as these writers sometimes liked to present it – with which they interacted. I show in later chapters that these writers were unmistakeably public figures around the Second World War, but that should not be taken to imply that they were necessarily marginal ones in the years around the First.

Current work in modernist studies suggests a growing readiness to think of experimental writers as figures of cultural authority. Defending the canonical and authorial focus of his illuminating historicist study *The Great*

War and the Language of Modernism, Vincent Sherry remarks with some reservations modernism's new 'populist provenance', a backlash against the old top-down, reverential and author-centred approach to the field. Rather than take sides in this quarrel between the ahistorical and the new historical, Sherry posits 'equivalent privilege' between high culture and the political establishment, a formula I find invaluable as a way to access the submerged relationships between modernism and political culture, where 'political' here conveys its old meanings of parliamentary, journalistic and diplomatic discourses.[31] Attempting likewise to align modernism with the public life of its times, T. J. Clark refuses to apologise for having 'rubbed [the] reader's nose' in the minutiae of political history, not when Politics ... is the form par excellence of the contingency that makes modernism what it is. This is why those who wish modernism had never happened (and not a few who think they are firmly on its side) resist to the death the idea that art, at many of its highest moments in the nineteenth and twentieth centuries, took the stuff of politics as its material and did not transmute it'.[32]

To perpetuate the severance of difficult texts from the political conditions of their production – even, as Clark is suggesting, when these conditions are thematised in the texts themselves – is to breathe life into the formalist canard that great art thrives in conditions of cultural insulation, and (as Sherry's comment about 'a populist provenance' suggests), modernist studies in the last decade have offered a democratising corrective to what Michael North justly dismisses as the old 'intellectual amber' version of modernism.[33] Still, it was surely a factor of modernism's early institutionalisation, when historicism would have been de trop, that we have never had the kind of criticism that could have done justice both to the amplitude of the period (rather than just a few canonical figureheads) and to the meaningful political engagements of individual literary intellectuals. Taking these engagements seriously can certainly tell us something about these authors' enduringly important careers, but it can also simultaneously help to explain how the period was experienced and imaginatively organised and why it continues to be remembered as it is.

What follows aims to give a context for experimental form and political impurity, showing how the consensus politics of the Second World War were productive of acutely self-aware literary forms. An adequate definition of modernism needs to take account of this self-referential and historiographic late phase: its critical national consciousness, its scrutiny of the links between creative and economic privilege and its rehabilitation of the private life against abuses of collective power. But I hesitate to call this book revisionist when reappraisal of the conventional periodising of modernism is so overdue: our institutional modernism was name-for-name already orthodox in the period I am discussing. Even as early as 1940, a reasonably perceptive critic like John Lehmann could summarise modernism without sounding a false note: the major novelists were Joyce, Woolf, Lawrence, Stein and Hemingway; Eliot was the major poet, with honourable mention of the older Yeats. From this distance of sixty-six years, Lehmann's retrospective summary of the high modernists of the 1920s is in no way contentious, and 'however much they fell out of fashion with the vanguard of the intellectuals in the next decade ... it is difficult not to conclude that their achievement was very great'; their books were milestones, he concludes, like *Tristram Shandy* and the *Lyrical Ballads* before them.[34] It is indicative of modernism's precipitate institutionalisation that Lehmann could describe so authoritatively a modernist canon and period identical to our own and felt able to sum it up as if it were as deadly historical as the eighteenth century. This was only 1940, and there was some life in modernism yet.

Recent years have seen some important attempts to account for modernism's closing stages. In using the phrase 'late modernism' in this book, I echo Tyrus Miller's 1999 study, *Late Modernism: Politics, Fiction, and the Arts Between the World Wars*, and I share Miller's belief that modernist studies have been disproportionately determined by a 'grand narrative of ... beginnings: "origins," "rise," "emergence," "genealogy"' that accords somewhat uncritically with modernists' own rhetoric of new beginnings.[35] The phrase 'late modernism' may sound faintly paradoxical (does its belatedness not mitigate its modernity?), but it certainly demonstrates how much weight 'modernism' carries as a period designation. To speak of late modernism is to signal unambiguously a move away from the manifestos of the 1910s and the climactic year of 1922, a shift that allows us to reconsider what modernism means as a description of distinctive aesthetic modes that were not monolithic or static but capable of development and transformation. Focusing on late modernism is a way of reading modernism through its longer outcomes rather than its notional origins, and Miller convincingly identifies unexpected aesthetic likenesses among writers of different backgrounds and generations – Samuel Beckett, Mina Loy, Djuna Barnes and Wyndham Lewis – who either began or continued to produce radically experimental work many decades after the first blasts of 1914.

Miller's choice of subjects suggests the main differences in our projects. His authors are American, Irish, English and Canadian by birth, and all have complicated individual histories with regard to national affiliation. The interest in politics declared by Miller's subtitle thus precludes considerations of national specificity, and of course it could be said that Miller's late modernism is, unlike mine, all the more convincingly modernist in having nothing to say about the national: Beckett, Barnes, Lewis and Loy left the countries of their birth as Joyce, Stein and Eliot had done before them. It might also be said, however, that what is being echoed here is not so much high modernism as one of the most troubling aspects of its institutionalisation. By this I mean that the impulse to isolate late modernism qua aesthetic from the strikingly varied and often very particular circumstances of its production always risks replicating the same manoeuvres that depoliticised modernism in the first place. Since modernism is so conventionally identified – and again one notes Miller's subtitle – with a period book ended by two total wars and institutionalised under the threat of a third, to think about modernist politics without registering the impact of world war and the stunning ideological force of the nation as a constellation of power in these circumstances is to come close to avoiding history itself.

Bearing the political stamp of the age that made it dogma, the dislocation of modernism in the process of its mid-century institutionalisation might most suspiciously be seen as a NATO of the critical imagination, asserting that high culture transcends nationhood by subsuming local differences and preoccupations into a general category of western literary modernism. Indeed, Fredric Jameson goes so far as to describe 'late modernism' itself as not only a second wave of modernism exemplified by experimental mid-century writers such as Nabokov, Beckett and Stevens but also as a retroactive theory of aesthetic autonomy that could only have emerged in all-too-historical post-war circumstances: 'It is an American invention', he writes of how late modernism rewrote its past as self-referential aestheticism, 'A product of the Cold War'.[36] Elsewhere Jameson elaborates on the 'now virtually universal stereotype of the great Western modernists as subjective and quietistic antipolitical figures', which came about when 'the power of the various aesthetic modernisms was, during the Cold War and in the period of their North American canonization, displaced and invested in essentially antipolitical forms of academic aestheticism'.[37] In contrast, reading modernism alongside its messily political contexts, national and otherwise, makes it impossible to see these writers as in any sense 'subjective and quietistic'.

The most recent reappraisal of late modernism takes national consciousness entirely and refreshingly seriously. Jed Esty's *A Shrinking Island: Modernism and National Culture in England* identifies in the late work of Forster, Eliot and Woolf an 'anthropological turn', an interest in Englishness as just one culture among others (rather than as the universal culture) that prepares the way for Birmingham School cultural studies and for the literature of the post-colonial diaspora of the 1950s onwards.[38] So long as one is willing to accept the premise that high modernism in England was not deeply interested in the national culture already – and there is a case for saying that Woolf and Forster, as well as Lawrence, West, Ford and others had been much preoccupied by domestic questions from the 1910s onwards – this is a work of tremendous explanatory power that bridges in the most ambitious way to date the neglected period between the two thoroughly institutionalised fields of modernist and post-colonial writing. The loss of the empire, then, is the engine that drives *A Shrinking Island*, and the war is relegated to two or three half sentences; that the war and the loss of the empire were closely connected – politically and economically, as well as imaginatively – is nowhere registered. Like Esty, I see diminution (rather than 'decline') as the crucial dimension of post-war culture, but feel that, to paraphrase Katherine Mansfield, we cannot just leave the war out. Marianna Torgovnick has recently described as a 'war complex' the extent to which the Second World War continues as unfinished business in American public culture.[39] Stronger terms even than this would have to be found to describe the relentlessness of the war in 'ordinary life' in the United Kingdom – by the hazardously experiential ordinary life I mean that it infiltrates public discussions of everything from football to international relations and offers a default setting for sitcoms and serious contemporary fiction alike. The endurance of the war in Britain is surely related to the island's shrinkage; it may even be the acceptable idiom for speaking of it.

The coming chapters use the afterlife of modernism to suggest that the war was experienced through aesthetic habits which were familiar from the 1920s that found their political realisation when modernism reached middle age twenty years later: Woolf's mitigated pastoralism; West's resurrection of the mythical method; Eliot's radical attack on gerontocracy; Green's use of high style as political neutrality; Waugh's rearguard defence of artistic individuality. This is an alternative history of a long modernism, where modernism is read backwards in an effort to bypass conventional historiographies of origins and emergence that promise an imaginative return to a time before modernism in order to reconstruct it from its beginnings. We can only read modernism from where we are. The teleological account of modernism demands a peak of achievement from which everything that follows disappoints, and, instead of relating a closing narrative of aesthetic retrenchment, this book focuses on revisionist acts through which British modernists outlived their canonical moment to reshape modernism itself. Late modernism puts to new political uses the imaginative structures of modernist writing – but it was too late to count. Modernism by then had ossified into a self-contained literary period and into an aesthetic achievement that could only be construed as political in the most problematic, even embarrassing, of ways.

Beginning with a canonical test case for the political engagements of late modernism, Chapter 1 shows how Woolf's pastoral representation of Englishness in wartime represents a move from her radical pacifism of the 1930s towards the politically centrist *Between the Acts* (1941). Her final novel demonstrates retrospectively the persistence of condition-of-England preoccupations across the high modernist era but also encodes a critical reflection on high modernism that brings her close to the rehabilitations of Englishness being advanced in mass and middlebrow culture. From this account of a hesitant late recovery of national affiliation, I go on to suggest that the longer career of Woolf's less familiar contemporary Rebecca West shows how more outspoken contraventions of the left/right demarcation could compromise critical reputations. I argue that when the political binaries of the 1930s finally collapsed, a familiar modernist structuring principle resurfaced as a way of superimposing order on the political confusion of the war's early years: the famous mythical method of Joyce and Eliot resurfaces as the nationalist myth itself. In her two-volume epic about the legacies of empire, *Black Lamb and Grey Falcon* (1941), this socialist and feminist author unpacked the community-making origins of myth in an attempt to recuperate nationality as a legitimate object of radical interest.

The discussion of West outlines a circle of controversial mutual acquaintances that included the ultra-fashionable Noël Coward and the Foreign Office heavyweight Robert Vansittart as well as more obvious political allies like Woolf and John Maynard Keynes. West's wide milieu is reconstructed here because it brings to the foreground an occulted middle ground between interwar right and left, and demonstrates the intimate connections that could exist between the centres of creative and political authority. However, that there is a potentially dangerous parallel between entrenched pre-war elites, political and artistic, is suggested by the 'old men' of T. S. Eliot's *Four Quartets* (1935–43). These seemingly least worldly of poems participate in the attack on governmental and cultural gerontocracies that had given the modernisms of the Great War their explosive rhetorical impact. Eliot's recourse to the trope of gerontocracy both directs the reader back to Eliot's by-then-famous Great War oeuvre (to 'Gerontion' and the failures of the old political order) and points outwards to the contemporary indictment of the decrepitude of Britain's interwar governing classes and also, finally, to the emergent literary debate about Eliot's canonical pre-eminence between and beyond the wars. These poems importantly reflect his unease about the transformation of modernism from a way of writing into a defunct institution.

If the figureheads of high modernism were occupying positions of political authority as elder statesmen and stateswomen of English culture, their younger followers were now trying to scramble up the crumbling ivory tower for all they were worth. A chapter on Henry Green offers to suture the expedient ruptures of the course catalogue ('The Auden Generation', 'The Thirties') by describing the multiple wartime instantiations of political neutrality in the experimental fiction of this atypical 1930s writer. Coolly apolitical, Green writes with a performed reluctance about the dominant public preoccupations of wartime – class division and economic inequality, the end of imperial power, and the problem of domestic reconstruction – and tries to deploy the evasions of autonomous high style against the currents of the hardening political consensus. In the end, disaffected mannerism collapses under the pressure of the post-war period's new standardisations, when 'we, the thin-blooded', as Green summarised the modernist generations, 'have not much left'.[40]

This capitulation was what the *Times* called 'The Eclipse of the Highbrow' as it gloated over the end of modernism in an editorial from the spring of 1941. Using Evelyn Waugh's wartime books as contemporary accounts of modernism's end, I suggest that the late modernist resistance to what was perceived as a post-war cult of philistine materialism points to something more complex and historically telling than a wholesale rightward turn. Reading the second-wave modernism of Green and Waugh alongside the mid-century dissolution of the *rentier* class from which modernism had emerged makes it possible to see why Waugh's wartime novels should have mourned the 1920s as a lost golden age. Linked by a recurrent character that Waugh identified as a composite of the interwar aesthetes Brian Howard and Harold Acton, *Put Out More Flags* (1942) and *Brideshead Revisited* (1945) represent modernism as the intersection of anti-middlebrow experimentation and anti-establishment dissent: the challenge to the chauvinistic and nostalgic nationalisms that, when his work got co-opted in the era of the new right and *Brideshead* became consummate heritage aesthetic, Waugh himself would come to epitomise.

Connected at many points, the intellectual worlds of these authors describe how the war was imagined from its anticipation to its aftermath. It is the story of a victory, of how literary modernism was culturally vindicated, which becomes a defeat when the prevailing political climate grows decreasingly sympathetic to the economic, social and cultural privilege underpinning modernism's literary triumph. Raymond Williams famously argued that any account of a period can only be true to its complexity by acknowledging the coexistence of 'residual' and 'emergent' forms circulating within the dominant culture. By residual, he meant elements 'effectively formed in the past, but ... still active in the cultural process'; by 'emergent', he meant that 'new meanings and values, new practices, new relationships and kinds of relationship are continually being created ... substantially alternative or oppositional to [the dominant culture]'.[41] The modernism of the Second World War is a point of transition, a missing link between imperial Britain and the devolved archipelago it turned into – and that is where this book ends. A coda describes how the collapse of the post-war settlement at the end of the 1970s provoked a reappraisal of the modernist collusion between high culture and privatised sensibility that the welfare-capitalist consensus had aimed to explode. Anchoring contemporary fiction to late modernist models of national imagining, the coda indicates the uses to which the war continues to be put. At the end of the century, novels such as Angus Wilson's *Setting the World on Fire* (1980), Kazuo Ishiguro's *The Remains of the Day* (1989) and Ian McEwan's *Atonement* (2001), revisiting both modernist culture and the Second World War, offered a counter to the dominant fin de siècle historiographies of the political right ('national decline') and left ('post-imperial melancholy').

Ultimately, I would like to suggest some of the ways in which modernism in England was bound to the national culture by throwing light on the historical moment at which modernism was simultaneously a way of writing (a formal and often a political challenge) and a way of reading (already an institution, a canon). This book argues that the importance of 1939–45 lies in the multilateral nature of its modernisms: the Second World War marks the moment when 'making it new' could simultaneously be the rallying cry of experimental poetry, popular cinema and parliamentary politics. Too often modernism has been seen as an alienated, alienating form of creative production – mandarin erudition admiring itself on the lofty transcultural heights – and, on exactly the same grounds, it has been institutionalised for its virtuoso magnificence and attacked for its rarefied elitism. Either way, to restate continually the marginality of modernism is to keep alive the illusion, and one that intermittently haunted these writers themselves, that political responsibility precludes high artistic achievement. This book is a study of public modernism: it aims to reinstate the complexity of mid-century British culture; it charts the depth, and attempts to measure the impact, of the late modernist engagement of it.

CHAPTER I

Virginia Woolf and the pastoral patria

> If the people who rule Britain are made of the same stuff as the little people I have seen today ... then the defense of Britain will be something of which men will speak with awe and admiration so long as the English language survives. Politicians have repeatedly called this a people's war. These people deserve well of their leaders.
> Ed Murrow, broadcasting from London, 18 August 1940.[1]

> London looked merry and hopeful, wearing her wounds like stars; why do I dramatise London perpetually? When I see a great smash like a crushed match box where an old house stood I wave my hand to London. What I'm finding odd and agreeable and unwonted is the admiration this war creates – for every sort of person: chars, shopkeepers, even much more remarkably, for politicians – Winston at least, and the tweed wearing sterling dull women here, with their grim good sense: organising First aid, putting out bombs for practise [*sic*], and jumping out of windows to show us how. We burnt an incendiary bomb up on the down last night. It was a lovely tender autumn evening, and the white sputter of the bomb was to me, who never listened to the instructions, rather lovely. I'd almost lost faith in human beings, partly owing to my immersion in the dirty water of artists [*sic*] envies and vanities while I worked at Roger [*Roger Fry*]. Now hope revives again.
> Virginia Woolf, writing to Ethel Smyth, 25 September 1940.[2]

As if it were liberating to escape the small circle of high modernist art in which her biography of Roger Fry had re-enclosed her, Woolf enacted what it meant to have a place in the country in the early years of the Second World War: the salute to the heroically ravaged city, the celebration of the tweedy ladies of the parish setting off bombs and springing from windows, the affectionate encompassing of social strata from Winston Churchill to charwomen. Woolf's gentle middlebrow moment prefigures the yearnings with which British culture looks back at the war as a moment of lost communality and unity, and modern cultural historians consistently rebuke this popular amnesia about the bereavement, poverty and insecurity that were presumably more credible experiences for civilians dragged into another war by a governing class that had not necessarily done much for them in peacetime. But Woolf's surprising participation in what have since become consolatory cultural memories of the war sheds a useful light on the late politics of a writer once thought apolitical and now routinely presented as a leftwing radical. Examining the shift to the political centre suggested by her comments to Ethel Smyth, this chapter returns Woolf's final writings to the discursive contexts of the war's early stages.

The project of rebranding Britain is the single most noticeable feature of mass and middlebrow culture in 1940, and was clearly impelled by the need to draw the neutral United States into a war that Britain could not win on its own. The 'people's war' mythology of classless civilian solidarity proved indispensable for this purpose. The documentary *London Can Take It!* (1940) is a representative example of the propaganda directed at potential American allies, and, like Ed Murrow's anti-isolationist broadcasts from London, it describes how a populace transcends its hardships just by pursuing under fire the ordinary business of life and work. The camera rests on civilians sleeping through devastating air raids ('These are not Hollywood sound effects', the American voiceover explains), getting up to clear the night's wreckage, pulling a pet cat from the rubble, hitching a ride to work through trashed streets. Focusing on the adaptation of everyday routines to devastating circumstances, the film's unmistakeable intention was to invite neutral audiences to find supportable what was being presented as a uniquely democratic civilian war. Fascinatingly, the British seem to have been willing to believe their own hype, and the film proved massively popular with domestic audiences when it was renamed *Britain Can Take It!*, as if the London Blitz (over 13,500 dead by the end of 1940) could be reflected back at the whole country in emblematic recognition of its hardships.[3] The film's honouring of the bombed metropolis partakes of exactly the same mood as Woolf's praise for a 'merry and hopeful' city in her letter to Ethel Smyth; however, although Woolf tends to be thought of as a metropolitan novelist, famously celebratory of London life, it is the other propaganda-rich synecdoche of wartime culture that speaks most clearly in *Between the Acts*. Structured around a village pageant, Woolf's last novel makes rural England stand for the whole country.

JAM AND JERUSALEM

For modernist writers in England, this particular substitution had always been so readily to hand that to look at Woolf's Pointz Hall, the setting for *Between the Acts*, in the context of wartime representations of a united national community is to be struck by the continuities between British modernism and the affective structures that earlier forms of fiction had bequeathed it. More than thirty years ago, Raymond Williams exploded the alluring fictions of escape that the pastoral has traditionally offered when he remarked the dissonance between Britain's rapid industrialisation and the rural settings of its literature. This gap between how people lived and what they wrote about only widened from the Victorians onwards:

> Rural Britain was subsidiary, and knew that it was subsidiary, from the late nineteenth century. But so much of the past of the country, its feelings and its literature, was involved with rural experience, and so many of its ideas of how to live well, from the style of the country-house to the simplicity of the cottage, persisted and even were strengthened, that there is almost an inverse proportion, in the twentieth century, between the relative importance of the working rural economy and the cultural importance of rural ideas.[4]

Supposing Williams had been thinking about modernism (he was not), his conclusions would still hold true.[5] For all that modernist writing is definitively identified with the metropolitan, the expatriate and the deracinated, English modernism consistently betrays an ongoing preoccupation with the meaning of rootedness, to the extent that many of its most canonical novels have at their centre the inheritance of a house in the English countryside: E. M. Forster's *Howards End* (1910), Ford Madox Ford's *The Good Soldier* (1915) and D. H. Lawrence's *Lady Chatterley's Lover* (1928) are obvious instances of how narrative innovation coexisted right across the high modernist era with traditionally realist interests in possession, lineage and entitlement. It could even be said that Woolf's own *To the Lighthouse* (1927) – Laura Marcus calls it the 'most significant precursor' to *Between the Acts*[6] – is still using an older literary currency in the significance it accords the endangered country house harbour. That so many major modernists, novelists whose literary radicalism has never been in doubt, continued to imagine a place in the country as Englishness itself suggests that there is potentially more to this trope than its superficially conservative appeal.

It would certainly be true to say, though, that a context of war exacerbates the conservative function of the imagined countryside. That rural Britain was 'everywhere hastening to decay', as the Liberal politician C. F. G. Masterman wrote in his proto-sociological survey *The Condition of England* (1909), is routinely cause for mourning in the literature of the early twentieth century; and Masterman himself would become head of the War Propaganda Bureau in the First World War, when soothing conceptions of English pastoral offered an open conduit for the sentiments of propagandists and combatants alike.[7] In the Second World War, idealised rural England once again became the literary mainstay of nostalgic longings for community and continuity, and it has often been noticed that the Victorian novelist Anthony Trollope made a wartime comeback, presumably because his serial representations of English country living represented a community that looked, albeit from a distance, enviably secure. Perhaps it is also symptomatic that no fewer than eight of the middlebrow novelist Angela Thirkell's additions to the chronicles of Trollope's Barsetshire were published between 1939 and 1945. Pointing directly to her books' sedative intentions, the first of Thirkell's novels to register the Second World War is the preposterously titled *Cheerfulness Breaks In* (1940).

As with the people's war propaganda of the London Blitz, rural England found a special political utility in the search for a serviceable Englishness to send across the Atlantic. Of exemplary silliness here are contemporary anti-isolationist tracts like Samuel Chamberlain and Donald Moffatt's *This Realm, This England ... The Citadel of a Valiant Race Portrayed by its Greatest Etchers*. Published in the United States in 1941, this collection of mostly late-Victorian renderings of the conventionally lovely begins with a chapter on London but soon turns to 'Villages', 'Farms', 'The English Countryside', 'Scotland' [*sic*], 'Rivers' and so on. The book opens with the declaration that the British are not urban people: 'The Englishman's heart is in the land, in the fields and waters and ancient forests of the countryside itself. There his spirit comes truly alive; there, if anywhere, he feels at home, his existence justified. His sense of kinship with nature is no mere poetic fancy. It is real, a part of his bone and blood and fibre.'[8] From this horrible first principle, the book puts together an explanation of what it calls the English 'race' that mounts an apology for the empire ('as much a spiritual as a material union') and for domestic social hierarchies ('the British concept of equality [is] one of the hardest things for an American to comprehend').[9] The none-too-subtle pretext for championing what American neutrals could surely be forgiven for thinking an unrepentantly class-bound empire is primarily a collection of Britain's scenic rural treasures.

While Woolf was clearly never going to indulge in cultural forgetfulness on that fantastical scale, the war generated strange meetings between social radicalism and pastoral patriotism that suggest how progressive aspirations might be articulated in a traditional idiom. Writing at the end of her career to an American audience, Woolf spoke from this centre ground in her essay 'Thoughts on Peace in an Air Raid' (1940) when she quoted from Blake's *Milton*: '"I will not cease from mental fight," Blake wrote. Mental fight means thinking against the current, not with it.'[10] This famous passage from Blake would be most familiar to an English audience as the Anglican hymn 'Jerusalem', which had been adopted as an assembly anthem by the suffragettes and by the ascendant Labour Party, but also by the proverbially rural and domestic Women's Institute (WI), formed in Britain during the Great War to mobilise countrywomen for food preservation. Popularly known as 'Jam and Jerusalem', the WI became powerful enough to send delegates to the League of Nations, and, on the League's failure, undertook war work once again (the chair of the WI was also the director of the Women's Land Army). Woolf herself became closely involved with the WI in 1940, when she became treasurer of her local group, and it likely provided the bomb-handy women of the letter to Ethel Smyth that I quoted at the start of this chapter. These were the 'battalions of willing ladies who have emerged from the herbaceous borders to answer the call of duty', whose good works ('cramming astonished yokels' heads into gas masks') the English writer Mollie Panter-Downes found so hilarious in her contemporary letters to America in the *New Yorker*.[11]

Woolf's use of 'Jerusalem' in her own 1940 letter to America illustrates how the same cultural property can be used to motivate both patriotic sentiment and progressive good deeds: as with the contemporary *Times* dictum about the need to put the national house in order in the process of winning the war patriotism becomes protest and vice versa. Given the contemporary convergence of reformist energy and the rhetoric of a green-and-pleasant-land, *Between the Acts* is understandably self-conscious about registering the mood of the *Times*. The local reporter, Page, ponders the ending of the village pageant that takes up most of the novel:

That was a ladder. And that (a cloth roughly painted) was a wall. And that a man with a hod on his back. Mr. Page the reporter, licking his pencil, noted: 'With the very limited means at her disposal, Miss La Trobe conveyed to the audience Civilization (the wall) in ruins; rebuilt (witness man with hod) by human effort; witness also woman handing bricks. Any fool could grasp that. Now issued black man in fuzzy wig; coffee-coloured ditto in silver turban; they signify presumably the League of. ...'

A burst of applause greeted this flattering tribute to ourselves. Crude of course. But then she had to keep expenses down. A painted cloth must convey – what the *Times* and *Telegraph* both said in their leaders that very morning.[12]

There is nothing blithely hopeful about this correspondence between the 'painted cloth' and the mainstream media, and not least because the reference to the 'League of ... [Nations]' recalls the last failed attempt at rebuilding civilisation after the Great War; a failure close to Woolf's heart since her husband had been committed to the League for the whole of the interwar period.[13] In any case, the reader has already been told what else the newspapers 'said ... that very morning': of the economic vulnerability of France that brings British defeat closer; and of the rape in the barrack room that represents a strident refusal on Woolf's part to give British militarism any moral exemption on the grounds of its nationality alone.

'DEFENCE OF ENGLAND; NOT ALL CLAPTRAP'

Though increasingly sensitive to what military defeat would mean, Woolf was scarcely ready to suppress her old contempt for the rhetorical contortions that it would take to legitimise another war; her generation had lived through the Great War and its trench nightmares, as well as the Boer War, another high water mark of British imperial jingoism. One of the pressing concerns of Miss La Trobe's pageant is the way in which literature colludes in establishment cover-ups. The comic Victorian policeman Budge ('*It's a Christian country, our Empire; under the White Queen Victoria. Over thought and religion; drink; dress; manners; marriage too, I wield my truncheon*' [162]), alongside the satirical playlet that he introduces ('*a lifetime in the African desert among the heathens would be ... Perfect happiness!*' [166]), offers Woolf's most powerful example of how the means of imposing domestic and imperial order get suppressed by the official languages of government and also by the unofficial literary vocabulary that uses the advancing of the British Empire as material for a conventional romantic plot. More, even, than that self-referential warning about the danger of discursive complicity, the novel's scenes beyond the pageant are dominated by acts of physical violence; these cannot be forgotten, even if to remember them properly would be to render the war totally unfightable.

This is why it matters 'what the *Times* and *Telegraph* both said ... that very morning'. Bart Oliver's eccentric use of his rolled-up newspaper as the snout of a sinister beast, 'a terrible peaked [beaked?] eyeless monster moving on legs, brandishing arms', is more than appropriate when both his son and daughter-in-law are prompted to violence by the contents of their morning newspaper (11–12). Their internal confrontations with militarism are often cited. Isa Oliver reads a newspaper story that has been shown to be 'startlingly, not invented',[14] which reports how a girl has been tricked into coming into military barracks by the 'fantastic' promise of seeing a horse with a green tail and is then raped by soldiers:

> That was real; so real that on the mahogany door panels she saw the Arch in Whitehall; through the Arch the barrack room; in the barrack room the bed, and on the bed the girl was screaming and hitting him about the face, when the door (for in fact it was a door) opened and in came Mrs. Swithin carrying a hammer. (20)

The hammer gets assimilated into Isa's 'imaginative reconstruction of the past,' to borrow a phrase from earlier in the novel (9), and she uses it to respond to the raped woman's victimisation with a fantasy of violent defence. When Isa imagines the woman beating her attacker 'about the face with a hammer', the hammer used to nail a placard for the traditional village pageant becomes inseparable from its violent potential (22).

In a psychological manoeuvre analogous to his wife's expropriation of the hammer from its harmless pastoral context, Giles contemplates how 'the whole of Europe – over there – was bristling like ... He had no command of metaphor. Only the ineffective word "hedgehog" illustrated his vision of Europe, bristling with guns, poised with planes' (53). Anodyne hedgehogs and hammers have become instruments of violent self-defence, because 'Had he not read, in the morning paper, in the train, that sixteen men had been shot, others prisoned, just over there, across the gulf, in the flat land which divided them from the continent?' (46). His response to this is to kill the 'monstrous' snake choking on a toad. Since 'The snake was unable to swallow; the toad was unable to die', this act of violence is almost arbitrary since he cannot save either of them: 'But it was action. Action relieved him' (99). Trapped by his consciousness of growing violence, Giles, 'manacled to a rock he was, and forced passively to behold indescribable horror' (60), recalls the description of Clara Durrant in Woolf's Great War novel, *Jacob's Room* (1922). Clara, 'a virgin chained to a rock', is the passive Georgian model of femininity whom Jacob, himself emblematic of English masculinity *c*. 1914, idolises.[15] As if reiterating Woolf's *Three Guineas* argument that feminism is the avant-garde of the war against fascism, the twinning of Clara and Giles across the two decades separating the novels in which they appear suggests that Nazism forces quasi-feminine passivity on everyone.[16]

Nonetheless, there are significant differences between *Three Guineas* and *Between the Acts*. Woolf wrote *Three Guineas* during the Spanish Civil War in which her nephew was killed, and the book restates over and over again the material and bodily effects of war, irreconcilable with any political ends they could possibly advance:

Here then on the table before us are photographs. The Spanish Government sends them with patient pertinacity about twice a week. They are not pleasant photographs to look upon. They are photographs of dead bodies for the most part. This morning's collection contains the photograph of what might be a man's body, or a woman's; it is so mutilated that it might, on the other hand, be the body of a pig. But those certainly are dead children, and that undoubtedly is the section of a house. A bomb has torn open the side; there is still a bird-cage hanging in what was presumably the sitting-room, but the rest of the house looks like nothing so much as a bunch of spilikins suspended in mid-air.[17]

The stunned reiteration throughout *Three Guineas* of blown-to-bits houses and bodies comes in support of an unequivocally pacifist argument. The progress of Nazism would cause that pacifism to slip away as she wrote *Between the Acts*, and came to recognise a little belatedly (there were other feminist intellectuals who had already reached this conclusion) that what Britain's patriarchal institutions did to middle-class women was not equivalent to what the Nazis were doing to the Jews. Events after 1938 would render unsound equations like 'dictatorship ... against Jews or against women, in England, or in Germany' and 'in Holloway or in a concentration camp'.[18] In any case, praise for the radicalism of *Three Guineas* should probably be tempered by the recollection that, first, it conflates two surely incommensurable forms of violence, and that, second, Woolf was simultaneously engaged in publishing 'The Duchess and the Jeweller', her story about an arriviste Jew ruined by his lust and social-climbing, and so unselfconsciously anti-Semitic that its transatlantic publication in April and May of 1938 suggests the limitations, at this stage, of Woolf's understanding of the Nazi within and without.[19]

In context, these limitations are noteworthy. To my mind, it is unthinkable that 'The Jew and the Duchess', as she refers to it, could have been written by one of her major women contemporaries, say by a Rebecca West or Storm Jameson, who spent the closing years of the 1930s travelling around Eastern and Central Europe as it collapsed to totalitarianism, and later working for continental writers and intellectuals in exile. I shall return to West at length in Chapter 2, but Jameson, the president of English PEN, is one of the politically minded writers at whom Woolf takes a swipe in her diary – 'old Prostitutes', she calls them in May 1938.[20] Months later, and right through the Munich crisis, she still considers the imminent war 'nothing that any human being ... cares one straw about ... merely a housemaids [sic] dream'; 'we know winning means nothing'; 'whats [sic] the point of winning?'[21] It is not until the summer of 1940, when she and Leonard are making plans to commit suicide in the event of the expected German invasion, that Woolf's diary reveals a grisly awakening. The week Paris falls, she writes that 'Now we suffer what the Poles suffered', an anticipatory identification with the earlier, Eastern European victims of Nazism that sounds more like Jameson or West.[22] Woolf's diaries now start to recall the Churchillian script: 'our wounded', 'our men', 'our majestic city', 'Armada weather', 'now we're fighting alone with our back to the wall'.[23]

The belatedness of Woolf's war awakening makes it impossible to superimpose the pacifist polemic of *Three Guineas* on her last novel. The typical over-reading that this elicits sees Giles as 'the tyrant or dictator who must be resisted in *Three Guineas*', or 'a natural killer, a frustrated man of war ... very close to the Fascist threat he fears'.[24] In fact Woolf emphasises how he has been made a victim of the caricatured versions of masculinity imposed on him by the novel's characteristically 'sensitive' female characters, from Lucy Swithin 'expressing her amazement, her amusement, at men who spent their lives buying and selling', even though 'Given his choice, he would have chosen to farm. But he was not given his choice' (47), to the failure of the others to acknowledge his emotional loyalties: 'At any moment guns would rake that land into furrows; planes splinter Bolney Minster into smithereens and blast the Folly. He, too, loved the view' (53). The presentation of Giles, with all his frustration, his inarticulate sensitivity and his thwarted uxorious love, does not convincingly support the equations of English masculinity and the European dictatorships that seem rhetorically so powerful in *Three Guineas*. In Miss La Trobe's pageant, these sympathies redeem people from their public failures: 'our kindness to the cat; note too in today's paper "Dearly loved by his wife"' (188). The diffident humanistic gesture anticipates Philip Larkin's pitch for private over public masculinities in 'An Arundel Tomb' (1954), where, with a long-range historiography like that of *Between the Acts*, the speaker marvels at the tomb of a medieval knight holding his wife's hand in effigy: tentative evidence that proves 'Our almost-instinct almost true: / What will survive of us is love'.[25]

By the newly anti-heroic, post-imperial standard for masculinity more familiar from later writers like Larkin, even Woolf's blustering Bart Oliver, a one-time colonial administrator, comes close to redemption when he goes in search of his son midway through the pageant because 'Giles was unhappy': 'Arms akimbo, he stood in front of his country gentleman's library. Garibaldi; Wellington; Irrigation Officers' Reports; and Hibbert on the Diseases of the Horse. A great harvest the mind had reaped; but for all this, compared with his son, he did not care one damn' (115–16). Woolf is again recalling material that she had used in *Jacob's Room*, where the same collection of books is used to sum up and indict the patriarchal culture – all Great Men and county squiredom – that brings Jacob to his death in the Great War.[26] But, unlike Jacob, Bart can see that his collection of masculinist and militaristic pomposity is no longer sufficient, is completely irrelevant compared to his son's despair. And Giles's own stamping on the snake-toad enormity, like Isa's violent seizure of the hammer, is more than a tritely masculine impulse towards aggression. For all that Giles is thoroughly implicated in the male monopoly on education, capital, professional life and domestic authority that Woolf had held up in *Three Guineas* as the foundation of militarism, she insists that they are 'all caught and caged; prisoners', that Giles's inexpressible feeling of being 'damnably unhappy' is silently shared by his wife and the gay poet William Dodge (176), that, despite the ostensibly impassable social gulf between the City stockbroker and the lesbian artist, Giles's self-consciousness about the blood on his shoes communicates itself in the otherwise entirely meaningless analogy used to describe Miss La Trobe's 'panic' when 'Blood seemed to pour from her shoes. This is death, death, death ... when illusion fails' (180).

In the novel's sheltered world of village pageants, bazaars and cricket matches, Giles's bloodstained tennis shoes are a powerful emblem of the fall from innocence that comes from reacting with violence to violence. More than that, they speak of Woolf's own fall from innocence in accepting that it was no longer possible to be an Outsider, as she had advocated in *Three Guineas*, attacking patriarchal instincts and institutions from the radical margins: insiders and outsiders, Giles, Isa, William and Miss La Trobe, are necessarily in it together. But although I obviously disagree with those who argue that 'Woolf's commitment to pacifism ... allowed no oscillation. This is the one issue on which Woolf did not waver', the book also complicates any easy debunking or the slick revisionism that suggests that fighting a war means forgetting how wars get fought.[27] This is the guilty compromise of its time, and it finds an echo close to home in Leonard Woolf's contemporary argument that 'the use of force is always bad ... But that unfortunately does not settle the matter. In human affairs the choice is rarely between what is good and what is bad; it is usually between what is bad and what is worse'.[28]

REBUILT IN A NEW STYLE

It seems to me that the critical commitment to Woolf's uncompromising (and therefore presumably uncompromised) pacifism partly comes of misunderstanding the differences in how the two world wars originated and were perceived at home. The year 1939 was no replay of the year 1914, and to argue that Woolf could imagine the Second World War fightable is not to evoke the kind of Great War nationalism that had motivated strangers to stone people's pet dachshunds in the park. After the propaganda abuses of the Great War, the new war aims of 1940 must have looked eminently supportable when, as the Blitz began, the bombs that indiscriminately hit city slums and royal residences became the figurative forces clearing away the stratified and corrupt Old England to make room for a new social order. Describing the bombed cityscape of 1941, Herbert Read noticed that it wasn't just 'the workmen's tenements and the warehouses' that had been destroyed, but 'also the Bank of England and the Royal Academy, the Church of England and *The Times* ... and if they survived at all, they would have to be rebuilt in a new style'.[29]

Rebuilding in a new style would become more than left-radical wishful-thinking when the political acceptance of the Beveridge Report, a peculiar sort of bestseller at the end of 1942, would change Britain enough for the defeat of Germany to look, smugly enough, a moral triumph for social democracy.[30] Mark Rawlinson rightly argues that this wartime rhetoric of building a new social order demands considerable sleight of hand: 'the transfer of reality from victim to an impersonal, and contingent, political structure'; or, as he later puts it, 'In Britain in the early 1940s these ideals were bound up with a rhetoric of omission and of the substitution of benign effects for flesh-breaking causes'.[31] Although this is perhaps a fancy way of describing any war, Rawlinson's use of 'contingent' is absolutely crucial and a pointed reminder that the Second World War as the catalyst for a new social order, ultimately one of the most influential of modern British culture's 'memories' of the war, barely amounted to a promise in 1941.

Between the Acts is surprisingly slippery on the issue of what the New England would be like, given how outspokenly Woolf declared her late political views elsewhere. I have already suggested that Woolf's use of

Blake in 'Thoughts on Peace in an Air Raid' implies aspirations towards social justice, and Janet Montefiore has characterised Woolf's contemporary lecture 'The Leaning Tower', as ' "one nation" leftish patriotism'.[32] John Mepham's critical biography describes how these last years of Woolf's life showed 'a very real desire on her part to overcome the narrowness of her social life' and goes on to describe how 'The Leaning Tower' makes a 'declaration of solidarity' with the working-class men whom it addresses that Mepham finds 'quite astonishing ... quite unconvincing'.[33] In *Between the Acts*, though, her social interests are only articulated in that imprecise formulation of 'rebuilding civilisation'. Unlike Woolf's earlier major novels, there seems to be a refusal here to engage questions of social class: perhaps an unlikely avoidance in a novel that is so much more explicitly public than her earlier, classically modernist, experiments in representing the inner life.

Because if it is above all a milestone in modernist autobiography and the narration of interiority, *To the Lighthouse* thinks out loud about social injustice. Mrs Ramsay embodies all the good intentions of a concern that motivates charity rather than political intervention, in what seems to start out as (but almost certainly is not), a satirical rendering of late-Victorian *noblesse oblige*:

The real differences, she thought, standing by the drawing-room window, are enough, quite enough. She had in mind at the moment rich and poor, high and low ... the things she saw with her own eyes, weekly, daily, here or in London, when she visited this widow, or that struggling wife in person with a bag on her arm, and a note-book and pencil with which she wrote down in columns carefully ruled for the purpose wages and spendings, employment and unemployment, in the hope that thus she would cease to be a private woman whose charity was half a sop to her own indignation, half a relief to her own curiosity, and become what with her untrained mind she greatly admired, an investigator, elucidating the social problem.[34]

Like her husband, who 'cared about fishermen and their wages', indeed, 'could not sleep for thinking of them', Mrs Ramsay partly defines herself through her public conscience and commitments:

Nor was she domineering, nor was she tyrannical. It was more true about hospitals and drains and the dairy. About things like that she did feel passionately, and would, if she had had the chance, have liked to take people by the scruff of their necks and make them see. No hospital on the whole island. It was a disgrace. Milk delivered at your door in London positively brown with dirt. It should be made illegal.[35]

But the grim late-Victorian social situation is encapsulated in the obscure misery caused by Mrs Ramsay's famous brown stocking, 'too short by half an inch at least, making allowance for the fact that *Sorley's little boy would be less well grown than James*' [emphasis added].[36] I have emphasised this because in the end Woolf could not, not when social inequality (why is Sorley's little boy less well-grown than James?) and existential suffering amount to the same thing, 'the eternal problems: suffering; death; the poor'.[37]

The tension throughout Woolf's work between her emergent public conscience and her ultimately class-constrained imagination is potentially most pressing in *Between the Acts* because the writing of the novel coincided with the widest-ranging public debate about social reform in Woolf's lifetime. In fact, the novel shows some unease about the values of the reconstructed England, about the likely materialism of its manifestations of social justice, or 'what after all the *Times* was saying yesterday': 'Homes will be built. Each flat with its refrigerator, in the crannied wall. Each of us a free man; plates washed by machinery; not an aeroplane to vex us; all liberated; made whole' (182–3). This foreshadows the fear expressed in Forster's wartime 'Does Culture Matter?' even as he conceded that life in a newly democratic England will be 'by no means a nightmare': 'There will be work for all and play for all. But the work and the play will be split; the work will be mechanical and the play frivolous. If you drop tradition and culture you lose your chance of connecting work and play and creating a life which is all of a piece'.[38] Writers with an essentially middle-class liberal sensibility, Woolf and Forster could undoubtedly think of far worse things than material equality, but they could not imagine 'wholeness' coming of it. This is the meaning of Woolf's play on words when she has an unnamed voice in *Between the Acts* suggest that 'What we need is a centre. Something to bring us all together', ostensibly some kind of community centre – but the novel's closing emphasis on disintegration and fracture is so extreme that no centre could hold these characters together.

The community centre will mean rebuilding England in a more literal sense than Woolf could bring herself to face. Again, Forster's comments are illuminatingly ambivalent because they articulate both the need for and the price of reform. His own pageant *England's Pleasant Land* (the title of course comes from the ubiquitous 'Jerusalem') was first performed in July 1938, and the *Times* reviewer there on the opening day hit immediately on its political insecurities, and was much amused by how the 'slightly pink interpretation of history' offered by its treatment of the

Enclosures was 'quickly suppressed' when the land finally passes from the gentry and the baddies sing their 'fiendish song of triumph called "Ripe for Development"'.[39] Forster's oscillation between the 'slightly pink' and a more anxious response to social change is characteristic. The narrative commentary he subsequently wrote for Humphrey Jennings's film *A Diary for Timothy* (1945) tells the story of the war's end as if to a baby born on the fifth anniversary of its outbreak. Still, the film transcends this heart-sinkingly sentimental premise when Forster's commentary tells the new baby that he is 'one of the lucky ones ... If you had been born in wartime Holland or Poland, or a Liverpool or Glasgow slum, this would be a very different picture'; and Forster goes on in this encouragingly radical vein when he interrupts the story of how the heroic airman Peter is recovering after being shot down over France, with news that Goronwy the coalminer has had a serious accident in the pit, because, baby Timothy is warned, 'People get hurt in peacetime same as in war, though that shouldn't be'. The upshot is a surprisingly brave parallel between total war and the ordinary condition of the working class that would be made many years later by Jennings's Mass-Observation collaborator Tom Harrisson when he suggested that the celebrated stoicism of the Blitzed urban poor was an ironic consequence of their appalling pre-Welfare-State conditions. 'Misery was accentuated, but it was not new', Harrisson dryly reflected, 'The loss of warmth, hot food, even furniture, was not a universal novelty.'[40]

Agreement, then, between Forster and the solidly lefty instigators of Mass-Observation, but it took a different kind of courage for Forster to describe after the war what social change would cost. To realise that social justice means social housing makes for a 'collision of loyalties' because 'I cannot free myself from the conviction that something irreplaceable has been destroyed, and that a little piece of England has died as surely as if a bomb had hit it. I wonder what compensation there is in the world of the spirit, for the destruction of the life here, the life of tradition'.[41] It is easy enough to deride Forster's nostalgia for the old feudal order, a yearning that is very much of his Edwardian time. Shared by writers in every other respect more avant-garde, such conservatism, as Louise Blakeney Williams has most recently argued, started many modernist contemporaries on a road that would lead straight to fascism.[42] Although Forster and Woolf were manifestly impervious to the originary fantasies of fascism, the lost pastoral remained their battleground for progressive optimism and its practical implications. And even when it is not a portent of rightwing reaction, the exaltation of the pastoral facilitates a self-interested blindness to historical process, as Raymond Williams forcefully pointed out:

> For there is no innocence in the established proprietors, at any particular point in time, unless we ourselves choose to put it there. Very few titles to property could bear humane investigation, in the long process of conquest, theft, political intrigue, courtiership, extortion and the power of money. It is a deep and persistent illusion to suppose that time confers on these familiar processes of acquisition an innocence which can be contrasted with the ruthlessness of subsequent stages of the same essential drives.[43]

Although Williams was writing in the 1970s, the argument has roots in Woolf and Forster's era; another Welsh socialist, Aneurin Bevan MP, had used it to defend the egalitarian ambitions of the first post-war Labour administration (1945–51) against Tory mystifications of private wealth: 'ownership of property is not a social service', Bevan expostulated, 'It derives from the power to exploit the exertions of others . . . a predatory power made possible by carrying over into modern society the concepts of barbarism, when theft, raid and pillage were accepted ways of acquiring property'.[44]

It is extremely significant in the context of this emergent debate that Woolf should try to cut the link between country-worship and plain old snobbery by accounting for Pointz Hall's sources of economic support. She rejects the ahistorical mystique of inheritance when she stresses that the money it takes to keep the country house going in 1939 is unglamorous middle-class money, the salary that comes with Giles's unwanted career as a London stockbroker. In fact, there is something nearly defensive about how the novel's setting is established; Pointz Hall is emphatically not an aristocratic country pile but 'a middle-sized house. It did not rank among the houses that are mentioned in guide books', and the Olivers have not been here forever:

> Driving past, people said to each other: 'I wonder if that'll ever come into the market?' and to the chauffeur: 'Who lives there?'
> The chauffeur didn't know. . . . Only something over a hundred and twenty years the Olivers had been there. Still, on going up the principal staircase – there was another, a mere ladder at the back for the servants – there was a portrait. A length of yellow brocade was visible half-way up; and, as one reached the top, a small powdered face, a great head-dress slung with pearls, came into view; an ancestress of sorts. (6–7)

The ancestress is a fake, although the Olivers also have a portrait of a real ancestor; and it is true that, as new money goes, a hundred and twenty years is not all that new. Much has changed, though, in the thirty years since

Howards End: the modern mobility which gave Forster such anxiety – the damage done by cars, the transfer of property from indigenous residents to prosperous incomers – is glossed over in that single sentence about passing motorists wondering if Pointz Hall will 'come into the market'.

If Woolf begins the novel with progressive good intentions, it becomes clear as she goes on that most of the unsightly processes that caused such anxiety for earlier modernists are not going to be visible from Pointz Hall. The parallel growth of consumer culture and social services that D. H. Lawrence blamed for the destruction of his native Nottinghamshire ('the new brick streets spreading into the fields, the new erections rising at the collieries, the new girls in their silk stockings, the new collier lads lounging into the Pally or the Welfare'[45]) is altogether suppressed from Woolf's Midlands panorama, which remains much as it was when it appeared in 'Figgis's Guide Book (1833)':

The Guide Book still told the truth. 1830 was true in 1939. No house had been built; no town had sprung up. Hogben's Folly was still eminent; the very flat, field-parcelled land had changed only in this – the tractor had to some extent superseded the plough. The horse had gone; but the cow remained. If Figgis were here now, Figgis would have said the same. (52–53)

Woolf simply does not want to deal with the uglification and vulgarising of the countryside by 'The motor bike, the motor bus, and the movies' that are only mentioned in passing (75).

Roughly speaking, however, had Figgis been there in person and called a roll call, half the ladies and gentlemen present would have said *"Adsum*; I'm here, in place of my grandfather or great-grandfather," as the case may be. At this very moment, half-past three on a June day in 1939 they greeted each other, and as they took their seats, finding if possible a seat next one another, they said: "That hideous new house at Pyes Corner! What an eyesore! And those bungalows! – have you seen 'em?"(75)

The changes are only on a minor scale; the continuities are far more pronounced. What is more, the author's surrogate refuses to approve even these minor alterations to the landscape, and the snobbish, anonymous complaint against the 'eyesore' new houses gets endorsed later on by Miss La Trobe's closing monologue, in which 'Mr. M's bungalow. A view spoilt for ever' is taken as evidence that 'the gun slayers, bomb droppers ... do openly what we do slyly' (187).

Here, Woolf is on extraordinarily (and literally) conservative territory. In 1939, a collaboration between the Ministry of Labour and the Pilgrim

Trust had instituted a project called 'Recording the Changing Face of Britain', a commissioned collection of watercolours to memorialise the architecture and landscapes endangered by the outbreak of war. However, Lord Macmillan, the Pilgrim Trust's chairman, retrospectively explained the rationale in such a way as to make the war only part of a bigger question about rural heritage because 'apart from the havoc wrought by the enemy ... the outward aspect of Britain was changing all too quickly before the War at the sinister hands of improvers and despoilers'.[46] (Macmillan was the first Minister for Information, occupying a similar post to that of the rural elegist Masterman in the First World War.) This equation of wartime and interwar 'violence' against the landscape had even emerged long before an Allied win could be taken for granted; a 1942 essay in *Horizon* had also argued that 'The ravages ... began long before the war':

The invention of the internal-combustion engine may be regarded with justice as the greatest single disaster in the history of mankind. Not only has it destroyed the security of England and made wholesale death and mutilation familiar things; it has also destroyed the beauty of England, killed quiet, and, with quiet, dignity. Take, for example, the case of Sussex. ... [47]

By the end of the article's extravagant first page, the horrors of aerial warfare and the horrors of suburban development ('London burst like a bomb and scattered its debris far and wide over the faces of Surrey and Kent'[48]) are already, as for Miss La Trobe, interchangeable. Ultimately, this is the problem with using the pastoral as shorthand for what-we-are-fighting-for: to imagine a timeless rural England brutalised by German bombs is necessarily to evoke the self-inflicted pre-war damage and to raise the possibility that the propaganda promise of post-war reform threatens the greenbelt with further butchery.

The debate creeps into *Between the Acts*, which is much preoccupied (as country-house novels usually are) by questions about continuity. In its lighter early stages, the novel stresses a comforting adaptability: how, after the Reformation, 'the chapel had become a larder, changing, like the cat's name as religion changed', but transformations become exponentially more threatening (32). When, for instance, Mrs Manresa's husband is introduced into the narrative as 'a Jew, got up to look the very spit and image of the landed gentry' (40), Woolf seems suspiciously close to the world of 'The Duchess and the Jeweller':

'Behold Oliver,' he would say, addressing himself. 'You who began life in a filthy little alley, you who ... ' and he would look down at his legs, so shapely in their perfect trousers; at his boots; at his spats. They were all shapely, shining; cut from the best cloth by the best scissors in Savile Row.[49]

This is the point at which the one-nation politics of *Between the Acts* risk clannishness and nativism, and Ralph Manresa's presumptuous makeover only acquires a more resonant character retrospectively when one villager asks: 'what about the Jews? The refugees ... the Jews ... People like ourselves, beginning life again. ... But it's always been the same' (121). The notion that change and uprooting have always happened is a consolatory myth, a way of minimising what's happening to the Jews and other refugees, and a strategy for warding off the sense of Armageddon. It is related to the story that a villager watching the Victorian play implies when she considers how 'change had to come, unless things were perfect', a naturalising of crisis as benignly fatalistic as the conclusion which the vicar draws from the pageant, that 'We act different parts; but are the same' (174, 192). None of these answers is presented as definitive, only as a fragment of public opinion overheard, as if by a Mass-Observer of 1939 'approaching the study of Britons rather as if they were birds, emphasizing seen behaviour or overheard conversations'.[50]

1922 REVISITED

Having lost her London residences in the Blitz, and hearing nightly the planes passing over her house in vulnerable Sussex, Woolf knew at first hand that modernist homelessness could become more than a metaphor. The ruining of the home might come, if not from Nazi bombs, from the accelerated social change that would follow a military victory. This is perhaps why *Between the Acts* is so obsessively ethnographic, with a long-range view of history that looks as far back as the Domesday Book and the last invasion of 'English' soil. As with the middlebrow pastoral that achieved a wartime apotheosis in *Mrs Miniver*, there are excruciating analogues for Woolf's ethnographic historiography.[51] These include the atrocious local pageants that Jed Esty has described so entertainingly (the Romans arrive at Colchester, 'first attracted by your delicious bivalves'),[52] as well as cinematic efforts like David MacDonald's contemporary film *This England* (1941), which opens with a voiceover explaining why 'The story of Rookeby's farm and the village of Clevely is the story of them all'. Like a pageant, *This England* uses the same actors over and over again to represent England's unbroken continuity with 'her' heroic past: scenes from the Norman Conquest, the Spanish Armada, the Napoleonic Wars, and so on. 'The keynote is "our glorious heritage"', Orwell summarised in his film column in the socialist weekly *Time and Tide*:

and as in nearly all patriotic films and literature, the implication all along is that England is an agricultural country and that its inhabitants, millions of whom would not know the difference between a turnip and a broccoli if they saw them growing in a field, derive their patriotism from a passionate love of the English soil.

Are such films good for morale? They may be, it is a fact that many of the events which the jingo history-books make the most noise about are things to be proud of ... And yet ... would it not be better to say a little more about the things that happen between the high-spots?[53]

Obliquely, Orwell's review of *This England* suggests the degree to which the ruralist *Between the Acts* participates in 'our glorious heritage', and the extent of Woolf's unease with it: stuffed full of references to the literary and historical high spots, but called *Between the Acts* strongly to signal the importance of what happens outside the 'jingo history-books'.

The pageant dashes through the canonical highlights of medieval, Elizabethan, Restoration and Victorian periods, while modernism is revisited in the novel's scenes beyond the pageant. Woolf herself was reflecting on the modernist project at the time; in a diary entry from two months before her suicide she remembers getting the typescript of *Ulysses*, recalling how Katherine Mansfield would read bits aloud alternately to ridicule and praise it, and describing how T. S. Eliot chattered raptly in Ottoline Morrell's salon about how no one would surpass Molly Bloom's final monologue. In January of 1941, Woolf looks back to modernism's annus mirabilis of 1922 and writes that 'This goes back to a pre-historic world'.[54] And *Between the Acts* closes in a more literally prehistoric world when, in an allusion to her revered Conrad, the novel ends 'in the heart of darkness, in the fields of night' (219), as if all the metaphysical desolation apprehended by the early modernists had finally been realised in Nazism's annihilating prospect; or as if the structural trauma of modernity could retrospectively be conflated with a single historical one.[55] Conrad's description, in *Heart of Darkness*, of London as formerly 'one of the dark places of the earth' finds other echoes in Second World War writing: 'Time might have gone back two thousand years', Evelyn Waugh wrote of the black-out, 'to the time when London was a stockaded cluster of huts down the river, and the streets through which they walked, empty sedge and swamp'.⁵⁶

This contemporary revisiting of modernism's founding conceits – above all, the idea that the progress of industrial modernity may be no more than a circular route back to the primeval swamp – suggests that the links between the high modernist *To the Lighthouse* and the late modernist *Between the Acts* go beyond their shared countryhouse setting. Haunted by the moment at which modern war will mean universal destruction, *Between the Acts* is as much a war elegy, however precipitate, as its predecessor. Even the famous vision of desuetude in *To the Lighthouse* re-materialises when the tortoiseshell butterflies of 'Time Passes' (which 'pattered their life out on the windowpane'⁵⁷) die once again in the library of Pointz Hall:

The fire greyed, then glowed, and the tortoiseshell butterfly beat on the lower pane of the window; beat, beat, beat; repeating that if no human being ever came, never, never, never, the books would be mouldy, the fire out and the tortoiseshell butterfly dead on the pane. (17)

Not an original figure for transience here, moths and butterflies appear routinely in Woolf's writing and nowhere more movingly than in the posthumously published 'The Death of the Moth', which uses a bomb-anxious idiom when it describes the moth's struggle to live as 'extraordinary efforts made by those tiny legs against an oncoming doom which could, had it chosen, have submerged an entire city, not merely a city, but masses of human beings'.⁵⁸ Prue and Andrew Ramsay and the moth all die, but narrators and others survive to record and mourn their loss. There are not these guarantees here: 'Empty, empty, empty; silent, silent, silent' is Woolf's non-description of Pointz Hall beyond the human and beyond rehabilitation (36).

All the humanistic individualising of high modernism's exploration of the private self has now given way to the determinism of fracture and difference: the 'scraps and fragments' or 'orts, scraps, and fragments' that keep returning in the course of the novel (39, 120, 122, 188); the artists 'who can't make, but only break; shiver into splinters the old vision; smash to atoms what was whole' (183). The diffuseness and iconoclasm of high modernist mimesis have become sinister, threatening and suicidal. Yet, even more frightening than these fractures is the indistinct or indistinguishable frontier: so much for the fluent crossing of boundaries that modernist writing once championed, 'a world in which the borders that separate us become permeable and sometimes disappear altogether'.[59] In *Between the Acts*, the inter-subjective procedures of high modernist narrative, as when the perspective oscillates between Bart and his grandson, animate strange monsters. The transgression of borders, the work of merging and connecting that Woolf celebrated when Mrs Ramsay or Mrs Dalloway did it, has dangerous connotations now because 'what's the channel, come to think of it, if they mean to invade us?' (199). The fuzzy effects of pacifist internationalism obliterate national specificities as surely as would the occupying totalitarian regime that it could do nothing to resist. Invasion remained a perpetual possibility in the last year of Woolf's life, and was believed imminent when the government did its blanket distribution in July 1940 of 'If the Invader Comes', the Ministry of Information's pamphlet of advice so phlegmatic ('stay put', 'use your common sense') that it almost belies the pamphlet's chilling title. The expected invasion might explain why spatial and territorial boundaries have become so desirable in *Between the Acts*, and why assimilation is imagined as a return to the swamp:

"Once there was no sea," said Mrs. Swithin. "No sea at all between us and the continent. I was reading that in a book this morning. There were rhododendrons in the Strand; and mammoths in Piccadilly." (29–30)

The 'aeroplanes in perfect formation like a flight of wild duck' now close the English Channel (193). A reversion to the original unity may be made forcibly by a Nazi occupation and bring a return to the desolate landscape of marshes and monsters that existed 'when the entire continent, not then, she understood, divided by a channel, was all one' (8).

And the novel from the outset makes the argument that prehistory and written history have conspired to unify Britain and continental Europe: 'From an aeroplane, he said, you could still see, plainly marked, the scars made by the Britons; by the Romans; by the Elizabethan manor house; and by the plough, when they ploughed the hill to grow wheat in the Napoleonic wars' (4). Here, the history of the relationship between the island and the continent is explicitly imagined as one of attempted invasion or successful conquest: the Roman occupation, the repulsion of the Spanish Armada and the aspirations of Napoleon to pan-European domination. From the aeroplane that will either produce the next vignette in a linear historical pageant or complete the historical cycle from swamp to civilization and back again, the 'scars' of all past struggles are visible on the quiet national landscape. It would be both sentimental and historically legitimate to point out that by the time this novel was drafted, the British Isles were in an extremely vulnerable position, only twenty-two miles or ten minutes' flying time from occupied Europe, and holding out against odds so dismal that the unremittingly propagandised American government could see no value in intervening. Woolf had written in *Three Guineas* that, 'as a woman I have no country. As a woman I want no country. As a woman my country is the whole world', but *Between the Acts* is closer than could have been thought possible to the familiar history of Their Finest Hour.[60]

CHAPTER 2

Rebecca West's anti-Bloomsbury group

> It is difficult, from the point of view of a small offshore island, to develop a sense of the integrity of Europe ... My grandfather's generation left these British islands only to fight in wars, wars which redrew the map of continental states but left the returning islanders lonely and injured and confirmed in their separateness.
> Hilary Mantel, 'No Passes or Documents are Needed' (2002).[1]

> How horrible, fantastic, incredible it is that we should be digging trenches and trying on gas masks here because of a quarrel in a far-away country between people of whom we know nothing.
> Neville Chamberlain, broadcasting on 27 September 1938.[2]

Hailed by *Time* as 'indisputably the world's No. 1 woman writer' when she appeared on its cover in 1947, Rebecca West is a surprisingly obscure figure compared to Woolf.[3] Closely involved with the suffragist *New Freewoman* before it became the modernist standard-bearer *The Egoist* (it was she who employed Ezra Pound), and a board member of the socialist journal *Time and Tide*, West had an interwar career with at least as much to say as Woolf's about the histories of radical cultural production in Britain. As a novelist and critic of modernist sympathies, in earlier years one of Ford Madox Ford's iconoclastic '*les jeunes*' and a famous name in left journalism, she had secured a formidable reputation by the time she published her mid-war and mid-career *Black Lamb and Grey Falcon: A Journey through Yugoslavia* (1941), a 1200-page essay on imperialism and its legacies in the Balkans.[4] Though West's suffragette beginnings and her interwar fiction and journalism have long attracted the attention of revisionist feminist scholars of modernism, critics have tellingly been less drawn to the political writing that began here and led to post-war work on war crimes and treason that was increasingly implicated in the anti-communism that estranged West from many of her own contemporaries on the left. If, as a declared anti-imperialist, socialist and feminist, West looks a perfect subject for a rethinking of modernist politics, there are important idiosyncrasies that make her an awkward fit for a straightforwardly recuperative agenda. Politically, she undertook advocacy for the primacy and inviolability of national sovereignty in years when the demystifying critique of the nation-state had hardened into left-liberal orthodoxy; creatively, she resurrected high modernist mythmaking to disavow the materialist cultural inheritance of her own progressive politics. This chapter describes how in *Black Lamb and Grey Falcon* West tried to rehabilitate nationality through the mythical method of the 1920s.

A JOURNEY THROUGH YUGOSLAVIA

The end of Chapter 1 showed how Woolf's tentative late rehabilitation of nationality emphasised an island history, conceived of European reunification as the most disastrous possible outcome of the war. In contrast, West's *Black Lamb and Grey Falcon* looked at the problem of endangered cultural identity from the other end of the continent to explain why Chamberlain's notorious 'people of whom we know nothing' might matter. Ending during the Blitz when 'there was nothing on earth to prevent the fall of England', the book details what a history of occupation has done to the Balkans by way of showing what it might mean for Britain to lose the war.[5] Its epigraph comes from the speech in *Henry V* where the (very) Welsh soldier Fluellen describes the similarities between one end of Europe and another, because 'I warrant you sall find, in the comparisons between Macedon and Monmouth, that the situations, look you, is both alike'.[6] What makes this an apt, but also a provocative, introduction to the book is its suggestion that war on the continent might force a robust national identification to grow into a more inclusive version of internationalism than had been available in the interwar years.

Although the interwar was a golden age for the travelogue as a distinctive genre, the book's diffident subtitle – 'a journey through Yugoslavia' – does not come close to classifying a book that ranges through European imperial history from the fall of Rome in the fourth century to the fall of France in 1940.[7] The principle structuring this mass of material is the binary of the book's title, two Serb myths that West encounters late in her journey when she gets to culturally overloaded sites in Macedonia and Kosovo. The 'black lamb' is derived from an annual event at which a lamb gets ritually slaughtered to procure the fertility of the community's women. What might have been occasion for primitivist rapture – a ritual of redemptive and primeval character – turns out to be both grotesque and familiar: 'a huge and dirty lie ... a penny-in-the-slot machine of idiot character. If one drops in a piece of suffering, a blessing pops out at once ... All our Western thought is founded on this repulsive pretence that pain is the proper price of any good thing'.[8] The accepted version of the Crucifixion becomes a death-driven con: someone tried to teach people how to live humanely on earth and 'we found nothing better to do with this passport to deliverance than destroy him' (827). Her use of the second myth in the book's title is similarly heretical. A Serbian epic poem that purports to explain why the Serbs fell to the Ottoman Empire in 1389 has the Serb leader, Tsar Lazar, visited on the eve of battle by a grey falcon, or the prophet Elijah in disguise. Offered the choice between winning and losing the battle, between an earthly kingdom and a heavenly kingdom, the Tsar Lazar chooses the latter. Again, the explanatory myth legitimises suffering and privileges the redeeming power of sacrifice, and again West engages in an act of debunking revisionism when she wonders if the Tsar might have done better than to consign the Serbs to 500 years of subjection in order to procure his personal salvation.

Black Lamb's religious framework is of immediate significance in the book's historical context because it transgresses an important frontier separating left and rightwing thinking between the wars, when writers' religious beliefs were politicised in ways that are unique to the period. Even if her rendering of the sacrificial myths of black lamb and grey falcon is theologically wayward, West was still more than culturally Christian, and attributes her enthusiasm for the Balkans to what she thinks of as its inhabitants' subscription to 'the only theory that renders the death of the individual not a source of intolerable grief ... to die, and to know a meaning in death, is a better destiny than to be saved from dying' (254). In the minds of West's leftwing colleagues, however, Christian allegiances were closely identified with reactionary politics, and, if the association was not exactly unfounded, it could be damningly overstated. Among the interwar spate of conversions from agnosticism to Roman and Anglo-Catholicism, T. S. Eliot's is probably the best known, and his tendency to turn the Church of England into a club for the intellectual aristocracy, along with the infamous self-advertisement linking Catholicism, Royalism and Classicism, had given Orwell reason to surmise that Eliot 'would probably choose Fascism' over 'some more democratic form of Socialism'.[9]

By the time Orwell wrote this in 1940, associations between political and religious conversion were determined by the recent Spanish Civil War, which had accumulated a religious dimension when the Church backed Franco against the anti-clerical and socialist Republic. Even before Spain, Eliot had complained that the critic with religious (rather than what he termed 'liberal-minded') views was being libelled as 'either a mediaevalist, wishful only to set back the clock, or else a fascist, and probably both', but that the Spanish Civil War only hardened the identification of religious feeling with reactionary politics is most explicitly registered in Cyril Connolly's *Enemies of Promise* (1938), a forensic survey of his and his generation's non-achievement.[10] Among the causes and symptoms of failure, Connolly included 'people of exceptional sensibility, poetically minded writers for whom the ugliness of materialism is a source of horror ... hiding under the skirts of one of the great reactionary political forces of the world ... the poet drawn to the confessional and the smell of incense finds himself defending the garrotte and Franco's Moors'.[11] In West's writing, however, spiritual commitment gets aligned with progressive radicalism in ways that complicate the left/right binary that Orwell and Connolly recall. In the starkly unlikely context of an early essay on Lloyd George, for instance, West wrote that Jesus was 'so practical a politician that he died on the cross': by implication, the levelling social gestures of the Chancellor have fallen far short of his radical promises.[12]

Like other socialists, but unlike many declared Christians among her acquaintances, West had 'taken sides' with the secular socialist republic in the famous *Left Review* survey which asked the intellectuals of 1937 'Are you for, or against, the legal Government and the People of Republican Spain? Are you for, or against, Franco and Fascism? For it is impossible any longer to take no side'.[13] Eliot, for instance, responded with a declaration of neutrality, while the newly Catholic Evelyn Waugh was somewhat ambiguously pro-Franco. In contrast, West's reply expressed her support for the republic through a recondite comparison between fascism and the reforms of the emperor Diocletian, which 'made many people temporarily happy, but failed in the end and added greatly to human misery'.[14] This reading of the present through historical precedent strongly anticipates the recursiveness of *Black Lamb*, and it goes with the Yugoslavian territory that the implication of religious values in political activism proves every bit as dangerous as it had in Spain. West explains early in the book that the crucial divisions between Croats (Roman Catholics) and Serbs (members of the Serbian Orthodox Church) are religious rather than territorial (a Serb could be Croatian, a Croat live in Serbia); nonetheless *Black Lamb* tends rhetorically to impose a more forceful correlation between region and religion because the religious specificity of Yugoslavia's different constituents lets West describe the wrecked cultures that empires leave behind them: the Catholic Austro-Hungarian Empire in Croatia, and the Muslim Ottoman Empire in Bosnia. The outcome is unequivocally partisan because the Serbian Orthodox Church can be presented as a liberationist outfit rather than the cultural residue of defunct empires.

This bias is obviously disconcerting given the events that intervene between West's writing and a modern reading (the break up of Yugoslavia likely created the market for the single-volume 1993 paperback that I am using here). To see European Muslims, as in Bosnia, as simply the legacy of empire makes for a racist essentialism; the belief that, for example, 'there could be no two races more antipathetic than the Slavs, with their infinite capacity for inquiry and speculation, and the Turks, who had no word in their language to express the idea of being interested in anything' (302). But the reason Muslim Bosnia interests West so much is that it allows her to represent imperialism as a cultural catastrophe for both the coloniser and the colonised; for West to show that Bosnia is depressed and depressing contributes to the book's central argument that 'the corpses of empires ... stink as nothing else' (280), a claim with as much bearing on the moribund British Empire as on any other, as I will show later. In an episode that illuminates West's attitude to post-imperial Ottoman culture, she visits a former Pasha's house in Herzegovina now kept as a kitschy theme park: fake concubines in a pretend harem affect to produce Turkish embroidery under the management of a lecherous conman masquerading as a Pasha. West notes with disgust that the supposed concubines wear the handkerchiefs of Christian Slavs rather than the customary veils of Muslim women and that they produce what she considers deracinated trash rather than the 'delicious' handicrafts of the Turks (278). This heritage-industry travesty of Islamic culture in its post-imperial context appals her as much as the cultural erosion of old Bosnia by the Turkish occupiers, 'pitiful in itself, and it was pitiful in its implications, if one thought of the fair-mannered and decent Moslem men and women in Trebinye and all over Yugoslavia ... dead and buried in their lifetime, coffined in the shell of a perished empire, whose ways these poor wretches were aping and defiling' (279).

West's privileging of cultural 'authenticity' might recall a familiar modernist romance with ethnography (D. H. Lawrence's travels would offer one canonical analogue), but the book acquires harder edges when West makes the cultural question secondary to the problem of unequal political power that it signals. She rather sniffily acknowledges her Islamophobia when she writes that her unease with the Bosnians who converted under Ottoman rule is that 'one sees them with a different eye when they are in a majority and could put at a disadvantage all those not of their kind' (315). Their privilege, however, is at an end: West records a state visit of Turkish officials to Bosnia, and, taking out their old Ottoman flags to welcome co-religionists from the former colonial power, the crowd of Bosnian Muslims is unprepared for the fact that post-imperial Turkey is a secular state. West describes the embarrassment with which the Westernised Turkish functionaries look on the crowds of people wearing the religious clothing outlawed in post-imperial Turkey; she imagines that to them this must seem a 'monstrous retrograde profusion of fezes and veils' (317). West embarks on one of the elaborate analogies that appear all through the book whereby imperial relations are imagined as sexual ones; in a characteristic late modernist equation of public and private experience, she writes that it is as if an elderly woman called out for her old lover and was answered by his son, who sees her only as 'a shameful passage in his family history'; witnessing which, West concludes, 'none of us would be able to withhold our pity' (318). History, then, has rendered irrelevant the privileges that came with conversion to the imperial religion, and where political inequalities have already been levelled West's attitude to cultural hybridity is vastly different. An appreciative account of the ethnically mixed city of Sarajevo describes how 'They greet delight here with unreluctant and sturdy appreciation ... they will let no drop of pleasure run to waste ... This tradition of tranquil sensuality is of Moslem origin, and is perhaps still strongest among Moslems, but also on Jewish and Christian faces can there be recognized this steady light ... an instruction necessary for the mastery of life' (298–9). This is only a short extract from an extended paean to the positive influence of Muslim culture in Bosnia. The racialised essentialism endures – Muslims are like this, Jews and Christians like that – but this passage about the long-term effects of the ancient cultural encounter is unqualifiedly celebratory of happy mixture.

What has happened in Sarajevo to provoke a positive version of the Ottoman legacy? Here she introduces new villains, the imperial rulers who made Sarajevo notorious as the place where the last world war had begun. In West's version of events, the Habsburgs are brutish and bloated oppressors who got their comeuppance at the hands of Gavrilo Princip. In West's legitimising psycho-biographical account of the 1914 *attentat*, the hunter is deservedly hunted: nationalists close in on Franz Ferdinand as his battues had cornered the thousands of animals artificially reared to satisfy his aristocratic bloodlust. West pits Islamic and Habsburg cultures against each other at the start of the Archduke's lethal visit to Sarajevo when Franz Ferdinand's morganatic wife goes to meet women from the main Muslim families of the city 'in order that she might condescendingly admire their costumes and manners, as is the habit of barbarians who have conquered an ancient culture' (345). Although West is polemically inverting the imperialist rhetoric of the civilised and the savage so that the sophisticated Catholic Viennese become 'barbarians' and the subjugated Bosnian Muslims representative of 'culture', there is something less predictably ironic about her appeal to the legitimacy of an 'ancient culture'. Seen alongside the arrogant Habsburgs, Muslim Bosnia gets promoted to the status of the authentically antique.

The idea of what it means to be an 'ancient culture' is thoroughly destabilised by this tactic: hardly newcomers on the Central and Eastern European scene, the Habsburgs become new-money Eurotrash gloating over their spoils. What prompts this surprise pro-Islamic propaganda is the book's wartime context: even if the Great War wiped out the Ottoman and Austro-Hungarian Empires, imperial Vienna has, for West, achieved a dangerous afterlife. In a contemporary letter, she described Austria as 'the nastiest of the old European powers, and in her present phase very willing to hold the bag for Nazi Germany', and throughout *Black Lamb* she conflates dead imperial Vienna and 1930s Berlin so that the illegal and inadequately protested *Anschluss* of 1938 is imagined not as a hostile takeover but as a reuniting of old partners in crime.[15] On this neatly symmetrical model – historically wobbly but imaginatively satisfying – Nazism is the renaissance of Habsburg hegemony by new means: 'Vienna is speaking again, through Hitler ... a message of self-infatuation and a quiver of hatreds for all but the chosen Teutonic people' (488); 'Hitler is not a German but an Austrian, and nothing he has brought to post-war Germany had not its existence in pre-war Austria' (1106); 'Hitler is simply an exporter of Austrian goods' (1107). It speaks of the book's own time that the Habsburgs come off much worse than the Ottoman Empire (against what West's noticeable religious prejudices would suggest), but Turkish power is defunct while Austria is a Nazi partner and this implicit contrast makes for the book's most productive insecurity. That is, if West wants to denounce what the Ottoman Empire did to Bosnian culture, she sees in fascist ideology the ugly reflection of her own modernist nostalgia for cultural 'purity': seen through the racist lens of 'the chosen Teutonic people', the mongrel formation of post-imperial Yugoslavia turns out to be a tremendous virtue after all. The book even ends with what would now be called the ethnic cleansing of multicultural Skoplje, then under Axis occupation, because the 'mixed population of such towns ... has irritated the racial purism of the Germans' (1148).

The haunting historical irony of that example suggests some of the problems with West's marked pro-Serb partisanship. Increasingly championing what sounds an inviting pluralism in a recent composite of a country, the book is forced to confront the tensions that attend it. Demands for federalisation are lengthily discussed in the section of the book where West describes Croatia as the region subject to the worst tyrannies of Habsburg exploitation, and where she might well have focused her anti-imperial outrage. The sticking point is Croatian grievances about Serbian predominance within Yugoslavia. In a clunky dialogue between a Croat federalist and a Serb functionary of the Yugoslavian state, West has the Croat expose the bogus liberationism of the Serb hierarchy by caricaturing it as the proposal that 'we are to let Serbs torture us Croats, because under Yugoslavia we are not to be tortured by the Italians and Hungarians' (88). This friction between West's championing of integrated nationality against transnational totalitarian violence and her knowledge that the appeal to national unity sanctions internal injustices makes for an absolute impasse in the book's valorising of national identification. West was not entirely willing to censor the hatred engendered by Serb hegemony, but, writing under the threat of Nazi encroachment, she had no reason to be confident that units smaller than Yugoslavia had a fighting chance of surviving 'modern conditions [that] make the independence of a small nation a bad joke' (531).

'I SPOKE OF YUGOSLAVIA TO BLOOMSBURY INTELLECTUALS'

From where West was standing, there was nothing inevitable about the break up of the post-Versailles successor states, which may be why she alludes in the book to her Anglo-Scottish ancestry since it suggested a model close to home for how unequal partners might transcend their differences in order to preserve strategic unity despite a terrible historical record. Denunciations of the imperialist strategy of divide and rule – 'that counsel of Hell' (97), 'that evil precept' (181), 'the fiendish rule' (642) – are a leitmotif of *Black Lamb and Grey Falcon*. Since the book describes across more than a thousand pages imperial efforts to keep neighbouring ethnic groups politically separate and universally oppressed, the obvious implication is that national sovereignty so hard earned ought not to be lightly surrendered; tactical unity is 'not a predestined harmony', but 'a necessity' (494). The Second World War was a high point of Scottish unionist feeling, and the reason why a British book addressed to America in 1941 (it was published in Britain the following year) should place such a premium on national unity is virtually self-evident: a country on the verge on implosion would be a poor investment for external shoring up. Still, it is noticeable that West should be trying to reclaim rhetoric of national integrity that, because it sanctioned internal suppressions, she knew could serve less than progressive ends.

This was a conscious compromise that would set her at odds with her most obvious allies, the stalwart readership of *Time and Tide* and *The New Statesman*, for whom she had always written. As Woolf's career makes plain, the liberal left had good reason to be suspicious of appeals to the 'national' after the Great War, and this is most obviously why speaking 'of Yugoslavia to Bloomsbury intellectuals' would be a waste of time (1101). As shorthand for a rarefied leftish liberalism, Bloomsbury provided an easy target for political writers of the 1930s, but West's critical address is more than an attack on *rentier* radicalism. Another contemporary Scottish woman author of serious political stature offers a useful contrast here to West's project and its politics: Naomi Mitchison's *Vienna Diary* (1934) is secondarily interesting as an instance of the 1930s genre of plain-speaking itinerant political writing (Orwell's *Homage to Catalonia* is probably the most canonical example) from which *Black Lamb* stylistically departs. *Vienna Diary*, too, makes snide remarks about theoretical left politics, as when Mitchison, writing of her attempt to smuggle money to the beleaguered Austrian Socialists, describes her cadre as 'like Bloomsbury, if it were possible to imagine a Bloomsbury in which it was really brave or dangerous to be a Communist'.[16] Mitchison sees Bloomsbury as only playing politics, a low-risk leftism unlike (the reader is to infer) her own committed activism.

In telling contrast, West takes Bloomsbury absolutely seriously as the measure of her compromised principles. The journey through Yugoslavia has proved a turning point in her relationship with the left, who 'want to be right, not to do right. They feel no obligation to be part of the main tide of life, and if that meant any degree of pollution they would prefer to divert themselves from it, and form a standing pool of purity' (912). Giving the game away by declaring herself carried by the 'polluted' tide, West argues nonetheless that the left has been seduced into a paradoxical, self-defeating insularity by its own seeming internationalism.

'Bloomsbury intellectuals, themselves freethinking' were ignorant about why the integrity of a small country should command their support:

> The left wing, especially, was sharply critical of the new states and all that they did. This was inconsistent in those who believed, often to a point far beyond the practical, that the individual must be free to determine his own destiny, and it was partly due to a theory ... that nationalism is always anti-democratic and aggressive, and that internationalism is always liberal and pacific. Yet nationalism is simply the determination of a people to cultivate its own soul, to follow the customs bequeathed to it by its ancestors, to develop its traditions according to its own instincts. It is the national equivalent of the individual's determination not to be a slave. The fulfilment of both those determinations is essentially a part of the left programme. (1100–1)

And this is why West despairs of talking about Yugoslavia to Bloomsbury intellectuals: even if 1930s commentators generalised spitefully about 'Bloomsbury', all the people who have been identified with the Bloomsbury group could agree wholeheartedly on the pernicious nature of national identification and its incompatibility with progressive politics.

Examples are easily come by: Forster's celebrated declaration that he would rather betray his country than a friend is characteristic of the Bloomsbury rejection of what Woolf called 'unreal loyalties' to the state.[17] As I have tried to show, her comments in 1938 were nowhere near her final position, but Woolf's response to the appeasement policy in its last agonies does not suggest a profound engagement with the problem of national sovereignty that it had brought into the foreground. Unlike the more colourful Yugoslavia, whose autocratic king had been assassinated in 1934, and whose ethnic divisions were already notorious, Czechoslovakia was the poster child for the post-war Peace: domestically liberal, a model citizen of the League of Nations, and by 1938 the only European democracy east of the Rhine; now its British and French allies were handing it over to Nazi Germany. Woolf's summary of the European scene:

> Chamberlain flying today to Gotesberg (?). A strong opposition has risen. Eden, Churchill & the LP [Labour Party] all denounce serving C. S. [Czechoslovakia] on the altar & bidding it commit suicide. C. S. very dignified and tragic. Everyone calling everyone else a pick pocket. The prospect of another glissade after a minor stop into abyss. All Europe in Hitler's keeping. What'll he gobble next? Thats [*sic*] the summary of us in Sussex.[18]

That Woolf was not much of an internationalist is clear in the reluctant concessions to national feeling that she had made at the time; it took an inward movement of the most unreflectively parochial kind for Woolf to propose that this 'pure, if irrational, emotion' of patriotism should make a woman 'give to England first what she desires of peace and freedom for the whole world'.[19] It is no wonder that West, like Woolf herself, should have found the Bloomsbury version of the nation inadequate by the time the war came around: for refusing to differentiate between imperialist nationalisms and the nationalities emerging out of imperial subjection, or between nations that aspired to pan-continental domination and nations that aspired to survive their incursions.

West's despairing comment that left-liberal intellectuals 'use the words 'nationalism' and 'imperialism' as if they meant the same thing' points to both the virtues and the limitations of the Bloomsbury rejection of nationality (1101). On the one hand, to reject British nationality is to reject the seemingly interminable violence of the British Empire; on the other, a degree of insularity underwrites the assumption that all nations manage their affairs in the same invulnerable and expansionist way as your own. The Anglocentric underpinnings of Bloomsbury anti-nationalism are plain in the work of the 'Bloomsbury intellectual' whom West would have had predominantly in mind when she was writing *Black Lamb and Grey Falcon*, John Maynard Keynes. Famously, Keynes had written *The Economic Consequences of the Peace* (1919) after leaving the Paris Peace Conference in disgust, and what remains most memorable about Keynes's book is its depiction of a vindictive and dangerous peace treaty. Keynes claimed to be simply showing, as an economic specialist, why the Treaty of Versailles would not be workable, but he gave an example that would have been close to West's heart when, discussing the Allies' inflated reparations demands, he serenely described how 'The losses of Serbia, although from a human point of view her sufferings were the greatest of all, are not measured *pecuniarily* by very great figures, on account of her low economic development'.[20]

Marking his distance from the chauvinists he abandoned in Paris, Keynes begins the book proclaiming that his time at the peace conference had made this Englishman 'a European in his cares and outlook'.[21] In retrospect, it is clear enough that compared to contemporaries with more extensively worked-out Europeanist sympathies, Keynes is not very interested in Europeans who are neither English nor German. One of the book's most edifying blind spots is its perfunctory dismissal of French fears about aggressive German expansionism, despite how badly France had come off against Germany in 1870 and 1914; edifying, I mean, because the belief that historical events should have no bearing on the present is one of the starkest differences between Keynes and West (who, in *Black Lamb*, wrote two volumes on why they do). The French Prime Minister foolishly believed that 'Nations are real things', and this, Keynes loftily summarised, 'is the policy of an old man, whose most vivid impressions and most lively imagination are of the past and not of the future'.[22] Related to this rejection of nationality, but surely even less surprising for West, was Keynes's chauvinism about the countries that had emerged as a result of the Peace Conference's least obviously self-interested aspiration, Woodrow Wilson's insistence on national self-determination for people formerly under the rule of the defunct great powers. Poland, for instance, would turn out to be 'an economic impossibility with no industry but Jew-baiting', while the other new European countries are dismissed *en bloc* as 'greedy, jealous, immature, and economically incomplete nationalist States'.[23]

The Anglo-American contingent in Paris should have looked forward to economics and not backwards to the older issue of nationality, Keynes argued, because 'the problems which claimed their attention were not political or territorial'.[24] Writing in the Second World War, the French commentator Etienne Mantoux took particular issue, pointedly expressed as a jab at Bloomsbury's easy irreverence, with the cruelty of Keynes's attack on Wilson's outdated emphasis on national sovereignty for Habsburg chattels: 'An eminent statesman – almost an eminent Victorian – had been gloriously and decisively debunked'.[25] Keynes's belief that nations and frontiers were passé would have amounted for West to a form of thoughtless British privilege. In a 1942 polemic in *Time and Tide* she criticised on these grounds the work of E. H. Carr, another Paris Peace Conference delegate and, like Keynes, a forceful critic of Wilsonian self-determination.[26] Carr may well write 'of self-determination and all its works with a peculiar whinnying scorn which suggests that it is a ridiculous invention of the doctrinaires', but the Great War had left millions of Europeans citizens of nowhere when 'the collapse of the State which had previously incorporated them left them a Stateless nation, and they had perforce to become a nation-State or sink into anarchy'.[27] The idea that national self-determination is a good thing is the point from which *Black Lamb and Grey Falcon* begins, and West resurrects this apparently antiquated issue of national sovereignty in order to advance a tentatively post-colonial sensibility when she defends national identification as 'an effort by a people to rebuild its character when an imperialist power has worked hard to destroy it' (843). As A. J. P. Taylor noted in his history of the origins of the Second World War, many liberals thought the post-Versailles states 'reactionary, militaristic, economically backward';[28] and there was surely nothing unusual about a statesman of Keynes's generation favouring traditional Anglo-Saxon *Macht* over the primitive Slavic east. Attributing childlike silliness ('greedy, jealous, immature') to the disenfranchised is the old trick of presenting colonised natives as unfit to manage their own affairs, and, entirely at odds with his pleas for Europeanist magnanimity, Keynes saw no difficulty in dismissing the new states in the timeworn epithets of the imperial apologist. 'But it matters', West writes at the beginning of her journey to the Balkans, 'what happened to these people matters a great deal' (57).

'THE PEOPLE WE SHOULD HAVE BEEN SEEN DEAD WITH'

It almost goes without saying that *The Economic Consequences of the Peace* would have looked different from the perspective of the early 1940s; that, as Mantoux sardonically put it, 'the legend of the Carthaginian Peace has, of late, worn a little thin'.[29] Mantoux's *The Carthaginian Peace, or The Economic Consequences of Mr Keynes* was published after his death in action in 1944, and many of his arguments overlap with West's. Above all, both identified 'the vehement and indiscriminate abuse' for Versailles as partly the discreditable product of western chauvinism:

The peace that brought liberation to millions did not bring the millennium. So to the many other millions who, free as they were already, could not understand the full meaning of this liberation because they could not experience it, it came as a sharp disappointment – disappointment being probably sharpest among those who had suffered least, for it was they who were expecting most.[30]

West used a more extravagant phraseology in support of this argument when she described how 'the treaties of Versailles and Trianon and St. Germain had set the small peoples free ... Finland, Estonia, Latvia, Czechoslovakia, and Yugoslavia, they were all like young men stretching themselves at the open window in the early morning after long sleep' (1100). And, in her attack on 'the mood of lazy and cynical self-criticism which has afflicted the powers that were apparently victorious in 1918' (365), West anticipates Mantoux's indictment of an Anglo-French culture of 'Meaculpism' that refused to take notice even when Hitler came to power on the back of Germany's victimisation with 'invective ... like some ghastly echo from *The Economic Consequences of the Peace*'.[31]

Another important record of the Paris Conference, Harold Nicolson's *Peacemaking 1919* was typical of what, after Keynes's first brave protest, quickly became the orthodox line that Versailles was a mean-spirited shambles (although that Nicolson should say so in 1933 has its own historical irony). However, when Nicolson reissued *Peacemaking* during the war, it acquired a preface that showed him ostensibly endorsing his earlier position, but all the while using a thoroughly un-Keynesian turn of thought in describing the need to 'eliminate from the German body this apparently endemic disease' of warmongering.[32] A diplomat, journalist and writer, Nicolson was also a political shape-shifter – the former Mosleyite who spent the war years as a Member of Parliament for the centre-left National Labour Party – and that makes him a useful barometer for highbrow left-liberal political opinion. The war evidently made it socially okay to cast doubt on the progressive optimism of the Keynesian assumptions, and, if I would not want to suggest that *Black Lamb* is emblematic of a rightward swing during the Second World War, the right-left lines were certainly starting to look blurrier than they had just a couple of years earlier. If the leftwing sounds surprisingly rightwing, the rightwing was sounding surprisingly liberal: the official position of even the Tory-led coalition was that Britain was at war with 'Hitlerism' or 'Hitlerite' Germany, and not with the Germans (the near-septuagenarian Churchill was attacked for sporadic lapses into the retro, comprehensive 'Huns').

By the time West published her book, it was a wartime commonplace that there were 'Two Germanies': the Nazi regime and the German people awaiting liberation from it. The phrase is taken from a 1940 article in the BBC magazine *The Listener* (the wireless was the defining medium of the Second World War), and the BBC got itself badly tangled in the benign doublethink that the idea of 'two Germanies' encodes when it banned the work of West's old friend Noël Coward.[33] A favourite anthem of Churchill himself, Coward's 'Don't Let's Be Beastly to the Germans' (1943) travestied the re-emergent Keynesian line:

> For many years –
> They've been in floods of tears
> Because the poor little dears
> Have been so wronged and only longed
> To cheat the world,
> Deplete the world
> And beat
> The world to blazes.
> This is the moment when we ought to sing their praises.[34]

Coward's song sends up the liberal softies and their buoyant platitudes that Nazism had no popular support ('It was just those nasty Nazis who persuaded them to fight') and that a richly cultured nation like Germany could never be as bad as all that ('their Beethoven and Bach are really far worse than their bite'); its satirical target was what Coward saw as an ineffectual meliorism colluding with Nazi violence by euphemising war guilt into invisibility: 'Let's be sweet to them – / And day by day repeat to them / That 'sterilization' simply isn't done'.[35] Noël Coward's song is only, if at all, remembered for the bizarre BBC ban imposed when a humourless censor thought it pro-Nazi, but the German establishment had clearly got the joke when they put Coward on the Gestapo's liquidation blacklist. Coward and West found a place there along with an old friend who had become literally synonymous with beastliness to the Germans: 'Vansittartism'. 'My dear', West wrote to Coward when the blacklist was discovered, 'the people we should have been seen dead with!'[36]

Their mutual friend Lord Vansittart was a diplomat, screenwriter, playwright and poet, but best known for his argument that only wishful thinking could make Nazism appear an aberration. By the mid-1930s he had been arguing that the Nazis were publicly and popularly rearming for Germany's fifth aggressive war in seventy-five years, 'And many people were angrier with me for saying it than with the Germans for doing it'.[37] In a contemporary article, Orwell noted with mixed feelings that Vansittart's pamphlet *Black Record: Germans Past and Present* (1941) 'sold like hot cakes'.[38] *Black Record* was based on a series of broadcasts on German militarism that Vansittart had delivered on the BBC at the end of 1940, and the ensuing controversy forced his retirement from the Civil Service. That Vansittart should have been vilified for being anti-German in the middle of a war that was acknowledged to have already killed over 14,000 British civilians reflects bafflingly well on the integrity of public debate in Britain, but Vansittart was by then something of an embarrassment – to the right, who had pursued appeasement; to the left, who did not want this Tory anti-fascist as an ally.[39]

That said, the left/right binary of 'writers taking sides' is not adequate to the complexity of a period in which jingo invective was off-limits even to rightwing thinkers, and when liberal relativism along the lines of who-are-we-to-condemn-Nazism had so successfully advanced the appeasement agenda. It is a salutary exercise to scratch the surface of the 1930s left to expose some the political contradictions within which late modernists were operating. However deceptive it finally turned out to be, the seeming straightforwardness of the Spanish Civil War – socialism against fascism; progress against reaction – must have come as a relief in a decade that was politically about as chaotic as it could be. One historian tracing the history of appeasement through the 1930s press finds the exemplarily progressive *New Statesman* 'meticulously inconsistent and confused' for most of the decade, describing how a single issue might carry articles 'variously and clamorously espousing British isolationism, pacifism, positive appeasement and military resistance to the aggressor states'.[40] The political uncertainty is typified by the now-forgotten public figures of the period. Among those who have worn particularly badly is the then-famous journalist and newspaper editor Hamilton Fyfe, whose wartime *The Illusion of National Character* (1940) starts off with a faultlessly liberal argument against nationalism which subsequently turns into an anti-Semitic rant: 'foolish and criminal' though anti-Semitism may be, 'there is no denying they have in large degree invited it ... Even when they are well treated, they make a grievance of it'; 'As an object-lesson in the unhappy consequences of deliberately forming and perpetuating a "national character" the Jews are Exhibit Number One'.[41] (For Fyfe, salvation from nationalism resides in the Soviet Union, whose implausible virtues under Stalin include 'government by and for the people', 'unfettered play of mind' and so on.[42]) Or, towards the other end of the political spectrum, there is the famous pacifism of Dean Inge, who from here looks confoundingly unpleasant: on Czechoslovakia ('dragged into war for a ramshackle republic, not twenty years old'); on Danzig ('which the Germans claim, reasonably enough, for the Reich'); on the origins of the war ('Jewish influence in the Press is being used against an understanding with Germany'); on Churchill ('he is not telling the truth. I do not see how we can win the war').[43] These apercus from Dean Inge come from a sympathetic biography by a fellow clergyman, who goes on to describe the Dean's hopes in the spring of 1942 for a settlement with Hitler.

While there were undoubtedly many bien pensant humanists, uncompromised by admiration for the Soviet Union or suspicions about 'Jewish influence', among the eleven million British people who signed the mid-1930s Peace Ballot to register their rejection of war and support for collective security, by the time the war came around even this high-minded enterprise looked like an extraordinary miscalculation of the continental situation. One contemporary commentator joked darkly that 'they might have voted that they were opposed to misery and want, opposed to death even, and in favour of collective happiness, collective prosperity, collective deathlessness'.[44] West made the same point about the Peace Pledge Union when she added her own question to theirs: 'Do you believe that you are going to abolish cancer if you get 100,000 people to sign a pledge that they do not intend to have cancer?'[45] Vansittart less ironically remonstrated that the Peace Ballot was 'a free excursion into the inane' because it had made an international declaration while Germany was known to be rearming that the British electorate would not support military intervention.[46] Himself soon to be discredited, Chamberlain had Vansittart moved from his influential position as Permanent Under-Secretary of State for Foreign Affairs in 1938 because, Chamberlain said, 'his instincts were all against my policy'.[47] The attacks made on Vansittart reflect the profound unease provoked by his strident anti-appeasement views; if the Conservative Chamberlain sacked him for refusing to support appeasement, it gives a sense of Vansittart's equally dire standing with the left that the *New Statesman* reviewed his *Black Record* under the uncompromising headline 'Evil Propaganda'.[48]

West broke with her own side on this issue. Writing just before the full extent of Nazi war crimes was acknowledged, she speculated satirically on the unease with which outright denunciations of the German regime were met. Like Coward, she wondered if there were self-flattering and classist aspects to the prevailing meliorism: 'Isn't there something rather coarse, rather too forthright, in saying that what the Germans have done is flatly abominable?'

That is the emotion which is suggested to them by the pro-Nazi propagandist who always puts it to the audience that there is a subtler way of regarding the evidence in question, a way that will testify to superior culture and wisdom. The emotion does not last long. A normal hard-headed audience realizes soon enough that there is no subtle way of regarding the dispatch of innocent people in cattle-trucks to starve on the frozen wastes of Lublin (where at this present moment they are awaiting winter as the descent into hell).[49]

Vansittart had been railing as early as 1940 against 'people here who, in smug insularity, refuse to credit, or ever to hear, these horrors ... The Channel has screened the modern Pharisees from agonies'.[50] The real infamy of *Black Record* derived from an allusion to Tacitus on the barbarity of the 'Germans', and nothing could have felt less in tune with what had become the received account of the war's causes than Vansittart's potentially mythmaking version of them. Even the absent W. H. Auden had taken a pre-emptive pot shot at foundationalist assumptions in 'September 1, 1939' when he concluded that 'I and the public know / What all schoolchildren learn, / Those to whom evil is done / Do evil in return'.[51] Auden's anti-essentialist explanation exemplifies the vulgarised Keynesian causality that Vansittart went full blast against. Even if the directives of Versailles were stone dead by the mid-1930s, it must still have been routine to invoke the victimisation of Germany when the centre-right *Daily Telegraph* decided to serialise Lloyd George's history of the peace in the summer of 1938. This would have been the only conceivable way for the arguments in his self-exculpatory *The Truth about the Peace Treaty* to find a mainstream audience.[52] Nearly a thousand pages long and prohibitively boring, it could not be more different from Keynes's version of events – economical, polemical, colourful, nearly twenty years old.

Vansittart, too, had been at the Paris Peace Conference, and although his autobiography corroborates Keynes's feeling 'that we could not both cripple Germany and expect her to pay', he concluded that *Economic Consequences* 'deserves notice less for its contents than for its consequences'.[53] Taking a swing at intellectuals' amateur diplomacy, Vansittart rhetorically wonders in *Black Record* what the Treaty of Versailles had to do with the Nazi 'burning of books, and the assaults on the universities', and marvelled at the efforts made to forget that Germany had been the aggressor in 1914:

No country had ever so well deserved defeat or asked more loudly for retribution; but she got off with a fraction of the penalties that she would have imposed on the world had she won. How loud the Germans cried about reparations. 'Poor, poor Germans', said all the tender-hearts. And some added: 'Besides, the figures are too big to make sense'. Well, the figures are nothing compared with those that the poor, poor Germans have now enforced on the poor, poor French.[54]

Orwell thought that 'Vansittart, badly though he writes, is an able man with more background than most of his opponents'; certainly, he would have been sympathetic to the thrust of Vansittart's argument.[55] Mid-war, Orwell would also observe that 'In all the denunciations of Versailles I listened to during those years I don't think I ever once heard the question, "What would have happened if Germany had won?" even mentioned, let alone discussed', a selective understanding of the Treaty's origins and consequences which West describes in *Black Lamb* when she refers to 'the strange propaganda against the Treaty ... year in year out by ordinary English people, who had never read a line of it' (1122).[56] It is perhaps not surprising that writers so heterodox in their politics as West and Orwell should have hesitated to climb aboard the anti-Vansittart bandwagon when many of their old allies did. West's review of Vansittart's posthumously published autobiography is effusive about his 'natural gifts, acquired accomplishments, experience of affairs and grace.

Sometimes it all seemed much too good to be true. But it was the truth', and she makes mordant reference, too, to 'what Vansittartism was supposed to be', alluding to the opprobrium dogging Vansittart's career.[57] If *Black Record* is overblown, so too was its characterisation as a crypto-fascist polemic: 'there have been potential reformers in Germany, but they have always been a weak minority', Vansittart wrote, 'That does not necessarily mean that it is hopeless *ever* to expect them to be in the ascendant'.[58]

'THE MYTHICAL METHOD'

But just as Woolf's hesitant recuperation of nationality in *Between the Acts* complicates any polemical division between herself and West – between Bloomsbury idealism and West's political worldliness – it muddles the Keynes/Vansittart dichotomy that I have implied to record that the old interwar left was infuriating even Keynes once the war came along. A famous letter he wrote to his colleague Kingsley Martin at the *New Statesman* expressed his fury at the magazine disseminating what he considered a dangerously unthought-out pacifism. A month into the war, the letter complains that those who had been adamant about the need to stand up to fascism now 'remember that they are pacifists and write defeatist letters to your columns, leaving the defence of freedom and of civilisation to Colonel Blimp and the Old School Tie, for whom Three Cheers'.[59] It was the same pacifist voice, specifically that of George Bernard Shaw, which provoked even the famously benign J. B. Priestley to rage in the first issue of *Horizon* against those 'who applauded Leftish writers like myself when we said that Britain should make a stand against the Nazis, [but who] now revile us as warmongers because we believe in the stand that Britain is now making. Why? Can you disintegrate the Gestapo by passing a few resolutions in Hampstead?'[60] Since the Molotov-Ribbentrop pact of non-aggression signed in August 1939 had rendered this another imperialist war, hard left-wingers were bound not to support it, and the pact seems to mark a critical moment in West's attitudes towards communism. She had always been forthright in her attacks on the British left's tendency to ignore Soviet abuses of human rights – twenty years earlier, she had written that their apologetics about Bolshevik 'efficiency' evoked 'Tory Imperialism in its most stupid and brutal form'[61] – but the Nazi-Soviet pact confirmed her most pessimistic fears because it 'put an end to the pretence that there is any real difference between fascism and communism'.[62]

The challenge for West and those on the non-communist left who wanted to argue in support of the war as she did in *Black Lamb and Grey Falcon* was discriminating between a corrupt Britain and a more corrupt Germany. This motivates a good deal of special pleading in the rallying conclusion of *Black Lamb*:

> My civilization must not die. It need not die. My national faith is valid, as the Ottoman faith was not. I know that the English are as unhealthy as lepers compared with perfect health. They do not give themselves up to feeling or to work as they should, they lack readiness to sacrifice their individual rights for the sake of the corporate good, they do not bid the right welcome to the other man's soul. But they are on the side of life, they love justice, they hate violence, and they respect the truth. It is not always so when they deal with India or Burma: but that is not their fault, it is the fault of Empire, which makes a man own things outside his power to control. (1060–1)

This evasive passage is, to use West's own idiom, humbug, but *Black Lamb*'s symbolic historiography makes it possible: as Austro-Hungary is to the Greater Reich (bad and reborn), the Ottoman Empire is to the British Empire (bad but defunct). By the time this book was published, British imperial power was almost as dead as the Ottoman autocracy: the Statute of Westminster (1931) had formally ratified the legislative independence of Ireland, Canada, New Zealand, South Africa and Australia, and the jewel in the one-time imperial crown would gain self-determination in 1947. 'Miss West, as a rule, disapproves of empires', wrote the *TLS* reviewer, noting that 'the British Empire ... is hardly in this picture ... because the author considers that it has largely ceased to be an Empire'.[63] This was a perceptive insight; when West refers to Britishness in *Black Lamb*, she writes as if the empire were already a thing of the past.

As West points out in *Black Lamb*, 'one empire is very like another' (280), and an early essay on her education makes evident how few illusions she held about what the British Empire had meant at its Victorian height:

> England black with industrialism, foul with poverty, iridescent with the scum of luxury, was held up to my infant eyes as the noblest work of God and the aristocracy. I was exhorted to glory in industrialism and pity such savage parts as Ceylon and Burma, where you may travel for years and never come on anything like Wigan and Burnley.[64]

In this satirical early account of the imperialist historiography of her late-Victorian upbringing, Dickens's utilitarian nightmare of Coketown has become the national achievement. Against Victorian empiricism and imperialism, West posits a different kind of national story: defensive rather than aggressive, self-scrutinising rather than expansionist. Suggesting the modernist championing of myth against materialism, but unpacking for the first time myth's nation-making origins and implications, she argues that groups unite defensively around the stories they invented to define themselves in the face of foreign occupation. Here, she describes why it matters that Croatia has (in her view) a weaker stock of national stories than its neighbour, myth-laden Serbia:

> As we grow older and see the ends of stories as well as their beginnings, we realize that to the people who take part in them it is almost of greater importance that they should be stories, that they should form a recognizable pattern, than that they should be happy or tragic ... Art is not a plaything, but a necessity, and its essence, form, is not a decorative adjustment, but a cup into which life can be poured and lifted to the lips and tasted. (55)

In an analytic move in advance of her time, West argues that nations invent themselves through imaginative and narrative structures. There would be no 'Englishness' without the mythical golden age under Elizabeth I, and there would be no 'Americanness' if the War of Independence had somehow refused to become a national mythology (56). Demonstrable historical truth is not the issue; what counts is that a population becomes a group in conceiving of its present as part of a long shared story.

It would be true, if somewhat pious given the circumstances, to say that West's advocacy of national myth over material and economic causality is problematic. The mythic-historical tactic was also how the contemporary Churchillian oratory had achieved its florid grandeur, superseding the greater caution of the Chamberlain rhetoric. Even if Chamberlain had been proud enough of his recent speeches to publish them in 1939, what he had offered his audience was a little Englandism that was no more progressive for being anti-heroic; and whereas Chamberlain's speeches have passed into popular memory as bathos ('Hitler has missed the bus'; 'people of whom we know nothing'), the Churchillian rhetoric imbued the crisis with the meaningfulness of historical epic. Written on this kind of scale, the main argument of West's book defies summary:

> Defeat, moreover, must mean to England the same squalor that it had meant to Serbia. Five centuries hence gentleness would be forgotten by our people; loutish

men would bind ploughshares to their women's backs and walk beside them unashamed, we would grow careless of our dung, ornament and the use of foreign tongues and the discoveries made by the past genius of our race would be phantoms that sometimes troubled the memory; and over the land would lie the foul jetsam left by the receding tide of a conquering race. In a *Denkmal* erected to a German aviator the descendant of his sergeant in the sixteenth generation, a wasted man called Hans with folds of skin instead of rolls of fat at the back of his neck, would show a coffin under a rotting swastika flag, and would praise the dead in a set, half-comprehended speech, and point at faded photographs on the peeling wall, naming the thin one Göring and the fat one Goebbels; and about the tomb of a murdered *Gauleiter* women wearing lank blonde plaits, listless with lack of possessions, would picnic among the long grasses in some last recollection of the Strength Through Joy movement, and their men would raise flimsy arms in the Hitler salute, should a tourist come by, otherwise saving the effort. In the towns homeless children, children of homeless children, themselves of like parentage, would slip into eating-houses and grovel on the dirty floor for cigarette-butts dropped by diners reared in a society for long ignorant of the nice. That is defeat, when a people's economy and culture is destroyed by an invader; that is conquest, that is what happens when a people travels too far from the base where it has struck its roots. (1119)

This is why, to recall West earlier phrase, 'the corpses of empires stink as nothing else', and her dystopian thought experiment about Britain's move from coloniser to colonised elaborates the America-addressed Churchillian imaginings when, in the famous speech on the retreat and evacuation at Dunkirk ('we shall fight on the beaches, we shall fight on the landing grounds' and so on), he used a high-risk rhetorical tactic to describe why the war needed to be kept going even as defeat looked likely; Churchill's strategy was to appropriate the projective historiography of the thousand-year Reich to imagine a horrible future for 'this island ... subjugated and starving'.[65]

In taking what she has seen of post-imperial squalor in Yugoslavia and transposing it on to an imagined post-Nazi England, West refuses to see English culture as a given but as contingent and vulnerable as the cultures that empires have always tried to obliterate. This relativistic strategy qualifies the seemingly universalising impulse towards myth that West shared with her canonical contemporaries, an impulse to which the title of the book points, and which is underscored by West's approval of what she sees as the Serbs' long cultural memory. In his landmark essay on *Ulysses*, Eliot had famously written that the old narrative methods had been supplanted by 'the mythical method' of Joyce, and if West wondered 'What is Mr T. S. Eliot's Authority as a Critic?' in an essay of that magnificently puncturing title, she clearly shared his admiration for this 'continuous parallel between contemporaneity and antiquity ... a way of giving a shape and a significance to the immense panorama of futility and anarchy which is contemporary history'.[66] Her myths link present crises to past ones as they link past empires to present ones. There is an anaesthetic element to this because it creates a promise of continuity that events of 1940–1 (the defeat of the allies, the likely defeat of Britain) do not warrant; on the other hand, West refuses to invoke recurrence as a way to diminish the significance of present political action: purporting to be universals, the black lamb and grey falcon have pressing and particular implications.

In the epilogue of the book, for instance, the cult of the necessary sacrifice finds its political corollary in *Weygandisme*. Notoriously, the Roman Catholics Weygand and Pétain had suggested that the fall of France might not be as disastrous as it looked.

> France, they said, was corrupt and must be regenerated by defeat. It is hard to guess what this could mean save that they were governed by the myth of Kossovo [*sic*], of the rock. There was nothing Christian in such speeches. Long ago the Church had declared that its altar required nothing but 'the reasonable and unbloody sacrifice' of the bread and the wine. This was the propaganda of black magic, of paganism. (1124)

Appeasement gets described as the same sacrificial heresy as collaboration: their interwar governments have left the British helpless, and 'the nation was to have its throat cut as if it were a black lamb in the arms of a pagan priest' (1121). But if the rightwing has failed, so too has the left. They have been seduced, like the Tsar Lazar, by the grey falcon who offers personal innocence and collective death: 'Lazar was a member of the Peace Pledge Union', she writes, and, like him, British liberals 'want to receive the Eucharist, be beaten by the Turks, and then go to Heaven' (911–12). She had used the same Serb analogies in an exchange with the materialist socialist Naomi Mitchison conducted through the letters pages of *Time and Tide* at the end of 1939, and Mitchison had taken her to task for 'thinking in dangerously nationalist terms', warning West, a propos her anecdotes of lambs and falcons, that 'One of the main war dangers to the intellect is to archaize (as in Rebecca West's moral story two issues ago)'.[67] What Mitchison misunderstood was that West's mythmaking is not intended as a transcendence of the historical but a way of reading bad responses – evasive and self-defeating responses – to the political present. The black lamb and grey falcon turn out to be offering, like the reformed

Auden in his post-war defence of the poet's contingencies against the politically doctrinaire, an 'antimythological myth'.[68]

When myth found its new life in the Second World War, it became simultaneously a qualifiedly nationalist ideology and a defence of a particular modernist aesthetic. 'The attribution of rationality to human nature, instead of enriching it, now seems to me to have impoverished it', Keynes confessed in his posthumously published retraction 'My Early Beliefs'.[69] In this paper for Bloomsbury's Memoir Club, Keynes outlined the disparity between his unworldly education at Cambridge and his view of the world as he wrote the essay in 1938. The Cambridge Apostles were, he wrote, 'among the last of the Utopians, or meliorists as they are sometimes called, who believe in a continuing moral progress by virtue of which the human race already consists of reliable, rational, decent people'.[70] Mantoux had spotted these assumptions in *Economic Consequences* when he ridiculed Keynes's confidence that humanity was 'a philanthropic institution' and that 'nothing but a conspiracy between privilege and superstition was blocking the way to the infinite perfectibility of the human race'.[71] In 'My Early Beliefs', Keynes conceded that this was a 'pseudo-rational view of human nature', and that it 'led to a thinness, a superficiality, not only of judgment, but also of feeling ... Some of the spontaneous, irrational outbursts of human nature can have a sort of value'.[72]

The occasion of Keynes's anti-Utopian epiphany was a paper in which he recounted his first meeting with D. H. Lawrence; herself an acquaintance and long-time admirer of Lawrence, West had always had less sympathy for the optimistic progressivism that the dominant strain of English modernism had inherited from late-Victorian liberalism. Indeed 'pseudo-rational' sounds like the kind of phrase West or Lawrence would have used, and neither would have thought it the basis of a meaningful creative or cultural endeavour. It is art, after all, that is most obviously under discussion in these comments on the 'pseudo-rational'. Steven Connor has recently offered a crystalline synopsis of myth and the modernists when he writes that "'Myth', in fact, becomes another of the many terms for 'art' and 'the aesthetic'".[73] This seems absolutely right, but when myth returns at the end of modernism there is something more at stake than just the status of artistic achievement: when they restore modernism's irrational element, Keynes and West undertake nothing less than an early examination of the politics of modernism. Defending the oblique against the transparent, West breaks with the intellectual inheritance of her own progressive politics, what Perry Anderson much later identified as 'the philistine narrowness' of the early twentieth-century left wing, which had inherited from Victorian progressives 'the deadly germs of utilitarianism ... [a] leaden legacy'.[74] 'Art', West writes, 'cannot talk plain sense, it must sometimes speak what sounds at first like nonsense, though it is actually supersense' (1128).

In its earlier incarnations, the modernist contempt for the utilitarian is well known. Writing one of the most famous of the 1920s manifestos, Woolf had denounced the prosaic materialism of realist contemporaries who had sacrificed the spiritual life to the drab detailing of socio-economic circumstance: H. G. Wells was reproached for 'taking upon his shoulders the work that ought to have been discharged by Government officials'; Arnold Bennett's characters 'live abundantly', Woolf conceded, 'but what do they live for?'[75] Here Woolf created a polemical distinction between novelists like herself whose declared aim was to tell the truth about individual life and writers such as Wells and Bennett who in her view conceived of fiction in terms of its social utility. Writing much later, however, Keynes suggests that the modernist inquiry ('But what do they live for?') is not simply a matter of fidelity to individual psychic life, as Woolf would have it, but a celebration of communal narratives:

And in addition to the values arising out of spontaneous, volcanic and even wicked impulses, there are many objects of valuable contemplation and communion beyond those we know of – those concerned with the order and pattern of life amongst communities and the emotions which they can inspire ... we carried the individualism of our individuals too far.[76]

In this defence of an art derived from 'the order and pattern of life among communities and the emotions which they can inspire' is the possibility of shared ground between Keynes, Mantoux and West. This might even be read as a rehabilitation of what Woolf had dismissed as 'unreal loyalties', because, as Mantoux pointed out in his refutation of Keynes's economic bottom line, it is one thing to say that nationality is constructed, but another to believe that it has no bearing on how people live: 'If the issues of nationality were 'unreal', how much simpler, then, it would have been to submit ... to the inevitable hegemony of the German people rather than disturb the admirable economic machinery of Europe. That would certainly have saved a great deal of trouble'.[77] And here are formulations of national imagining that would only be theorised decades later, as more than a spiritual whitewash with which hegemonic power conceals its own cynical interests. It is now a critical cliché to invoke the other Anderson brother in this context, but his comments are entirely apt: '*In themselves*', Benedict Anderson wrote, 'market-zones, "natural"-geographic or politico-administrative, do not create attachments. Who will willingly die for Comecon or the EEC?'[78] And when Anderson described how nationalism's concern with 'death and immortality ... suggests a strong affinity with religious imaginings', he was both acknowledging the experiential reality of national identification as well as its discursive constructedness, and suggesting the ways in which its articulations can be, and not simply in a pejorative way, archaic.[79]

Angus Calder has written that 'The heroism of the British under bombardment was quasi-Christian – its great symbol, after all, was St Paul's dome flourishing above the flames'.[80] Calder's *The Myth of the Blitz* is just one of the important accounts of the war that emphasises the transformation of history into myth, or how the war's uncertainties and incoherence were transmuted into a satisfying aesthetic and moral shape; others include Clive Ponting's counterfactual, polemically revisionist *1940: Myth and Reality*, and Malcolm Smith's more relativistic *Britain and 1940: History, Myth and Popular Memory*. Certainly, the Blitz has lent itself easily to heart-warming retrospection, but it is worth pausing on the fact that the relevant mythmaking has nothing to do with imperial power and everything to do with disempowerment, displacement and vulnerability. In a profoundly Churchillian account of the Blitz, West describes the horror of ordinary citizens emerging from nights underground to see 'the annihilation of dear and familiar things':

> They worked, they fought like soldiers, but without the least intoxication that comes from joy in killing, for they could only defend themselves, they could not in any way attack their assailants. In this sobriety, men and women went out and dug among the ruins for the injured while bombs were still falling, and they turned on fire, which it is our nature to flee, and fought it at close range, night after night, week after week, month after month. There have been heroes on the plains of Troy, on the Elizabethan seas, on the fields of Flanders, in the Albanian mountains that go down to the sea, but none of them was more heroic than this. (1130)

And here West's book shows how the war could be almost literally mythologised in real time: in elevating passive defence and civilian courage to a register so lofty that it isn't immediately clear what she's actually talking about, West is making room for unnamed London citizens and the unwritten heroisms of the Balkan mountains in the familiar pantheon of Troy, the Armada and (Woolf would never have gone this far) the Great War.

In all outward aspects an interwar iconoclast – socialist, feminist, anti-imperialist – West's compromised and self-conscious rehabilitation of nationality was a way of imposing creative meaningfulness on the political confusion of the period. Privileging nationality over what she considered illusory forms of internationalism, and arguing for modernist myth over the reductive promises of materialist realism, this mid-career book seems further evidence that West had turned away entirely from the radical politics with which she had been closely associated between the wars; and when she subsequently denounced communism as outspokenly as she had condemned fascism, she was accused of exactly that. But there appears to me to be something more historically significant in her compromise than one minor novelist retreating into reactionary mystifications of violence. Before turning to Eliot in Chapter 3, I want to mention one of his *Criterion* contributors as a final remarkable instance of how the war collapsed the political binaries of the 1930s. The Scottish nationalist and communist poet Hugh MacDiarmid had even less reason than West to collude with cosy fictions about how plucky little England won her heroic war: the rhetoric of social reform was at best promissory; the language of the war effort so stubbornly Anglocentric that even writers who knew better continued to use 'England' and 'Britain' interchangeably. MacDiarmid had spent most of the interwar period mocking the rallying cry of saving civilisation, attacking with perhaps unparalleled vitriol even the Great War dead ('professional murderers'): 'In spite of all their kind some elements of worth / With difficulty persist here and there on earth'.[81] So much for the refusal to mourn, MacDiarmid's subsequent elegy 'To Those of My Old School Who Fell in the Second World War' tells an altogether different story. Reusing lines he had originally written for – of all things – the International Brigades in Spain, MacDiarmid created his own antimythological myth:

> Neither legends nor lies are needed,
> The truth is enough. It should stiffen the spines
> Of all who fear for human liberty. You, comrades,
> Who froze and starved and rotted in this War,
> Were not superhuman; you merely preferred
> Suffering and death
> Rather than bend your knees
> To persons and principles you rightly despised.[82]

CHAPTER 3

The situational politics of Four Quartets

> You will be astonished to find how like art is to war. I mean 'modernist' art. ... I have set out to show how war, art, civil war, strikes and coup d'états dovetail into each other.
> Wyndham Lewis, *Blasting and Bombardiering* (1937)[1]

> War is not a life: it is a situation,
> One which may neither be ignored nor accepted
> T. S. Eliot, 'A Note on War Poetry' (1942)[2]

Published on T. S. Eliot's seventy-fifth birthday, and the product of the poet's own sifting and salvaging, *Collected Poems 1909–1962* offers illuminating insights into how Eliot viewed his career in its closing years. The last major work in the collection is *Four Quartets*, the sequence of poems that started in the mid-1930s with *Burnt Norton*, the poem which developed the model for those Eliot wrote in wartime: *East Coker* (1940), *The Dry Salvages* (1941) and *Little Gidding* (1942). But these are not the four last things the reader encounters in the *Collected Poems*; they have a postscript in the group of 'Occasional Verses' at the very end of the book. A poem written in celebration of Walter de la Mare's seventy-fifth birthday has a self-referential flavour; by far the best known of the five is Eliot's closing dedication to his wife; and the remaining three occasional poems are propaganda from the Second World War: 'Defense of the Islands' (1941), 'A Note on War Poetry' (1942) and 'To the Indians Who Died in Africa' (1943). The encounter with these poems just after *Four Quartets* generates unexpected echoes: 'A Dedication to My Wife', for instance, has a familiar ring in its references to 'The roses in the rose-garden which is ours and ours only', which recall the journey to the rose-garden of *Burnt Norton*, an encounter typically read as based on a visit Eliot paid to a derelict country house with an old girl-friend.[3] The meaning of this coincidence – a private joke with his wife (addressed to her in public)? – has a certain biographical interest, but the relationships between *Four Quartets* and Eliot's other saved 'occasional' work, propaganda poems, raise an issue of a different order about Eliot's late career.

Summarised in head notes in the 1963 collection, their original contexts reveal the purposes the three war poems were written to serve: '*Defense of the Islands*' was commissioned to accompany an exhibition of British war art at the Museum of Modern Art in New York; 'A Note on War Poetry' was also destined for the neutral United States, this time in Storm Jameson's *London Calling: A Salute to America* (1942), where it appeared with an essay from the Cambridge historian G. M. Trevelyan on one side and a story by the middlebrow favourite Angela Thirkell on the other. The last of the three, 'To the Indians Who Died in Africa' sounds perhaps even less promising; it was written for a publication titled, with a belated imperial flourish, *Queen Mary's Book for India* (1943) . To suggest that there may be relationships between these minor propaganda poems and the complex and elegant *Four Quartets* is certainly not to say that Eliot's late modernist masterpiece could be conceived of as propaganda, but only to propose that if the cultural and political work *Four Quartets* performed in their own time has been systematically bypassed, it is not because their author was interested in concealing it.

'*Defense of the Islands* cannot pretend to be verse', Eliot writes in his preamble to the poem, 'but its date – just after the evacuation from Dunkirk – and occasion have for me a significance which makes me wish to preserve it'.[4] The dire date helps to explain the poem's replication of all the clichés of one-nation propaganda; the poem consists of a catalogue of the different constituents of the nation at war: on the ocean ('British bone on the sea floor'); in the air ('fight the power of darkness in air / and fire'); on land (those who 'followed their forebears to Flanders and France'); and, this being the People's War, there's a tribute to the civilians, whose 'paths of glory are / the lanes and streets of Britain'.[5] That the poem is completely of its time is probably what is wrong with it; indeed, the more reflective occasional poem that follows it, 'A Note on War Poetry' opens with the cautionary injunction that war poetry not be 'the expression of collective emotion / Imperfectly reflected in the daily papers'.[6] Nonetheless, 'A Note on War Poetry' has something positive to say about timeliness too: 'The enduring is not a substitute for the transient, / Neither one for the other'.[7] Topicality may render a poem as ephemeral as 'the daily papers', but the transitory and provisional gets its due, and need not be wholly subordinated to an ideal of timeless durability.

The situational politics of Four Quartets

'Does *The Waste Land* Have a Politics?' Michael Levenson asks in an article of that playfully ingenuous title.⁸ It does, he concludes, but only if we jettison crude binaries of reactionary and progressive politics and listen less impatiently for the topical notes struck in a poem written in the unsettled aftermath of the Great War. Modernist ears are better attuned than they once were to the topical political nuances Levenson identifies, thanks in so small part to the vast body of scholarship on the literature and culture of the First World War. So, for example, Vincent Sherry's recent contribution to the long-running conversation about modernism's relation to the Great War opens by reading the botched Treaty of Versailles in the 'cunning passages, contrived corridors / And issues' of Eliot's 'Gerontion' (1920).⁹ The little old man of the poem's title confesses that he has not fought at the 'hot gates' of Thermopylae, nor has he been 'knee deep in the salt marsh . . . / Bitten by flies'; for Sherry, he is representative of the moribund generation who misused their pens to defend a war in which they were too old to fight.¹⁰ In its argument that modernist obliquity emerged as a response to the crisis in public reason brought about by Liberals' textual defences of the indefensible, Sherry's book is both an allegory of modernist origins and a reconstruction of their political context. But knowing so much less about the discursive culture of the Second World War, how can readers know what late modernists did with their textual surroundings? What is this 'transient' material that Eliot refuses to replace with the 'enduring'? To put it another way, does *Four Quartets* have a politics?

THE WISDOM OF OLD MEN

It helps that some of the topical material has a familiar resonance from the last war. To disavow political commitment in these poems is to be an old man, and the old men of Four Quartets are just as treacherous as they were in the poetry of the Great War trenches. Not obviously an *enfant terrible* in 1940, Eliot nonetheless distances himself very trenchantly from the old men's failures of feeling and imagination:

> Do not let me hear
> Of the wisdom of old men, but rather of their folly,
> Their fear of fear and frenzy, their fear of possession,
> Of belonging to another, or to others, or to God.
> The only wisdom we can hope to acquire
> Is the wisdom of humility: humility is endless.¹¹

There is no doubt what 'the wisdom of old men' had amounted to in 'Gerontion'. A racist, an anti-Semite and a pontificating bore (so far, so familiar), Gerontion is an unqualifiedly negative figure as he awaits death in his rotten material and dynastic 'house'.[12] And contrary to the many readings that render the *Four Quartets* spiritual to the exclusion of the political, Eliot's speaker in *East Coker* rejects without hesitation the dissociated passivity that old men like Gerontion have to offer. Their antipathy to commitments – commitment to action, to other people and to moral obligation – ought not to be mistaken for a somehow superior 'wisdom' of political disengagement.

Eliot was so conscious of his own eminence at the time of the *Quartets*' writing that he could likely assume that the empty-headed old men in *East Coker* would direct the reader back to 'Gerontion' and to the post-1918 political failures that the earlier poem diagnoses. Pulling rank in 'A Note on War Poetry', Eliot recalled his long and illustrious career to caution the novice war poet of 1942 that 'A poem is not poetry / That is a life.'[13] Still, even if Eliot was attentive to how a body of work, a life, might be read indivisibly, the guilty old men of *East Coker* had a discursive existence outside Eliot's already iconic oeuvre. The failures of the gerontocracy are a recurrent trope in political discourse during the early years of the Second World War. The old men of Eliot's poem strongly resemble the elderly pro-appeasement Tories and accomplices being savaged in the contemporary press. In a best-selling philippic precipitated by the evacuation at Dunkirk, Neville Chamberlain (d. 1940), Ramsay MacDonald, Sir Samuel Hoare, Stanley Baldwin, Lord Halifax and Lord Simon were grouped as the interwar 'Guilty Men'. Published in 1940 by a group of journalists calling themselves 'Cato', *Guilty Men* indicted the parliamentary coalitions of the 1930s for a devastating catalogue of crimes: for lying about the need for rearmament in order to win the General Election of 1935; for the calamitous appeasement policy and for leaving Britain so unprepared for war that Dunkirk had exposed a probably fatal disparity between German and British strength: 'Peace in Our Time', these journalists concluded, was an 'old man's dream'.[14] The allusion, as ironic as Eliot's twenty years earlier, is to Cardinal Newman's poem (1865) and Edward Elgar's oratorio (1900), *The Dream of Gerontius*, in which the just soul contemplates his imminent death.

Orwell's contemporary essay on socialism in Britain, *The Lion and the Unicorn*, is compulsively repetitive about the Guilty Men's advanced age: Chamberlain was 'a stupid old man'; England was 'ruled largely by the old and silly'; their mouthpieces were 'old duds' and something had to be done about 'inefficiency, class privilege and the rule of the old'.[15] Also exactly contemporary, though a shade further to the right, Malcolm Muggeridge's mordant survey of the 1930s uses the same rhetoric of decrepitude when it reaches the climactic failure of Chamberlain's inept foreign policy and ventriloquises derisively that 'A chat with Mussolini or with Hitler, even a friendly nod to Stalin, would make all the difference. Chamber of Commerce Quixote, Knight of the Woeful Countenance, bearing umbrella instead of lance, his chivalry Rotarian, his accoutrements funereal, he set forth hopefully to save the world from an impending catastrophe'.[16] Like Eliot's foolish old men, this bizarre Quixote will not realise that his moment has passed. More malign, finally, are the 'old men' of Angus Wilson's eccentric invasion allegory, *The Old Men at the Zoo* (1961), which, as the older Evelyn Waugh pointed out in an effort to explain the novel to its baffled reviewers, was not a futuristic fiction, but 'a study of 1938–42'.[17] In Wilson's re-imagining (with bestiality, cannibalism, Roman circuses) of C. P. Snow's administrative novels, the 'Uni-Europeans' invade on 'British Day' to the music of Gilbert and Sullivan. Their conquest has been prepared for by the old men in the novel's title, civil service mandarins who are either privately sympathetic to the authoritarian politics of the invaders or so much blinded by imperial nostalgia that they will not see how Britain's weakness makes their realisation inevitable.

East Coker details the total cultural collapse that Wilson's novel retrospectively delineates; rejecting the wisdom of the old men, Eliot goes on to catalogue their disintegration. If the allusion to Milton's *Samson Agonistes* suggests a transhistorical condition of blindness, the quotation gets mangled in important ways: 'O dark dark dark', Eliot begins with Milton's Samson, but amends Samson's lament for his own blindness to make it about the blindness of others: 'They all go into the dark' (*EC*, 185). The associative and thoroughly topical joke here, beyond what might be seen as an ironic evocation of the black-out, is that the pillars which Samson will suicidally bring down are the pillars of society, and Eliot embarks on an inventory of interwar civic life – its military, political, cultural and industrial supports, an obituary for the societies eclipsed by the regimes that they could not hold back:

> The captains, merchant bankers, eminent men of letters,
> The generous patrons of art, the statesmen and the rulers,
> Distinguished civil servants, chairmen of many committees,
> Industrial lords and petty contractors, all go into the dark,

> And dark the Sun and Moon, and the Almanach de Gotha
> And the Stock Exchange Gazette, the Directory of Directors,
> And cold the sense and lost the motive of action.
> And we all go with them. (*EC*, 185–6)

Using arch aural pedantries like the 'Directory of Directors' to intensify his exhaustive list, Eliot debunks with iterative boredom the familiar bureaucratic infrastructure whose certainties he wants to throw into question. 'Had they deceived us', Eliot wonders, 'Or deceived themselves?' These deluded and self-deluding old men knew only 'dead secrets / Useless in the darkness into which they peered / Or from which they turned their eyes' (*EC*, 184–5). Like more predictably dissenting commentators, Eliot indicts a geriatric establishment, both ludicrous and damnable, for its collective incompetence and quiescence.

The old men have nothing to offer because circumstances impel the reappraisal rather than the recycling of pre-existing knowledge. In Eliot's anti-manifesto for situational thinking over retrenchment into obsolete certainties, there is 'only a limited value / In the knowledge derived from experience':

> The knowledge imposes a pattern, and falsifies,
> For the pattern is new in every moment
> And every moment is a new and shocking
> Valuation of all we have been. (*EC*, 185)

At the risk of reading this sometimes prosey poem in too prosaic a way, it might be said that this critique of entrenched habit has a pointed political meaning in the context of 1940. If pattern 'falsifies', it could be argued that Chamberlain's business-as-usual policy in the tensely expectant early months of the war, the so-called Phoney War of September 1939 – May 1940, had meant exactly that. Of course, in what amounts to the postponement of slaughter, 'hope would be hope for the wrong thing' (*EC*, 186). But the most symptomatic aspect of Eliot's seeming religiosity is that this *via negativa* is not the mystical fugue of *Burnt Norton* – 'Internal darkness, deprivation ... / Inoperancy of the world of spirit' (*BN*, 179) – but a product of the political extinction that precedes it; the public authorities 'all go into the dark ... / And we all go with them'. These represent a pan-European establishment since the *Almanach de Gotha* is the authoritative snob-book of continental heredity, but in going on to liken the hiatus to mechanical failure in the London Underground, Eliot turns to the unmistakeably domestic and demotic, against what his own customary snobberies would make likely. These were notably in evidence even as late as the first of the *Quartets*: in *Burnt Norton*, for instance, 'eructation of unhealthy souls' fouls the London air in which 'Men and bits of paper' are blown about as if they were equally worthless (*BN*, 179). In contrast, *East Coker* confers value on the involuntary entrapment of the urban populace when Eliot promises that 'the faith and love and the hope are all in the waiting' (*EC*, 186). In what might be read as another evocation of Milton, blindness and those excluded from executive power (that they also serve who only stand and wait), the poem makes a spiritual virtue out of an inescapable circumstance.

Even discounting the ubiquitous diatribes against the paralysing gerontocracy at the time of the poem's writing, support for identifying the old men with the particular political contexts of the war comes when they return in the London Blitz. In *Little Gidding*, the fire-watching poet meets his spectral mentor: a compound figure of obviously poetic provenance (Dante, Yeats, Mallarmé and Pound are all plausible identifications), the old man shares his wisdom about the 'gifts reserved for age':

> And last, the rending pain of re-enactment
> Of all that you have done, and been; the shame
> Of motives late revealed, and the awareness
> Of things ill done and done to others' harm
> Which once you took for exercise of virtue.
> Then fools' approval stings, and honour stains. (*LG*, 204–5)

Eliot's biographer Lyndall Gordon sees in this opaque confession Eliot's guilt about his first wife, Vivienne Haigh-Wood, committed in 1938 to the asylum where she spent the last nine years of her life.[18] Admittedly, biographical readings are invited by poems in which Eliot is doing the police in nobody's voice other than his own; on the other hand, what a straightforwardly biographical gloss on this passage has to ignore is the decisively public language of morality that Eliot borrows to describe a popular policy turning into a source of shame. Breast-beating about stained honour and the approval of fools does not seem remotely appropriate to marital failure because it is recognisably the oratory of public guilt and its allusion to unearned honour recalls above all 'peace with honour' and what the dissenting Tory Vansittart called 'appeasement's sudden change of meaning from virtuous endeavour to craven immorality'.[19] In 1938, Chamberlain had been feted by everyone from the royal family to the waiting London crowds for what appeared his extraordinary statesmanship and for what subsequently became the most shameful policy of the decade. I agree that this passage feels like autobiographical confession, but it is both spoken in a public, political register and it specifically evokes the poetic rather than the private life (Dante, Mallarmé, Yeats, Pound). With all these strands – autobiographical, political, poetic – in mind, it might be said to be a self-condemnatory identification with discredited forms of quietism: 'While I am naturally sympathetic', he had written in his polite refusal to take sides on Spain, 'I still feel convinced that it is best that at least a few men of letters remain silent'.[20]

The explicitness with which Eliot rejects the quietistic old men of 1940 necessarily qualifies the orthodox reading of these poems. Leaning too heavily on the mid-1930s's *Burnt Norton*, readers have turned the *Quartets* into an escape from secular history without acknowledging that *Burnt Norton* more strongly resembles in content the 1930s religious dramas with which it shares lines than it does the poems which Eliot only later realised might formally be modelled on it. Eliot himself recollected that *Burnt Norton* began as scraps from his play *Murder in the Cathedral* and that the writing of the next three quartets was the entirely situational outcome of wartime circumstances.[21] While there is something uncomfortably ex post facto about John Xiros Cooper's use of Eliot's Cold War spokespeople as a stick to beat the poems' own politics, he is surely right to draw attention to the unworldly formalist practices of *Four Quartets*'s most distinguished advocates. Cooper has a field day with Dame Helen Gardner's 1950 study:

Buoyed by such warm exultation, I hesitate lugging the discussion back to earth, to the political dilemmas of the 1940s when these words were written. I suppose I must say that I know of no better example from this period which so capably, but unconsciously, delineates the epistemological slant and hothouse ambience of the mandarin enclave. It is a criticism which has been so thoroughly colonized by the work of art under examination that it can no longer operate on its own, but needs the poem as primary life system. It circles back on itself tracing the lineaments of the poem's self-referring, inward-gazing elements, strenuously recommending Eliot's mastery, and his impenetrable polish, in the highest possible terms.[22]

The ferocity is bracing, but Cooper chose an easy target when he made Gardner's old book exemplary of 'hothouse' ahistoricism; the political contexts of *Four Quartets* are still sidestepped even in readings that see the war as crucial to the poems. Thus, for example, Sebastian Knowles's argument that Eliot rewrites Dante in order to render the war metaphorical evades rather than acknowledges material history on the grounds that the evasion is Eliot's, and seems a little susceptibly to assume that this sovereign transcendence of local culture – even if that is indeed what Eliot was after – could ever come off.[23]

Cooper is right to marvel at how *Four Quartets* was turned into a formalist masterpiece of the Cold War; more surprising is that, sixty years on, a student of his late work could learn a phenomenal amount about the poet's intellectual and religious life but not necessarily realise that three of the four poems were written from the losing end of a war. Refusing to exalt *Four Quartets* to transcendent vacancy, Jed Esty and Steve Ellis represent fine exceptions, though I would want to reinstate some of the poems' most immediate political contexts to their readings. Of course, I do agree with them about the poems' 'antichauvinism', that Eliot is 'insisting on England as a relative rather than an absolute value' and that Eliot deploys 'a Churchillian rhetoric purified of mere patriotism by the appeal to eternity'.[24] I wonder, though, what they are comparing Eliot with, since the wholly disgraced propaganda of the Great War had rendered Hun-bashing denunciations and imperial bigotry off-limits for the second war. Even Eliot's own ultra-conservative *The Idea of a Christian Society* (1939) argues that there is no reason whatsoever for English smugness when it squares up to the continental totalitarian regimes, because 'We conceal from ourselves, moreover, the similarity of our society to those which we execrate.'[25] That is to say, Nazism was, for Eliot, as for less obviously conservative writers, offering a mirror image of domestic values – one analogue would be Woolf, wondering in *Three Guineas* what the difference was between Continental fascism and the British establishment – and 'What is more depressing still is that only fear or jealousy of foreign success can alarm us about the health of our own nation; that only through this anxiety can we see such things as depopulation, malnutrition, moral deterioration, the decay of agriculture, as evils at all.'[26]

THE DEATH OF COLONEL BLIMP

The Great War had discursively been 'fundamentally conservative ... fought not for change but to protect the values at the heart of [Britain's] greatness'.[27] In contrast, there is a sense in which the Second World War was the really modernist war, since it provoked the widespread critical introspection whose absence in the earlier war had ostensibly made social modernism necessary. Modernist studies have, for obvious reasons, been too much determined by the 1910s and 1920s for anyone to trace the closing gap between English culture and its interwar avant-garde. 'Patriotism, religion, the Empire, the family, the sanctity of marriage, the Old School Tie, birth, breeding, honour, discipline –' Orwell in 1940 had no difficulty listing the old values, 'anyone of ordinary education could turn the whole lot of them inside out in three minutes'.[28] Fifteen years younger than Eliot, Orwell had been educated during and just after the Great War, in years when these sacred tenets had presented a deserving focus for righteous radical outrage. I am thinking here of, for instance, the monstrous patriarch in Katherine Mansfield's 'Daughters of the Late Colonel' (1922) who dies glaring through one bulging eye at his down-trodden girls, 'purple, a dark, angry purple in the face'; and of Woolf's first-draft Dalloways in *The Voyage Out* (1915), whose 'talk was all of valour and death, and the magnificent qualities of British admirals'.[29] If modernist women were on the vanguard (as it were) of anti-militaristic politics, by 1940, the kinds of reactionaries that they had identified as a dangerous enemy only existed even in English mass culture – not exactly progressive at the best of times, let alone in times of war – as the target of popular satire. This is the 'Colonel Blimp' of David Low's contemporary newspaper cartoons, whose overdue pensioning-off is the subject of Powell and Pressburger's mid-war film comedy.[30]

Obviously this is not to suggest that one should ignore the Tory foundations of *The Idea of a Christian Society* (1939) and *Notes Towards the Definition of Culture* (1948) in order to show that Eliot was on the side of the angels after all. Eliot was above all a conservative thinker, and the organicist and ruralist dogmas of his 1930s and 1940s discursive writings very strongly suggest the nostalgic *Horse & Hound* politics underpinning much of the anti-isolationist propaganda sent to neutral America by sympathetic Anglophiles. These approximated the strain of Church of England thinking that Eliot reinforced when he spoke at the Anglican conference at Malvern in January 1941, although Stephen Spender had already reviewed *The Idea of a Christian Society* in similar terms when he wittily described it as 'curiously out of touch ... like one of those letters in *The Times* in which the bald head of some Bishop is seen for the first time emerging from the egg-shell of a lifetime's complacency'.[31] The conclusions drawn at Malvern were much the same as Eliot's public declarations about the condition of England, that the problem with contemporary society was the deleterious effect of urbanisation; as Esty winningly summarises it, 'Like all true organicists, he takes seriously the origins of the term "culture" in agriculture.'[32] Of course, this privileging of the rural is as much a product of the contemporary context as a reaction against it since war in Europe historically threw the country back on its own agricultural resources ('Dig for Victory', as the government campaign had it). Britain's archipelagic vulnerability to blockade meant that the world wars gave an excuse for Eliot's organicist politics and their temporary vindication. Again, and like the *via negativa* offered by the deferrals of the Phoney War, there is a potentially situational dimension to Eliot's political thinking, a tendency to make virtues out of necessities.

What is more, *East Coker* qualifies the backward-looking ruralist politics of the bald-headed bishops in ways that Eliot's own declarations do not lead the reader to expect. Given their apparent political differences, it is unexpected that Woolf in her final novel and Eliot in *East Coker* should simultaneously have hit on a similar language for tracing 'Englishness' back to its putative origins. The medieval pilgrims in Woolf's village pageant chant that they '*Ground roots between stones . . . Ground corn . . . till we too . . . lay under g-r-o-u-n-d*'; while Eliot, too, hears the 'Mirth of those long since under earth / Nourishing the corn' (*EC*, 183).[33] But Woolf's pageant represents a recognisably Tory-modernist historiography of decline, progressively debunking as it approaches the hypocritical Victorians and the novel's fractured present of 1939: she begins with early England as 'a small girl, like a rosebud in pink', and there is nothing to suggest an antagonistic distance.[34] The pre-modern is, as her wistful contemporary essay 'Anon' leads the reader to expect, easily the blandest scene in the pageant; what ensues is a steady deterioration into materialism. There is a shade of William Morris in her nostalgia for the pre-industrial, an era from which everything that followed has meant corruption and loss: Maypoles, Midsummer, Mummers and all, the communal culture that gave rise to 'Anon' is subsequently wiped out by the privatised textual modernity of the printing press.[35] Eliot's historiography is more sceptical than this.

East Coker gestures towards a pageant in its opening stages, when it eavesdrops on a lost England mediated through the poet's near-namesake, Sir Thomas Elyot:

> If you do not come too close, if you do not come too close,
> On a summer midnight, you can hear the music
> Of the weak pipe and the little drum
> And see them dancing around the bonfire
> The association of man and woman
> In daunsinge, signifying matrimonie –
> A dignified and commodious sacrament.
> Two and two, necessarye coniunction,

> Holding eche other by the hand or the arm
> Whiche betokeneth concorde. (*EC*, 182–3)

And so on, until the poem describes the yokels dancing, their 'Earth feet, loam feet, lifted in country mirth' in what must be the happier and simpler time of Woolf's idealised 'Anon' (*EC*, 183). But the borrowings from Thomas Elyot represent the first time that the poem's language actually changes; and, unlike, for example, the sections that quote Milton, this passage is glaringly, kitschly archaic. This is the Merrie England that a decade later provokes the comic disaster of Kingsley Amis's *Lucky Jim* (1954): asked to deliver an undemanding public lecture, the historian protagonist tries to replicate consolatory truisms about the 'integration of social consciousness' and the 'identification of work with craft', but collapses in the drunken recognition that 'Merrie England ... was about the most un-Merrie period in our history. It's only the home-made pottery crowd, the organic husbandry crowd, the recorder-playing crowd, the Esperanto ... ' – he is too drunk to finish the thought, but he does not have to elaborate on the spuriousness of interwar fantasies of a medieval golden age.[36] If it seems incongruous to link Eliot with Amis, it's worth recalling that Eliot dismissed bogus history absolutely scathingly in the famous *Ulysses* essay, where he distanced what he thought of as Joyce's groundbreaking classicism from the contemporary exhumation of 'mummified stuff from a museum'.[37]

In fact, when the poem projects into the past the kind of organicist fantasy that Eliot's cultural criticism tends at its least inviting to indulge, it puts unambiguous caveats in place first. As the reiterated preface 'if you do not come too close' makes explicit, you can only have this trite and comforting relationship with the past if you stand well back. The warning is necessarily rhetorical because the poem proceeds with thunderously repetitive lines, mimetic of the rhythmic clomping of rustic feet and the consolations of the seasonal cycles: the promise of universal harmony that Eliot had whimsically postulated in *Burnt Norton*, where he invoked a pre-modern cosmogony to imagine that 'The dance along the artery / The circulation of the lymph / Are figured in the drift of stars' (*BN*, 177). But this closer relation to peasant history only generates the less comforting throwback to the *contemptus mundi* of the middle ages, when the dance turns from spectacle, to the promise of earthly reconciliation, to an altogether Augustinian darkness:

> Keeping time,
> Keeping the rhythm in their dancing

> As in their living in the living seasons
> The time of the seasons and the constellations
> The time of milking and the time of harvest
> The time of the coupling of man and woman
> And that of beasts. Feet rising and falling.
> Eating and drinking. Dung and death. (*EC*, 183)

The hateful ending is the end point of the dance itself; in other words, to satisfy ruralist yearnings with the cyclicality and collectivity of pastoral ritual is to see that history amounts to a dourly democratic archaeology of 'flesh, fur and faeces ... / ... Dung and death' (*EC*, 182–3). If you really look at this apparent golden age as a materialist, Eliot's argument implies, you do actually have to see its material, a compost of purposeless corporeal waste.

Importantly, the next scene of Eliot's pseudo-pageant refuses to reinstate the divine harmony that would presumably restore transcendent meaning to the brute facts of human life and death. In a passage that has opened with time frighteningly out of joint, Eliot attempts to resurrect the omens of early-modern drama:

> Thunder rolled by the rolling stars
> Simulates triumphal cars
> Deployed in constellated wars
> Scorpion fights against the sun
> Until the Sun and Moon go down
> Comets weep and Leonids fly. (*EC*, 184)

This piece of sham prefatory omen provokes the poem's famous disavowal of a 'periphrastic study in a worn-out poetical fashion' (*EC*, 184), because not only is it impossible to believe in the universal unities that implicate the heavens in the destinies of human beings, it also happens to be bad poetry to try and dig them up again. And if Eliot rejects outright any idea that the past was a better time, or even that its theological promises of harmony were more hopeful, he is prompted to return to the pre-modern for different reasons. In place of Merrie England and its fantasies of a lost heaven on earth, he posits medieval mysticism: *The Cloud of Unknowing* ('the voice of this Calling' [*LG*, 208]) and Julian of Norwich's *Revelations of Divine Love* ('all shall be well ... ' [*LG*, 206]). At a time when political medievalism had long since been revived by avant-garde contemporaries – by the Catholic poet-artist David Jones, for instance, whom Eliot championed at Faber, and by

Jones's anti-capitalist and co-religionist collaborator Eric Gill – Eliot rejects it. In contrast, what interests him is its unknowingness, its modernist capacity for exploratory and epiphanic thinking.

A new degree of violence attends the late modernist epiphany. Returning to the famous description of the 'evening ... spread out against the sky / Like a patient etherised upon a table', he likens the numbness of the Phoney War to 'when, under ether, the mind is conscious but conscious of nothing' (*EC*, 186).[38] The ambiguity of the 'an-aesthetic' pinpoints the identification of art with pain, and Eliot brings into play the duality of 'operations' as military and medical interventions; in a rare echo of his old baroque, he not only runs the surgical and the military together in what feels like an improvised field hospital but also turns post-Crucifixion Jesus into a war-damaged physician:

> The wounded surgeon plies the steel
> That questions the distempered part;
> Beneath the bleeding hands we feel
> The sharp compassion of the healer's art
> Resolving the enigma of the fever chart. (*EC*, 187).

Eliot goes straight from this into his description of 'the years of *l'entre deux guerres*', in what is virtually an admission that he is participating in a familiar interwar rhetoric of pathology (*EC*, 188). Suggestions of sickness in and around the national body are commonplace in the writings of the 1930s; as Auden famously put in *The Orators*, his 'English Study' of 1932, 'What do you think about England, this country of ours where nobody is well?'[39] Again, the literary trope has parliamentary analogues: the Baldwin-MacDonald coalition had gone to the country asking for what they called 'the Doctor's Mandate', a request enough in tune with the times to get them elected. (Baldwin was presumably playing on the same psychosomatic disquiet when he took as his slogan the pre-emptive 'Safety First'.)

The familiar idiom takes a surgical turn in the Second World War when 'civilization is on the operating table', as Cyril Connolly put it in his inaugural *Horizon* editorial of 1940.[40] In the lurid imaginings of the period's younger poets, the war is explicitly identified with surgical violence: in J. F. Hendry's 'Midnight Air-Raid', for instance, 'Sensitive fingers of searchlights pick the pockets of dark / They are surgeons' pitiless forceps imprisoning in their grip'.[41] Or in his collaborator Henry Treece's argument that the war had 'all the terror and inevitability of cancer; the nightmare had to proceed, however much the patient screamed'.[42] Treece's 'Towards a Personal Armageddon' has the war poet as surgeon:

> The shapes of Truth are no man's history
> Or hope; born in the horny womb of Time,
> They die with the daylight, ere the Surgeon's hand
> Can grasp the knife to solve the mystery
> Of feeling and the half-formed word.[43]

Loosely affiliated with more established writers like Dylan Thomas and George Barker, Treece and Hendry were at the centre of the dominant post-Auden movement in British poetry, the New Apocalypse or neo-Romantics. As modernist manifestos go, theirs was a little impoverished: mechanisation is bad, and so is left/right ideology; aesthetic and economic freedom is good, and so is myth; most of the 1920s survivors would have agreed with them on all counts.[44] Far more significant is the attack on Eliot's classicism that drove the endeavour: 'One may only find truth by exploration', their leaders recapped in 1949, 'But the Classical mind, or what we would call the staid and restricted personality, for whom life's adventure has ceased, has no time, no necessity, and no energy for such a freedom of search.'[45] Given Eliot's use of the motif of exploration in *Four Quartets* – 'Old men ought to be explorers' (*EC*, 189) – it is tempting to see this assault on classicism *ad hominem*, specifically as an attack on a tired old man.

Spearheaded by the neo-Romantics, the wartime vogue for writing the dark unconscious in verse that was obscure in all the wrong ways haunts the later of the *Quartets*. Eliot had his own *grand guignol* of sprouting corpses and baby-faced bats in *The Waste Land*, but *Four Quartets* refuses to play with the surrealist gothic of the Apocalyptic poets. In *The Dry Salvages*, Eliot ridicules their cult of the subconscious by listing psychoanalysis alongside the more familiarly bogus ways of trying to access occult knowledge that were enjoying renewed popularity in wartime – as Mass-Observation recorded, astrological journals had a far higher circulation than those of the *New Statesman* and *Time and Tide* because 'when rational forms of reassurance had broken down, the irrational was at a premium'.[46] For Eliot, psychoanalysis takes its place alongside astrology and the rest of the 'usual / Pastimes and drugs':

> Observe disease in signatures, evoke
> Biography from the wrinkles of the palm
> And tragedy from fingers; release omens

> By sortilege, or tea leaves, riddle the inevitable
> With playing cards, fiddle with pentagrams
> Or barbituric acids, or dissect
> The recurrent image into pre-conscious terrors –
> To explore the womb, or tomb, or dreams. (*DS*, 198)

This looks like throwing stones in a greenhouse, since a Christian poet might want to avoid ridiculing practices for accessing supernatural wisdom, but it speaks to an aspect of Eliot's religiosity that is central to the textual procedures of *Four Quartets*: spiritual inquiry becomes something other than an effort at uncovering the kinds of certainty pledged by these other divining rituals. Eliot's dismissal of the others does not propose that religion is somehow more rational than these other sense-making methods, not when *The Dry Salvages* has its own primitivist streak in its attack on 'superficial notions of evolution' that are 'a means of disowning the past'. The past ought not to be disowned because it recalls the timelessness of violence: the ruinous coastal rock of the poem's title reminds us that 'moments of agony / ... are likewise permanent' (*DS*, 194, 195). Just as Rebecca West appeals to archetypal patterns in order to legitimise political choices that feel painfully particular to the Second World War, Eliot makes it the business of his late poetry to uncover comparable intersections 'of the timeless / With time' (*DS*, 198).

'NOT THE EXPRESSION OF COLLECTIVE EMOTION ...'

This language of creative and spiritual inquiry turns into the language of military achievement when Eliot writes that we 'are only undefeated / Because we have gone on trying' (*DS*, 199). The creative victory may or may not be possible; the military one was still looking unlikely in 1941: this is the poetic corollary of anti-collaborationism (France, notoriously, had not 'gone on trying'), but deliberately anti-triumphal with it. And if there were any danger of forgetting its war context, Eliot gave the game away in 'Defense of the Islands', his poetic supplement to a propaganda exhibition in New York. Of immediate interest in relation to 'The Dry Salvages' is the passage for those at sea:

> those appointed to the grey
> ships – battleship, merchantman, trawler –
> contributing their share to the ages' pavement
> of British bone on the sea floor.[47]

Of interest, that is, because so much of *The Dry Salvages* is about being drowned in the Atlantic:

> Pray for all those who are in ships, those
> Whose business has to do with fish, and
> Those concerned with every lawful traffic
> And those who conduct them. (*DS*, 197)

Those lost sailors, to point out the obvious, evoke the fishermen and merchant seamen, the 'lawful traffic' and the convoys which 'conduct' them, being sunk by presumably unlawful German traffic (at Nuremberg the Allies would consider criminalising the submarine warfare which had been the focus of popular Anglo-American outrage). In this, the American quartet, Eliot moves from the Mississippi of his St. Louis childhood, to the east coast of his adolescence, to the Atlantic waters in which British and American sailors are, at the moment of the poem's writing, being drowned. If 'Defense of the Islands' is a straight propaganda effort, the much subtler *East Coker* does qualitatively similar ideological work; given the ongoing hard sell of the war to the United States, there could not have been a better time for this transatlantic public intellectual to drive the point home that he was an American too.

This statesmanlike self-presentation obviously mattered to Eliot, even as the *Quartets* simultaneously insist that the public prerogative of 'old men' is something to be questioned. Drawing on the authority conferred by the poet's American origins, *The Dry Salvages* elegises a perpetual cycle of Atlantic losses in which 'the gear of foreign dead men' gets washed up always on the coast, even as it speaks agonisingly of its own transatlantic time: 'Not fare well, / But fare forward, voyagers' (*DS*, 192, 197). These voyagers are not to think of 'the fruit of action' (*DS*, 197), a phrase which Eliot reuses the following year in another propaganda poem, 'To the Indians Who Died in Africa': a poem which, like *The Dry Salvages*, describes 'action with a common purpose, action / none the less fruitful if neither you nor we / Know, until the moment of death, / What is the fruit of action'.[48] Critically, this minor poem is also a text about death in wartime exile and about the subject's relation to the foreign earth in which he may be buried: 'Where a man dies bravely / At one with his destiny, that soil is his'[49] has the inadvertently (and in this context inappropriately) imperialist ring of Rupert Brooke's corner of a foreign field that is forever England. What 'To the Indians Who Died In Africa' also importantly does, however, is to reprise the strategies that bridge the watery homelessness of *The Dry Salvages* with the relativistic homeliness of *Little Gidding*: 'England and nowhere' (*LG*, 201).

Documenting death by Atlantic water, *The Dry Salvages* ends with Eliot's hope for a land burial in an English churchyard, or 'Not too far from the yew-tree' (*DS*, 199). The most American of the quartets, then, ends with the most English of resting places, by way of prefacing the last and most emphatically domestic of the *Quartets*. The first run of *Little Gidding* went to almost 17,000 copies; to look at this well-produced first edition with the acute mid-war paper shortage in mind is to wonder at the abundance of unused white page and the generosity of the allocation – the surprising priority accorded to what could be predicted to be a demanding poem gives some measure of Eliot's status as a public figure.[50] The war had not yet turned in Britain's favour by the time *Little Gidding* was published, and the poem, like its precursors, refuses to pledge consolatory certainties. Opening in 'the dark time of the year', Eliot's stripped landscape recalls John Donne's elegy 'A Nocturnal upon S. Lucy's Day, Being the Shortest Day' (*LG*, 200). It is appropriate enough, given that Little Gidding is the site of a sanctuary destroyed in the Civil War, to recall this seventeenth-century apostate, but in contrast with Donne's universal midwinter – 'I am every dead thing'[51] – Eliot goes on to relativise his position by invoking other sites, other deaths:

> There are other places
> Which also are the world's end, some at the sea jaws,
> Or over a dark lake, in a desert or a city –
> But this is the nearest, in place and time,
> Now and in England. (*LG*, 201)

These seas, dark lakes, deserts and cities represent, as many have pointed out, other places of pilgrimage; they also suggest more contemporary versions of the world's end: death by Atlantic water for those who 'Ended their voyage ... / ... in the dark throat' (*DS*, 198); death in the desert war, ongoing when this quartet was published, with 'Dead water and dead sand/ Contending for the upper hand' or in the bombardment of the city when 'Dust inbreathed was a house' (*LG*, 202). *Little Gidding* relativises across time as well as space when Eliot asks, 'Why should we celebrate / These dead men more than the dying?' (*LG*, 206). Probably forgetful of the immediate context, Ronald Schuchard glosses Eliot's 'dying' as 'living', theologically plausible but it would represent unthinkable callousness at the beginning of 1942.[52] Indeed, Eliot's question about why the long dead should be memorialised over the currently dying anticipates, if it does not quite forestall, attempts to make *Four Quartets* an escape from war. What Eliot offers by way of an answer is not so much a conclusion as the deferral of one, the somewhat anti-climactic assurance that historical perspective makes conclusions inevitable when all the participants are dead, 'folded in a single party' (*LG*, 206).

This inconclusive conclusion is the necessary outcome of *Four Quartets*' central argument about fighting, writing and spiritual struggle that 'For us, there is only the trying' (*EC*, 189). Anticipating many later commentators on modernism, Eliot anchors the modernist effort solidly to the experience of war, and he makes the parallels between interrogative form and anti-collaborationist context explicit in the famous description of twenty 'largely wasted' interwar years in a passage that records the inbuilt obsolescence of the modernist artefact: once you make it new, you have to keep making it new (*EC*, 188). It is a familiar story that war and modernism are connected: introducing his 1937 autobiography of writing and fighting, Wyndham Lewis had, after all, promised that his reader would be 'astonished' to discover how alike they were. Here Eliot, however, offers something other than macho blasting and bombardiering when he replaces the young men conventionally at the heroic centre of modernist and military achievement with the pathos and vulnerability of advancing age.[53] With an expressive stylistic infelicity, the idiom of military weakness recounts his efforts 'Trying to learn to use words':

> And so each venture
> Is a new beginning, a raid on the inarticulate
> With shabby equipment always deteriorating
> In the general mess of imprecision of feeling,
> Undisciplined squads of emotion. (*EC*, 189)

Here, the objective correlative is the subject rather than the substance of the poem, in what might be read as a valedictory reappraisal of Eliotic dogma about the monumentality and impersonality of the poetic work: in modernism's end, aptly enough, is modernism's beginning.

This, finally, is why old modernists, like old men, ought to be explorers. In his important study of the literature and culture of the Great War, Samuel Hynes argued that the outcome of 1914 was radical discontinuity 'between generations, between fighting soldiers and those who controlled their lives, between the present and the past'; these he summarises as 'two terse propositions: the old betray the young: the past is remote and useless'.[54] Eliot's situational thinking in *Four Quartets* is a late legacy of what was already a decades-old disjunction: mindful of a stature and authority that he associates with a treacherous gerontocracy, an old poet renounces dead certainties as his generation had been forced to in the previous war. Writing when the milestones of high modernism have already achieved their canonical status, Eliot valorises modernism's critical and creative procedure rather than its portentous products. His parenthetical, prosey, confessional and self-correcting final work renders its conclusions obsolete in the moment of their formulation: 'Quick now, here, now, always – / A condition of complete simplicity / (Costing not less than everything)' (*LG*, 209).

CHAPTER 4

The neutrality of Henry Green

Every politician who has made a speech since September 1939 has ended with a peroration in which he has said that we are not fighting this war for conquest; but to bring about a new order in Europe. In that order, they tell us, we are all to have equal opportunities, equal chances of developing whatever gifts we may possess. That is one reason why, if they mean what they say, and can effect it, classes and towers will disappear. The other reason is given by the income tax. The income tax is already doing in its own way what the politicians are hoping to do in theirs.
   Virginia Woolf, 'The Leaning Tower' (1940)[1]

In the [1914–18] war people in our walk of life entertained all sorts and conditions of men with a view to self-preservation, to keep the privileges we set such store by, and which are illusory, after those to whom we were kind had won the war for us. That is not to say the privileged did not fight, we did, but there were too few of us to win.
   Henry Green, *Pack My Bag* (1940)[2]

Woolf's 'The Leaning Tower' takes its title from her argument that writers of the 1930s lacked the stable centre of an ivory tower from which to write well about their surroundings. Although I only mentioned the essay earlier by way of suggesting the unpersuasive self-positioning – 'quite astonishing', John Mepham called it, 'quite unconvincing' – that Woolf had to perform in order to imagine a future in which her own class privilege would no longer obtain, its most penetrating insight is political. In an oddly ominous expression, Woolf accuses the decade's best-known writers of 'profiting by a society which they abuse ... flogging a dead or dying horse because a living horse, if flogged, would kick them off its back'.[3] What initially seems an attack on the bad faith of Oxbridge communists, a legitimate but unambitious target, amounts, more suggestively, to the claim that these writers were only making noisy declarations of what most people knew already, that the interwar social order was on its last legs. What Woolf describes is eminently recognisable as the 'Auden Generation' who dominated critical accounts of the 1930s for the half-century that followed; what she implies is that these writers were largely a triumph of self-promotion.

Only now that the old orthodoxy of 'the Auden generation' has come into question does Woolf's argument show its force. In the last decade it has become something of a truism that the institutional dominance of Auden and the poets whom he influenced made it difficult to see the diversity of 1930s writing, and if women authors notoriously represented the worst critical blind spot, the conventional readings of the period conspired to exclude fiction writers of both genders who didn't conform to a pattern of formal prosiness and political left-mindedness. An opaque stylist and a throwback to Tory radicalism, Henry Green is a misfit on both counts, and the most useful efforts to place him have looked to the modernist canon rather than to his public-school-and-Oxford contemporaries. Jeremy Treglown's invaluable biography of Green takes this tack from the outset, because 'there are ways in which he can be compared ... not only with Lawrence and Woolf but with Franz Kafka, Gertrude Stein, William Faulkner. But what is most important about him is how unlike anyone else he is'.[4] Perhaps it is because Green is not like anyone else that he is more legible in relation to an idea of modernism that has always been committed to unlikeness (the similarities between Woolf and Kafka, or Stein and Faulkner, do not go far beyond the modernist epithet), canonising on the basis of the one-off style. If being posh, precocious, and full of class guilt gave Henry Yorke the perfect biographical profile for the 1930s writer, the novels he wrote as 'Henry Green' bore no resemblance to the hectoring and self-regarding tone that Woolf considered definitive of the 1930s.

In this context, it is noteworthy that the passages from Woolf and Green that I quoted as epigraphs should make Woolf sound rather more 'leaning tower' than Green. Of particular interest are her topical references to the ongoing debate about taxation – Keynes had published his socially progressive pamphlet *How to Pay for the War* only three months earlier, an effort (he said) at 'marking the line of division between the totalitarian and the free economy'.[5] Where Woolf is deliberately down-to-earth in identifying with the beneficiaries of the war's practical, levelling effects, Green remains an obdurate toff, and, even allowing for the different audiences to which her lecture and his memoir are addressed, they suggest radically different ways of approaching the possible social consequences of the Second World War. Although Woolf's essay puts in place qualifiers about whether or not 'they' mean what they say, 'The Leaning Tower' imagines the Second World War climactically, as an

The neutrality of Henry Green 93

ending and potentially a new start. In contrast, Green's mode is recursive, and he approaches the imminent war by writing what Rod Mengham has called 'a memoir of the First'.[6] In this anecdote about his parents turning their country house into a convalescent hospital for shell-shocked officers, Green stays on his high horse when he describes how 'people in our walk of life' (landed aristocracy), took in 'all sorts' (the vulgar and the colonial). The description of this coldly conservative tactic 'to keep the privileges we set such store by' sets up an indictment of the Great War hierarchy, which Green evades altogether with the sly provocation of calling its privileges 'illusory'. In other words, whereas Woolf is prepared for the Second World War to effect material transformation, Green coolly returns to the Great War to point out that it, too, generated temporary disruptions in the social order. This chapter argues that Green used recursive effects of neutrality in order to invalidate prevailing stories about the Second World War's home front, and describes why it matters that these effects failed.

'THE MULTITUDINOUS RANKS OF *THOSE TO WHOM THINGS HAPPEN* ...'

The Woolfs' Hogarth Press published *Party Going* in the month the war broke out.[7] Like Virginia's final novel, Green's war-anxious *Party Going* describes a festivity turning into a funeral; the main characters are bright young things fogbound in a London terminus en route to the continent, in a non-plot that either anticipated or supplied the metaphor Leonard used when he later likened the war to 'endlessly waiting in a dirty grey railway station waiting-room, a cosmic railway station waiting room, with nothing to do but wait endlessly for the next catastrophe'.[8] The note of doom is struck in Green's opening sentence when a pigeon falls dead from the sky; an elderly woman inexplicably washes it, and falls ill of something that might, or might equally not, be causally related to her act of arbitrary kindness. Most of what follows takes place in a hotel overlooking the railway station, from which the spoiled central characters see the stranded masses trying to get home from work: 'thousands of Smiths, thousands of Alberts, hundreds of Marys'.[9] Julia Wray's walk to the station to meet her millionaire playboy lover Max Adey coincides with the journey of the workers leaving the city for the suburbs. Leaving her house, the socialite Julia 'lost her name and was all at once anonymous':

Fog was down to ground level outside London, no cars could penetrate there so that if you had been seven thousand feet up and could have seen through you would have been amused at blocked main roads in solid lines and, on the pavements within two miles of this station, crawling worms on either side. (*PG*, 388)

From above, these people are 'crawling worms', but to be 'seven thousand feet up' in *Party Going* you would have to be the narrator, or, alternatively, a bomber – because a panoptic elevation is increasingly a sinister thing: 'What targets', a bystander comes to remark, 'what targets for a bomb' (*PG*, 483). These masses are 'swarming ponds of humanity ... water beetles ... that swarm of people' (*PG*, 395), and terrifying in their multiplicity; as the stationmaster tells one of the vacationing party, 'we found that when they really began coming in, nine hundred and sixty-five persons could enter this station by the various subways each minute' (*PG*, 424).

The seething populace of *Party Going* recalls the high modernist fascination with the crowd, and the ominous political tenor is now unmistakeable: what is to be done with these faceless masses? Wyndham Lewis seems almost explicitly evoked in Green's description of the people on the station floor: 'for is it not what most people desire ... to be looked after, disciplined into insensitiveness, spared from suffering by insensibility and blind dependence on a will superior to their own?' Lewis asked in *The Art of Being Ruled* (1926).[10] Green's workers would surely count as 'the multitudinous ranks of *those to whom things happen*' described by Lewis in another of his interwar books: 'the masses, who are the cannon-fodder, the cattle outside the slaughter-house, serenely chewing the cud ... *those to whom things are done*, in contrast to those who have executive will and intelligence'.[11] Lewis's bovine image returns in *Party Going* when the partygoers are told that at least they can 'take rooms and be a bit comfortable like instead of 'aving to stand like butchered cattle waiting to be slaughtered in that yard beneath', although Lewis's 'executive' power – which might have redeemed them – is altogether voided by the democracy of the fog (478). Hesitantly, because they remain as much types as individualised characters, Green tries to resist the dehumanising implications of these 'masses' by surveying the scene not just from above, but also from the point of view of Thomson and Edwards; the menservants who guard the partygoers' luggage have romantic interior lives as real as those of their employers. Distinguished by name at least, they cease to be just 'targets for a bomb'.

If by 1939 these modernist masses were a familiar imaginative construct, so too was the novel's play with the definitively 1930s altitude of seeing the partygoers themselves from above and 'all at once anonymous'. Valentine Cunningham's landmark study of the decade assembled an enormous catalogue of instances to support his argument that the aerial view is in every sense the dominant one of a period which believed that, to borrow the Prime Minister Stanley Baldwin's unnerving axiom, the bomber would always get through.[12] (In preparation for the expected apocalypse, the Home Office had estimated that 20 million square feet of timber would be needed each month for coffins.[13]) Perhaps the iconic example of the 1930s aerial aesthetic is by Green's admirer Auden, in the untitled poem which reproves the doomed wealthy from the vantage point of 'the hawk or the helmeted airman':

> Financier, leaving your little room
> Where the money is made but not spent,
> You'll need your typist and your boy no more;
> The game is up for you and for the others
> . . . .
> You cannot be away, then, no
> Not though you pack to leave within an hour,
> Escaping humming down arterial roads.[14]

Directed at the same sort of social privilege that gives *Party Going* its ostensible subject, Auden's poem is a comparatively nasty piece of work because it retains its lofty perspective throughout. In its replication of recognisable tropes of interwar writing, the almost determinedly trivial *Party Going* generates unease and fear through the new urgency in 1939 of mass-consciousness and the aerial view. This is now an oppressive dramatic situation, and one which encodes the threat of revolution.

Green, who believed that the writer has 'no business with the story he is writing', shifts backwards and forwards between the hotel and the station floor with an air of neutrality.[15] But although they render explicit the doubly imprisoning effects of class immobility, the hotel doors that get shuttered to keep the hordes out become scarier for the partygoers that they keep locked in. One maid asks her mistress 'Do you think it's the revolution, Madam, and I have your bath-salts unpacked and your bath is ready for you now' (*PG*, 468), an ostensible non sequitur anticipated by the hotel's painting of Nero fiddling while Rome burns. The privileged characters recognise the danger from below and are forced to revisit their own part in it. An exchange between Julia and the inexplicably damaged Alex as they look down from the window suggests the vulnerability of their privilege:

She wondered if this were what you saw when you stood on your wedding day, a Queen, on your balcony looking at subjects massed below . . . Alex came up and said what they saw now was like a view from the gibbet and she exclaimed against that. (*PG*, 430)

The nature of the spectacle depends on whether the people below are going to venerate or execute her – since these (to her) faceless masses are almost by definition an indeterminate, unknowable agent, Julia is kept in ignorant passivity by the same forces of stratification that keep her wealthy. She asks Max how he deals with begging letters:

'After all,' she said, 'one must not hear too many cries for help in this world. If my uncle answered every begging letter he received he would have nothing left in no time'. It was extraordinary how quiet their room became once that window was shut. (*PG*, 438)

To retain your wealth means a perfect willed stupidity, a deliberate decision to shut out the demanding noise from below, a noise that is, as Michael Gorra summarises it, 'both impossible to ignore and impossible to confront'.[16] But it's a struggle, because the characters capable of obliviousness are just unhappy in a different way. This, perhaps, is 'illusory' privilege, the possibility of living as blindly as Max: 'When he thought, he was only conscious of uneasy feelings and he only knew that he had been what he did not even call thinking when his feelings hurt him' (*PG*, 441). Alex, positively introspective compared to the other partygoers, supposes he knows what it all means, in a passage that offers to elucidate the otherwise inexplicable relationship between the death of the pigeon and the moribund condition of the elderly woman who performed its last rites:

Here he pointed his moral. That is what it is to be rich, he thought, if you are held up, if you have to wait then you can do it after a bath in your dressing-gown and if you have to die then not as any bird tumbling dead from its branch down for the foxes, light and stiff, but here in bed, here inside, with doctors to tell you it is all right and with relations to ask if it hurts. Again no standing, no being pressed together, no worry since it did not matter if one went or stayed, no fellow feeling, true, and once more sounds came up from outside to make him think they were singing, no community singing he said to himself, not that even if it did mean fellow feeling. And in this room, as always, it seemed to him there was a sort of bond between the sexes and with these people no more than that, only dull antagonism otherwise. (*PG*, 493)

Alex's blunt didacticism is partly legitimate because the novel is so clearly about the difference between having money and not; but it is also misleading because, halfway through, the passage turns from self-incrimination into self-pity. Incapable of crossing the barricades (supposing he wanted to, and he does not), Alex has nothing other than a vague, idealised sense of the workers' compensatory 'fellow feeling'; the noise from downstairs is only 'to *make him think* they were singing' (my emphasis). It proves an inconclusive epiphany because the revolution is postponed when the fog dissipates and the trains start running again. Relieved, Julia swallows her tears: 'Dear good English people, she thought, who never make trouble no matter how bad it is, come what may no matter' (*PG*, 525).

This is the comforting story that would accrue its tenacious significance in the Blitz, of the decent, plucky Londoners all coming together, and afterwards, when these 'dear good English people' would attain access to greater social opportunities without the violent revolution that looms like the fog over *Party Going*. But the novel is not going to sanction Julia's smugness any more than it allows Alex's sentimental imaginings of working-class camaraderie to be taken at face value. Even if these 'dear good English people' do not turn violent, their sheer volume ensures that they cannot help but be destructive. The steel doors have only been closed because last time the workers were trapped in the station they smashed the hotel up with their sheer mass, and a boy was permanently injured in the crush. Facetiously, Green's 'crippled' victim is identified as 'little Tommy Tucker' (*PG*, 437), whose improbable presence (Tiny Tim?) in the novel points toward, and dismisses, the gestures of middle-class sympathy elicited by the realist fiction that *Party Going* emphatically is not. Green's working-class characters, and they are the main characters in many of his novels, have a complex interiority that disavows authorial sentimentality. Was it because of their class politics that Green blurted out in a late interview that Tolstoy and Dickens were 'impossible – entirely impossible'?[17] The interviewer did not ask.

What Green's persistently under-read novels contribute to political readings of late modernism is this: a sympathetic fascination with the working classes is not, it turns out, exclusively the preserve of left politics in the 1930s; rather, a liking for the cultural specificities of class difference becomes almost tautologically compatible with an interest in their perpetuation. The issue arises most pressingly for *Living* (1929), a novel based on Green's experiences in his father's foundry, where he worked from the shop-floor upwards after leaving Oxford, and which is almost entirely about the lives of the workers. It's an obvious point, perhaps, that sympathetic representation can be a conservative (in the most literal sense) response to social change as well as a radical one, and not least when what's being represented is in the process of radical transformation. The General Strike of 1926 and the beginnings of the depression threatened to redefine the class identities from which *Living* is composed, while *Loving*, which I shall discuss at length later, details the end of the master/servant model of class relations hastened by the war. Even the much-remarked gerundive titles of Green's novels have something of the diorama about them – *Living, Loving, Party Going, Concluding* and *Doting*. Their fieldwork may well be determined by the diligent accretion of ethnographic trivia legitimised by the leftwing Mass-Observation, but they also offer a domestic parallel to the elegiac nostalgia at the heart of the aristocratic Bronislaw Malinowski's pioneering modernist anthropology: 'Just now, when the methods and aims of scientific field ethnology have taken shape, when men fully trained for the work have begun to travel into savage countries and study their inhabitants – these die away under our very eyes.'[18]

'IT BRINGS EVERYONE TOGETHER, THERE'S THAT MUCH TO A WAR'

This passing away of the pre-war is elegised in a more ostentatiously private way in Green's memoir *Pack My Bag*, written in the years leading up to the war and published in 1940. It opens with the assertion that only the fear of death and the imminence of war drive Green to autobiography:

I was born a mouthbreather with a silver spoon in 1905, three years after one war and nine before another, too late for both. But not too late for the war which seems to be coming upon us now and that is a reason to put down what comes to mind before one is killed, and surely it would be asking much to pretend one had a chance to live. (*PMB*, 5)

In this deeply ambivalent self-positioning, Green becomes simultaneously an outsider and an insider, capable of colloquially ridiculing his 'silver spoon' birth in the impersonal effacements of upper-class English ('asking much to pretend one had a chance to live'). Its sweetly morbid impulse keeps returning in the book, the idea that 'there must be a threat to one's skin to wake what is left of things remembered into things to die with' (*PMB*, 54). Through it, Green acts out the 'holy falseness'[19] with which Richard Roe in *Caught* prematurely bids farewell to his loved things, as in

Pack My Bag Green announces the likelihood of his own death by fire, 'speaking as the Auxiliary Fireman I have now become' (*PMB*, 162).

Representing in a more indirectly collective form the class antagonisms of *Party Going*, the two central characters of *Caught*, Pye and Roe (the punning allegory of their names is often noted), are firemen from different classes whose histories are personally and professionally mixed up with each other because, anterior to their meeting in the Phoney War, Pye's unstable sister has kidnapped Roe's son. In the artificial intertwining of the two class-divided lives, Green offers an acutely non-realist rendering of the familiar story that social boundaries collapsed on the home front. One critic has recently drawn the conclusion that 'class distinctions [are] erased and true individual merit made obvious'; and, while rightly conceding that Green may well have had mixed feelings about social change, he argues, 'That true merit does ultimately shine through suggests the possibility of a real democracy, which seems to Green a plausible outcome of the war.'[20] But class distinctions finally collapse only in a closing parallel between Roe and Pye that is anything other than reassuring: Roe has a neurotic breakdown and Pye commits suicide, suspected of paedophilia and convinced that he has raped his own sister. It would be a little bleak to see this as exemplary social levelling.

Indeed, in *Caught* as in *Party Going*, Green registers with suspiciously pre-emptive clarity the novel's susceptibility to allegorising interwar class politics. The narrator glosses a conversation between Roe and a colleague with 'They had neither of them come across anyone in the least resembling the other' (*C*, 66). The influx of volunteers puts the fire station supervisor Pye in a newly superior position to those of a higher class, while Roe's manual labour is a downward step, as the narrator points out in an authoritative explanation straight from Green's personal experience: 'War puts men in this position, however, that they can do little about their own affairs, they have no prospects, their incomes fluctuate wildly, heavier taxation is always threatened' (*C*, 5). However, Roe's ultimate mistake is to take at face value his downward mobility:

In his dirt, his tiredness, the way the light hurt his eyes and he could not look, in all these he thought he recognised that he was now a labourer, he thought he had grasped the fact that, from now on, dressed like this, and that was why roadmen called him mate, he was one of the thousand million that toiled and spun. (*C*, 51)

This is much more slippery than social assimilation; as with Alex's meretricious clarity about the 'fellow feeling' of the workers on the floor of *Party Going*'s railway station, Green's 'he thought' is not just the report of a character's beliefs, but exactly what proves them false. This 'he thought he recognised … he thought he had grasped' implies very strongly that whatever Roe is thinking, he's wrong. His slumming is only an interim self-dramatising because 'It brings everyone together, there's that much to a war', as he disingenuously remarks to 'Chopper', in an equally disingenuous replication of his workmate's demotic syntax; Chopper agrees, but Roe does not hear the answer from one of the women in the group: 'When it doesn't put blue water between' (C, 48).

What is happening across the blue water between Britain and the Continent is recorded in narrative interventions such as 'The news from Norway was worse', set aside as a whole paragraph in the middle of an account of the cook's resignation from the fire station, as if the characters have all begun to forget the war itself, and as if private events will always matter more than events of conventionally historical and global significance (C, 136). Most hideously, the war appears in the fantasy life of the kidnapped Christopher Roe ('I'm a German airman, I'm bombing' [C, 173]) when he drives the birds from the garden of his father's country house:

'They're Polish people', Christopher said, 'and I'm a German policeman, rootling them about.'

'Well, if that's so, hadn't you better carry on the good work where it's drier? Why not go back to the stables and see if you can't kill some more mice with a spoon? You could think they were Czechs', his father said. (C, 188–9)

Conceivably, a passage like this points pejoratively to the unreality of the war on the home front, or to Nancy Astor's contemporary indictment of the 'subconscious Hitlerism in the hearts of men'.[21] What it certainly indicates is the indirection with which historical events get experienced in Green's novels, and Lyndsey Stonebridge's reading of *Caught* as a mitigated form of trauma theory *avant la lettre* is especially inviting given the novel's emphasis on resisting premature closures.[22] The anti-climactic resolution of Christopher's kidnapping is a powerful instance of this: lured from a toyshop by Pye's sister, he is returned uninjured, 'And then all was over, forgotten seemingly, done with … But if that were so, why was it that the boy could never play with a sailboat again?' (C, 17). The novel insists that the past relived in all the distortions of memory is what causes the real damage, however history-making the present moment: Christopher's kidnapping is articulated in Gestapo identification, in his replacement of sailing boats with sadistic war games; Pye survives a career as a fireman but kills himself by putting his head in the oven. And as in the now-familiar account of trauma, war damage exceeds bodily harm. At the end of the novel, Roe himself has collapsed: 'A bomb came too close. It knocked him out. He was sent home, superficially uninjured. They called it nervous debility' (*C*, 172). By always getting inside, the war shows the dangerous permeability of the boundaries between insides and outsides.

Increasingly, this permeability makes the attempted evasion of war impossible, and the collapsing boundaries of *Caught* become unmistakeably political. Though the 'home front' by oxymoronic definition effaces the distinction between the site of battle and a place of safety, less expected is the parallel between the Blitzed cityscape and the countryside that gets associated for both characters with their repressed private histories. Commenting on Roe's 'nostalgia for a past life that never really existed', Andrzej Gąsiorek suggests that Roe's memorial reinvention of his mediocre family life on the country estate is 'the corollary of the public myth that rural England somehow represents the 'heart' of the country, that it embodies the values for which the nation fought the war and the virtues that enabled it to emerge victorious'.[23] The rural is also the scene of Pye's semi-invented past, the site of his fantastical incestuous encounter with the girl (possibly his sister) whom he thinks of, somewhat surreally, as 'Mrs. Lane's little girl' because they've had sex in 'that winding lane between high banks, in moonlight, in colour blue, leaning back against the pale wild flowers' (*C*, 42, 40). But this seeming idyll is horribly similar, rather than nostalgically antithetical, to the scene of wartime London, and once Pye begins to remember Mrs Lane's girl and his sister, past and present, country and city, public life and private become the same nightmarish landscape: 'Oh God she had been so white and this bloody black-out brought you in mind of it with the moon, this blue colour, and with the creeping home': 'What d'you make of this moonlight, I mean in the black-out ... D'you mistake objects in it, 'ave you taken one person for another?' (*C*, 41, 157). The black-out turns city into country once again for Pye; correspondingly, Roe's pastoral past is re-imagined as black-out when Roe thinks back to the manor that he's about to lose:

At night shutters, and in front of these, curtains covered by a Morris design, closed all sound of the cedar out as it groaned under the weight of snow or, in other weather, absolutely black in moonlight as the wind outside swept through and through. (*C*, 69)

It is as if his country house has been sealed in permanent darkness, perpetually on its war footing (the socialist curtains are a nicely ironic touch). By the end of the novel, Roe's place in the country is a 'beastly, decaying place'; 'The furniture he knew was sheeted, the soot deep in each cold fireplace' (*C*, 184, 173). As in Forster's lament that something has been lost 'as surely as if a bomb had hit it', what the war began, social reform is going to finish.

Retrospectively, it seems obvious that the destiny of the country house and the prosecution of the war have been mixed up in one another from the beginning of the novel. When Roe and his son go walking on their estate, the new fireman masochistically enjoys the prospect of self-extinction:

> Then, as they turned to come back, going out of their way to climb along a fallen tree, another herd of deer moved off into the veil, heads up, one of them coughing. He wanted to know if it was going to die. Asking this he struck so close to the note this sad day played over and over, with the wet, the silence once broken, flying low over tops of trees, by a warplane which he did not even look up to watch, neither did the deer, and to the note repeated which was this separation that war had forced into their lives, all these sounded the closing phrase of a call to depart, and Roe said the deer would die, that it was sure to. (*C*, 10)

Roe is here not just the second half of 'pyro', but is also the dying roe deer, a necessary cull for the health of the group. But, in his thoroughly self-dramatising identification with the doomed male elder, Roe cannot see that the war will mean disrupted lineage and lost proprietary continuity. Roe, caught up in his own self-presentation, has anticipated his own death, and has even enjoyed his social slumming, but the other endings that the war brings about come as a ghastly shock. Attributed his author's celebrated facility for replicating working-class dialogue, he is happy to assume temporarily the argot of his workmates when he introduces them to his son – 'It's all right, cock ... it's only my nipper' – but he expects everything to return to the pre-war structure: 'there's no nursery now', his son's childminder has to tell him, 'The days of nurseries are over' (*C*, 145, 175).

But Green seems not to have seen it coming either. In *Pack My Bag*, he had recalled the betrayals of the Great War in order to cast a sceptical eye on the propaganda claim that the war would be fought for structural change: 'The phrase then was "we gave our sons." "For what?" was the cry in 1923. It will be the same this time' (*PMB*, 194). The same refusal to be duped is given voice in *Caught* by the fire station's cook, who suggests that 'It's all on account of the rich, they started it for their own ends', and by Pye when he refers snidely to Roe's wealth, 'the dough 'e won't 'ave much longer, when we get this new world they say we're fighting for' (*C*, 114, 107). The desolation of Roe's country house at the end of the novel shows their suspicions misplaced because the war seems to have brought ruin on the class to which Roe and his author belonged. Green's Hogarth Press champion John Lehmann much later remarked that 'Richard Roe bears a strong resemblance to Henry Green, to Henry Yorke'.[24] This is autobiographical fiction as self-parody: Green's bogus classlessness and his imaginative faking of his own death come back to meet him in this novel; perhaps that's why he called it *Caught*.

'THE MOST CELEBRATED EIGHTEENTH-CENTURY FOLLY IN EIRE THAT HAD STILL TO BE BURNED DOWN'

That Green implicated himself so completely in the failed transgression of social boundaries cautions against over-reading the radicalism of his next novel *Loving* (1945), as I think Michael North perhaps does when he calls it 'a satire on the great house myth, which is simply the identification of an insular privileged way of life with civilization itself'.[25] Kinalty Castle is not a country house of the kind that Henry Yorke had known from birth, but an Anglo-Irish Big House. Set 'in Eire where there is no black-out', the novel's main characters are the English servants who are torn between their dislike of their peripheral location and their fear of returning to the British mainland during the Blitz.[26] The novel opens with the death of Eldon the blackmailing butler; his replacement Raunce is falling in love with the maid Edith; Edith's friend Kate is falling in love with the Irish lampman Paddy; a ring goes missing (twice) and is found (twice); by the end of the novel Raunce, the new blackmailing butler, is dying. The circularity of the book is driven home by the 'Once upon a day' that opens it and the correspondingly fairy-tale ending of 'happily ever after' (*L*, 18, 204).

That the neutral Republic of Ireland was something of a fantastical never-never land during what its politicians euphemised as 'The Emergency' is a recurrent theme in contemporary Irish writing. In Kate O'Brien's *The Last of Summer* (1943), for instance, a deracinated Franco-Irish ingénue strays in from an Elizabeth Bowen novel to find herself in rural Ireland on the outbreak of war. O'Brien describes the strange solitude of a heavily censored country in which, one character says, de Valera ensures that Ireland 'is Heaven's ante-room ... whether we like the idea or not'.[27] The novel's primary subject is a thoroughly dysfunctional family unit (a mad priest as a retainer; a mother in love with her adult son) whose unspoken but unmistakeable private strains correspond to accelerating tensions elsewhere in Europe, and the desperate international context generates a conflict in the novel between parochialism itself ('Danzig's a long way from Drumaninch') and the anxieties that parochialism simultaneously induces ('Being neutral will be precious little help to the imagination').[28] Henry Green's aborted memoir of the war had begun with himself and his wife on holiday in the Republic of Ireland at the time of the Munich Crisis. The fragment that survives as 'Before the Great Fire' speaks in affectionate anecdotes about the Irish vacation, but it makes reference, too, to the narrow-minded facets of Irish neutrality, to the belief that 'nothing could ever happen to the great Little Republic'.[29] In *Loving*, Green's insistence on aesthetic neutrality has to confront political neutrality in its most widely debated wartime instantiation.

Even if the fairytale register of *Loving* seems wilfully aslant, a straight evasion of the blitzed cityscapes of *Caught*, the novel ultimately points to the impossibility of escaping the insidious effects of war. In a subplot that recalls the traumatised cruelties of the kidnapped child in *Caught* ('they're Polish people ... and I'm a German policeman'), an urban evacuee strangles one of the peacocks beloved of the Irish lampman Paddy O'Conor. His scandalised aunt proclaims that 'Children is all little 'Itlers these days':

'Oh I screamed out but 'e 'ad it about finished the little storm trooper. There wasn't nothing left to do but 'ide the dead body away from that mad Irish Conor.'
'Yes he's taken up with the things that man,' Miss Burch agreed. 'As to that I've only to pluck it,' Miss Welch said, 'and 'e won't never distinguish the bird from a chicken they're that ignorant the savages.' (*L*, 53)

And despite that Green's writing about the English class system in wartime from neutral Ireland seems a characteristically evasive undertaking, there are hard-to-ignore political implications of being 'over in Eire as we are or whatever they call this country of savages' (*L*, 149). This familiar account of Ireland as a 'country of savages' keeps being reiterated in the novel because, as Raunce's employer tells him, this is 'enemy country. ... We simply must keep things up' (*L*, 23), an idea that she expands in a comically self-regarding conversation with her daughter-in-law:

'But in a way I regard this as my war work, maintaining the place I mean. Because we're practically in enemy country here you know and I do consider it so important from the morale point of view to keep up appearances. This country has been ruined by people who did not live on their estates. It might be different if de Valera had a use for places of the kind. Why he doesn't offer Ireland as a hospital base I can't imagine. Then one could hand over a house like this with an easy conscience. Because after all as I always say there are the children to consider. I look on myself simply as a steward.' (L, 169)

Mrs Tennant is obviously an absurdity: her paternalism forgets the historical obvious (that her home is a legacy of the British occupation), and that the newly self-determining Republic of Ireland has less than no reason to put itself at the service of the British Army, least of all when she herself continues to thinks of the native Irish as 'enemies'.

As Green suggests through the idiotic Mrs Tennant, the real significance of this being an Irish, and not an English, manor is that the Anglo-Colonial setting recalls the 'dirty hands' argument that anti-imperialist writers as different as Woolf and Orwell raised and renounced as the Second World War arrived: that Kinalty Castle exists at all recalls the forms of foreign occupation engaged in by the British, and which now threaten Britain. The link between British imperialism and Germany's territorial ambitions is made explicitly when the characters contemplate a Nazi invasion:

'But let 'im satisfy me in this respect,' Raunce cried, 'what the condition of Ireland has to do with it? For one thing if it wasn't rotten land fit only for spuds we'd've been 'ere to this day, our government I mean. No we gave Ireland back because we didn't want it, or this part anyway. Nor Jerry doesn't want it. Then what is 'e after? I'll tell you. What he requires is a stepping stone to invade the old country with. Like crossin' a stream to keep your feet dry.' (L, 98)

The perceived threat posed by Irish neutrality was exacerbated by the fact that the IRA had commenced a bombing campaign of the British mainland early in 1939, and because of widespread fears that Republicans were making common cause with Berlin against the British. The refusal to allow Britain the use of Irish ports to defend the North Atlantic convoys was considered an especially foolhardy instance of cutting off your nose to spite your face, as a David Low cartoon from November 1940 indicates: depicting a U-boat off the coast of Ireland (signposted by a notice prohibiting British refuelling – a bone of contention between

Churchill and de Valera), its caption reads 'God bless Eire's neutrality – until the Führer gets there'.[30] Although a purposeful gesture of the new state's national sovereignty, Irish neutrality was imagined as a strategy that could only, and perhaps suicidally, help the Germans.

The novel comically exploits the atmosphere of paranoia surrounding Irish neutrality in the early phases of the war. At the end of 1940, the *Times* carried the story of a bizarre international incident in which a wireless address to the United States by de Valera had appealed for support to protect Irish neutrality, and notwithstanding insistence from Dublin that the Irish leader had spoken of 'a crisis which would force our people once more to battle desperately for their liberty', the official Columbia transcript had recorded this as 'incitement which would force our people once more to battle against Britain and the British'.[31] And if it reached histrionic proportions in less liberal circles, anti-Irish feeling remained strong enough for even the high-minded *Horizon* to publish an Irish number at the beginning of 1942. Cyril Connolly's own Anglo-Irish background may have had something to do with the unusually long (and, unusually, signed) editorial in which he argued that 'Nobody should express any views on Ireland till he has read some Anglo-Irish history ... our record in Ireland is one of seven centuries of cruelty, injustice, intolerance and exploitation'.[32] The same point was made more acidly in an article in the same issue of *Horizon*, which described how 'The people of Eire have little faith in British democracy ... they cannot, by any stretch of imagination, bring themselves to regard Britain as the sole champion of international good sportsmanship or as the saviour of small nations'.[33]

Green later explained that his intention in *Loving* had been to take 'a crack at the absurd Southern Irish and at the same time a swipe at the British servants, who yet remain human beings. But it is meant to torpedo that woman and her daughter-in-law, the employers'.[34] But *Loving* appears hopelessly complicit in its colonial subject matter. There is no direct speech from Paddy ('that mad Irish Conor') in the novel, the joke being that everybody else finds his accent impenetrable. In love with him, at least in the absence of better romantic prospects, the housemaid Kate translates Paddy's speeches for the other characters. When her abilities fail, and sometimes even when they don't, the reader is completely excluded:

He muttered something. For once she could not have understood. (*L*, 88)

'Can a person eat them eggs?' she asked. He answered excitedly. 'That's all right,' she said. 'No need to get worked up. I only asked didn't I?' He muttered something. (*L*, 91)

Grubby and incoherent, 'Paddy' appears a nasty caricature, except that the novel's joke is to debar the (implicitly English) reader alongside the chauvinistically English characters from the kind of intimacy that Kate, because she takes Paddy seriously, enjoys, and which the others have no right to share.

In any case, Paddy's status as a representative and agent of post-colonial rebirth is made obvious when Edith and Kate come upon him sleeping in the derelict hunting stables of the Big House:

It was a place from which light was almost excluded now by cobwebs across its two windows and into which, with the door ajar, the shafted sun lay in a lengthened arch of blazing sovereigns. Over a corn bin on which he had packed last autumn's ferns lay Paddy snoring between these windows, a web strung from one lock of hair back onto the sill above and which rose and fell as he breathed. Caught in the reflection of spring sunlight this cobweb looked to be made of gold as did those others which by working long minutes spiders had drawn from spar to spar of the fern bedding on which his head rested. It might have been almost that O'Conor's dreams were held by hairs of gold binding his head beneath a vaulted roof on which the floor of cobbles reflected an old king's molten treasure from the bog. (L, 56)

Surrounded by gold as he sleeps in a stable that has fallen, alongside British power, into dilapidation, Paddy becomes a richly romantic figure of Irish renaissance. As Mengham notes, the 'hairs of gold' recall Gulliver on his first night in Lilliput – and Gulliver's Irish authorship seems particularly relevant here.[35] Held down by insubstantial restraints, Paddy is imagined as one of the dead kings of Ireland, who are continually alluded to through the archaeological digs nearby (to the Big House owners these are only an excuse for adulterous assignations), and newly arising as the Anglo-Irish aristocracy enters its terminal decline.

Insistently deflationary, the novel draws attention to its refusal to write in grand terms either British colonial power or its imminent conclusion. If Green was – and it becomes increasingly clear in the course of his career – basically conservative in his thinking about domestic politics, he was almost theatrically uninterested in the imperialist dimensions of Tory politics. The Anglo-Irish house will soon succumb, the reader is constantly reminded, to nationalist violence: 'For this house that had yet to be burned down, and in particular that greater part of it which remained closed, was a shadowless castle of treasures'; it is 'the most celebrated eighteenth-century folly in Eire that had still to be burned down' (L, 64–5, 182). The narrator's arch prolepsis is supported by Raunce's predictions, because pure self-interest allows him to read the writing on the wall: 'We're livin' under a shadow these days'; 'The way things are shapin' it wouldn't come as a surprise if places such as this weren't doomed to a natural death so to say' (*L*, 146, 195). Most of the house has been locked up and at least half the staff are dying (Eldon, Burch, Nanny Swift, Raunce), but unlike, say, Elizabeth Bowen's *The Last September* (1929), a novel set in the same Anglo-Irish milieu which ends with the burning down of the Big House, Green's novel never represents the conflagration that finally destroys the Ascendancy way of life. But this Big House world was Bowen's own, and no wonder she felt more troubled by its loss (she published *Bowen's Court*, a memoir of her ancestral pile, during the war). Green can afford to engage in his light, blandly disinterested premonitions; an arch form of counter-neutrality that allows him to foretell an apocalyptic conflagration, an ironic Blitz equivalent, which he needn't really bother to narrate.

'ONE OF THE LUCKY ONES ... BACK'

Green's unusually frivolous version of the modernist resistance to closure generates the novel's reiterative plotting: the dramas are not only totally inconsequential, but have an anti-climactic tendency to get recycled. Things go missing, get found, get lost again: the gardening gauntlet that Edith has borrowed to collect her stolen peacock eggs; the waterglass that she steals to preserve them; the peacock that is illicitly strangled, plucked, buried and dug up again; the ring that keeps being lost, stolen and returned. But it is mostly dialogue that gets appropriated and misappropriated. When Mrs Tennant tells Raunce not to keep calling her 'Madam' on the grounds that 'repeating a thing over and over rather seems to take away from the value' (*L*, 156), once again she is totally wrong. A limited range does all Green's work.

Charley seriously said, and at the same time imitated Mrs Welch's nephew, 'Maybe she put'm down and forgot to pick'm up.' (*L*, 66)

'Well Charley what'd you say?'
'I tell you this won't do,' he answered. 'Put 'm back where you found 'm.'
'Put it back where I found it,' she echoed as though dumbfounded. (*L*, 119)

The endless comic reverberations in *Loving* work to create a community in which characters infinitely borrow each other's speech habits, imitate each other and absent characters, and quote each other constantly and in hilariously unexpected circumstances. More stylised even than this in its constant repetitions, Green's final war novel reverses comprehensively these effects of intimacy and community.

Repatriated from a German prisoner of war camp in 1944, Charley Summers is 'one of the lucky ones ... back', but his return to England is made difficult by the death of his married lover, Rose, whose name speaks of both romantic love and resurrection.[36] Charley is reminded of Rose at every turn: by the name of a barmaid, by the past tense of 'rising' ('rising prices ... they've rose' [B, 39]):

He fled Rose, yet every place he went she rose up before him; in florists' windows; in a second-hand bookseller's with a set of Miss Rhoda Broughton, where, as he was staring for her reflection in the window, his eyes read a title, *Cometh Up as a Flower*, which twisted his guts; also in a seed merchant's front that displayed a watering can, to the spout of which was fixed an attachment labelled "Carter's patent Rose." (B, 63–4)

The first sentence in which 'Rose ... rose' indicates the textual transmissibility of Charley's nausea, asking the reader to surpass his traumatic fixation. War damage is imagined as a kind of mad reading, and Charley even ignores a young boy who might be his son because he 'spelled nothing to him' (B, 5). This misreading mimics Charley's loss of context in a highly bureaucratised end-of-war society, which has officially been made strange by the prevalence of acronyms that Charley does not know, and which the novel refuses to explain. Rose's husband tells him that 'everything's initials these days', a line soon repeated verbatim by Rose's father, Mr Grant (B, 10, 20); as Mengham points out, 'Britain in 1944 is literally *unreadable*'.[37] Mr Grant makes matters worse by setting Charley up with Rose's illegitimate half-sister, Nancy, whom Charley takes for Rose herself.

The next thing Charley knew he was by a church. He found himself reading a poster stuck up on the notice board outside, which went, "Grant O Lord," then said something about a faithful servant. The first word shook him. He cried again, "The bastard," right out loud. (B, 66)

Rose's husband sends Charley a story from a magazine whose mistaken identity plot echoes his predicament, and, although Charley is attracted by the similarity between his situation and that of the story, his final reaction is less invested than his habitual weird reading would make likely: 'Ridiculous story' (B, 120). But, like *Back* itself, it almost has to be a ridiculous story, because realist narrative modes are presented as being completely inadequate to the war experience. As Gerard Barrett writes in his graceful essay on the novel, *Back* is 'more interested in symbolic than mimetic values'.[38]

Qualitative distinctions of a similar kind had been made earlier in the war by Mass-Observation's Tom Harrisson when, in an amusing précis of the novels produced between 1939 and 1941 ('Never have I felt that I owed so little to so many'), he described how he had been 'totally, immeasurably bogged, engrossed in bad reading. Ninety-five per cent of it is stuff I would never have read, or even imagined could be written, before'.[39] Still, he finds some novels to praise when he argues that 'the isolations of war, the retreats and imprisonments, the tensions of loneliness have produced some of the worthwhile war literature so far'.[40] It is tempting here to substitute 'realist' and 'modernist' for the distinctions Harrisson is drawing, and *Back* is emphatically a war writing that validates the damaged interior life ('the isolations of war') in its disorientating tactic of having a plot replicate so completely the protagonist's mental illness: it turns out that Charley's landlady, Mrs Frazier, knows Mr Grant (Rose's father), who knows Middlewitch (Charley's old friend), who is Nancy's neighbour, who knows Ernie Mandrew (who has stolen Charley's girlfriend), who also knows Nancy (Rose's sister). Even beyond Charley's pathological search for connections, the novel's bizarre shrinkage traps him into paranoid alienation, the sense in which this New Britain is not simply unreadable but conspiring actively against him. As Mrs Frazier tells him, 'Once you start on coincidences why there's no end to those things'; Charley stops listening to the story that follows, the punch line of which is 'For they were as like as two peas' (*B*, 37) – and Rose and Nancy turn out to be so similar that he comes to believe that Nancy is Rose. Given that Nancy knows she's 'a sort of walking memory to other people' of her half-sister, her early conversations with Charley are gratuitously inane, as when he describes the child in the cemetery, her nephew Ridley:

'I've seen Ridley, Rose', he said. He watched her as he spoke, as a dog sits up for a bone.
'There you go, more riddles. And who's Ridley?'
He looked at her idiotically. (*B*, 86, 58)

The sickness is continually present, but its cause is hauntingly inexplicit. Charley feels a 'nausea, which had recently begun to spread in his stomach whenever prison camps were mentioned' but the novel never explains what happened there (*B*, 19).

When his secretary challenges him about Rose he calls her question a 'cruel shock, this searchlight on a naked man', and runs out 'in case he should have to vomit', the slippery focalisation makes it impossible to determine whether his sickness is caused by the mention of Rose or by the prison camp metaphor into which Charley has converted it himself (*B*, 129). Charley's experience in the camp is absent for most of the novel, but towards the end it threatens to resurface as Mr Grant dies in an upstairs bedroom:

And he saw the cat curled up asleep. It didn't even raise its ears. Then, at the idea that this animal could ignore crude animal cries above, which he had shut out with his wet palms, he nearly let the horror get him, for the feelings he must never have again were summoned once more ... they came rumbling back, as though at a signal, from a moment at night in France. But he won free. He mastered it. (*B*, 218).

The reader never finds out what is meant by this 'something in France which he knew, as he valued his reason, that he must always shut out' (*B*, 218); indeed, knows nothing about Charley's captivity other than that he had a pet mouse in the camp. Wondering if the mouse is the key to it all, Nancy asks if the guards took his mouse away from him; they didn't (*B*, 234). Green is not about to offer a key that might be used to open up – which is to say, close down – the novel.

That Nancy should be in pursuit of the suppressed cause for his symptoms represents just one of the novel's speedy and discredited diagnoses of Charley's madness. All the men around Charley, for example, are fully conversant in popular war psychology: 'All you're doing is to perpetuate the conditions you've lived under, which weren't natural'; 'there's compensations in not remembering'; 'Why only the other day in my paper I read where a doctor man gave as his opinion that we were none of us normal' (*B*, 32, 38, 102). In its casual familiarity with popularised psychoanalytic discourse, the novel raises the essentially second-wave-modernist issue of what happens after psychoanalysis – since it was the clinical problem of shellshock after the Great War that brought it into common view, psychoanalysis ought to make war trauma in the next war comprehensible. Barrett calls *Back* 'the decade's finest representation of a condition [PTSD] that has only recently acquired a name', and Kristine Miller's recent article on the novel amplifies the gendered undertones of Charley's psychological predicament ('the pressure of sustaining a masculine identity that relies so heavily on the repression of emotional pain').[41] Nonetheless, what emerges from *Back* is that an understanding of trauma does not necessarily help; on the contrary, the official recognition of trauma becomes as evasive as the traumatic experience is elusive. This is why the novel insistently makes the Second World War bleed into the First: Rose's mother mistakes Charley for her brother who was killed at seventeen in the Great War: 'She will insist it's the last war'; and Charley's self-perception is articulated in what, by 1944, must have felt an antediluvian turn of phrase: 'Charley considered he was as dead as if he were six feet down, in Flanders, under the old tin helmet' (*B*, 18, 94). '"They're coming back nervous cases, like they did out of the last war,' he repeated to himself, and thought that, in that case, then everything was hopeless' (*B*, 128).

Why the insistence on the last war? There is a clue to the significance of Charley's dead lover Rose in Paul Fussell's remark that roses were 'indispensable to the work of the imagination' in the First World War: a healing wound is a rose; a medal is a rose; a splash of blood is a rose; sacrifice, fidelity and England are roses.[42] And Fussell's comments about the prevalence of red roses in British war cemeteries reminds us that the novel opens in the rose-filled churchyard where Rose lies buried. Only if Charley's Rose had been a Poppy could her symbolic and memorial function be clearer, and she redirects the reader away from the present conflict and back to the war in which Green was too young to serve. The dominant aesthetic of Second World War writing is recursive: even the titles of Woolf's *Between the Acts* and Eliot's *Four Quartets* signal the texts' emphasis on the circular and reiterative rather than on linear forward movement, while Rebecca West thought she could trace the causes of the Second World War back to the source of the first (and her behemoth of a book perpetually threatens endless regress). To some extent this recursiveness simply makes an aesthetic virtue out of the brute historical fact that this was the second total war these writers had lived through, and if the war experience is almost truistically a limit case for the communicable ('unspeakable', 'indescribable'), it's no surprise that writers should return to what is already known.

Potentially, confronting the Second World War by looking back at the previous war, against the same country, and won, offers a reassuring strategy and a promise of more of the same. But the deflationary tactic of returning to the Great War makes *Pack My Bag* a progressively uncomfortable read:

We hated Germans and at school we did believe they were so short of food they boiled the dead down to get the fats, that they crucified Australians, and that they were monsters different from us. It is interesting to see how these atrocity stories are coming back today; as I write there are tales of concentration camps as bad as any told when Belgium was invaded in 1914. Again a month or two ago in September 1938 there was that authentic note of wild hysteria to recapture which you need only look at any war-time *Punch*. (*PMB*, 72–3)

In a horrible by-product of Green's interest in recurrence, atrocity narratives are seen as a pack of lies. This is a consequence of the same rhetorical impulse towards cool and anti-political neutrality that would make it possible in *Party Going* to describe impartially social classes with nothing to say to each other, or in the later *Loving* to describe with a studied lack of interest the end of English power in Ireland. The prevalence of this deflationary scepticism in the early stages of the war is borne out by contemporary sources such as Mollie Panter-Downes, who was jauntily telling her American readers that 'Atrocity stories that everyone over thirty remembers from the last war have turned up again, as good as new but with different details'.[43] There is, Green suggests, nothing necessarily unprecedented about this war, or unprecedently frightening about this particular enemy.

It could be seen as almost to the credit to the liberal conscience that some resisted the propaganda coming from the top, and it probably speaks well of the difference in the quality of public debate sanctioned during each of the wars that Panter-Downes felt able to write this to a country whose support Britain badly needed. But the problem was that in their grotesque conception and the industrial scale of their operation, the gas chambers that would come later really did recall one of the most prevalent anti-German fantasies of the Great War, the story to which Green alludes, that the Germans had corpse-rendering factories where they boiled the dead down for tallow. Appalling consequences followed from the refusal to be swept up again in the anti-German fantasies that the government and the popular press had encouraged in the Great War. In his seminal effort to explain why Britain, despite 'relatively generous' treatment of German Jewish immigrants in the 1930s, should have failed them so badly at the end of the decade, Bernard Wasserstein blames 'a general feeling that atrocity propaganda during the First World War had been shown to be greatly exaggerated'; 'until the end of 1942 many British officials refused to believe most of the reports of atrocities which were presented to them. They recalled the atrocity propaganda of the First World War... Churchill, with his broader imagination, was almost alone in his grasp of the magnitude of the disaster'.[44] Orwell had made the same case exactly in the middle of the war when he pointed out that the 'disgusting hypocrisy and self-righteousness' of Great War propaganda, 'the systematic lying of 1914–1918', had made it impossible to believe Tory politicians and their press allies when they described fascist and Nazi atrocities. In a deadened lexis that enacts the futile reiteration it describes, he wrote: 'These things really happened, that is the thing to keep one's eye on. They happened even though Lord Halifax said they happened . . . they all happened, and they did not happen any the less because the *Daily Telegraph* has suddenly found out about them when it is five years too late.'[45] Among those who got it right, then, where the people who believed capable of anything the nation they still thought of as Huns.

'WITH TWO WARS AND EVERYTHING IN BETWEEN, YOUR GENERATION'S HAD QUITE A PASTING'[46]

Reflex refusals to believe in anything that sounded like Great War rhetoric were perhaps symptomatic of a more widespread scepticism about political power in the period. Even if Green would participate in real life in the war effort, his wartime writing emphatically valorises the private experience that refuses to be surrendered to, and potentially abused by, the political authorities of the day.

> And if there are things we seek to share, hunched now on the office stool, facing a slow death in the shelter they have made our basement into, we might as well turn back to when we stumbled home through the dark, our faces still burning with the day's sun and then tell ourselves as the syren goes and frightened we begin to forget, because we do not know if we are going to be killed, how we did once find this or the other before we go to die to take with us like a bar of gold. (*PMB*, 53–4)

This passage makes a case for privacy, even if it is dressed up as a communal pooling: '*we* seek to share', '*our* basement', 'before *we* go to die'. Both Green and Woolf were engaged almost simultaneously in the thoroughly bourgeois activity of writing their memoirs, but however much Woolf feared appeals to the collective *Pack My Bag* suggests Green's stronger resistance to her famous wartime assertion of ' "I" rejected: "We" substituted'.[47]

Hostility to the public takeover imposed by war is explicit in Green's reference to 'the shelter *they* have made our basement into', a surely disingenuous identification with the disenfranchised, with those of us 'hunched on the office stool'. Recalling Woolf's insistent rhetorical 'they' in 'The Leaning Tower' to differentiate herself and her working-class audience from the political decision-makers, this marks a strange posture for a wealthy aristocrat and industrialist; Green's is the same unspecified (but unambiguous) 'they' who are routinely alluded to in the contemporary publications of Mass-Observation. But, as Woolf's essay anticipates, Green's point looks less strange retrospectively when the powerful 'they' who have failed to prevent the war get replaced within a couple of years by the equally threatening 'they' who are held responsible for the expropriative taxation of the post-war period and the associated incursions of the state on the lives of its citizens. This is another reason why it would be a mistake to consider Green's 'proletarian' novel, *Living*, or at the contemptuous look that *Party Going* takes at the pointless privileged, and either see the political force of democratic socialism or minimise Green's own investments in the pre-war order. Unremittingly, Green's novels come to articulate a resistance to the state's appropriating powers, and the loss brought by the post-war settlement to Henry Yorke's class was personally felt. In a suggestive identificatory reading, the novelist Angus Wilson, who had known Green's class and generation at close quarters, remarked 'that note of disintegration of the old ways of living that obsessed Green'.[48] Quoting Green's claim that 'these times are an absolute gift to the writer. Everything is breaking up', Wilson suggested that, in the end, 'the break-up did for him'.[49]

Green gave an extraordinary interview to the American magazine *Life* in the year he published his final novel, *Doting* (1952). Since he mysteriously stopped writing in his forties though he lived another 20 years, this late interview might be illuminating were it not for some unintended ambiguities. The interviewer writes that 'Unlike Henry Green, he [Henry Yorke] does not wish "to be ruled by intellectuals, and so I always vote for the Tories"'.[50] The fusion of reported speech and authorial comment makes this either a good joke by Green or an instance of really unprecedented snobbishness. If Green was alluding to an earlier comment that the real intellectuals are the working-class people he 'revered' when he worked with them, he's saying that he votes Tory so that he can only be ruled by the posh.[51] If Green literally meant 'intellectuals' (and the mid-century Labour government was full of former university teachers), then he was betraying an inflated anxiety familiar to his contemporaries: the triumph of materialistic technocracy would leave the modernists behind. Forster had defiantly declared this position in a 1942 essay – defiant, because the essay was for Storm Jameson's 'Salute to America' – in which he confessed that promises of a new order chilled him: 'each time

Mr. Wells and my other architectural friends anticipate a great outburst of post-war activity and world-planning, my heart contracts. To me, the best chance for future society lies through apathy, uninventiveness, and inertia'.[52] Privileging social and material utility above all else would render the artist irrelevant, Forster went on: 'the Bohemian, the outsider, the parasite, the rat – one of those figures which have at present no function either in a warring or peaceful world. It is not very dignified to be a rat: but all the ships are sinking, which is not dignified either ... I would sooner be a swimming rat'.[53]

The Labour government of 1945 presented itself as, one political historian writes, 'the party of the 'useful people', those who made an active contribution to the economy – not parasites who lived off the work of others, be they lumpen scroungers or upper-class drones'[54] Not only might the *rentier* modernists be construed as such (as Forster feared), but the 'upper-class drones' had always been the staple subject of Green's fiction, and he had a final fling with their (and his) class in *Nothing* (1950), which is set in the world of the superannuated new poor who sell their jewellery to pay for their children's twenty-first birthday parties and who are utterly baffled by these children with their real – *for money* – jobs in the expanded State sector. These socially useless elders being heavily taxed aren't a desperately sympathetic cause, and, true to apolitical form, Green doesn't make them any less trivial in middle age than their equivalents had been in *Party Going* a decade earlier. On the other hand, Green had a definitively liberal sense that social utility isn't all that matters. Their priggish bureaucrat children ('intellectuals'?) are as appalling in their own callous way, and believe that their parents 'all ought to be liquidated': 'They're wicked darling', one tells another, 'They've had two frightful wars they've done nothing about except fight in and they're rotten to the core'.[55]

Although this chapter has tried to describe how Green's instinctively dialectical fiction aspired throughout the war years to the evasive neutrality that he associated with high artistic disinterestedness, there is ultimately little doubt whose side Green was on in this new narrative of generational incomprehension. I want to finish by quoting from a short and eccentric (even by Green's standards) article first published in 1961. In what is notionally another essay on what became the familiar post-war subject of the condition, predicament or crisis of the English novel, Green turns the whole genre upside down by writing a very funny series of unrelated and completely inconsequential thoughts about modernist and contemporary novelists: a car crash Hemingway had in London ('a quarter of an inch of blood on the floor'); why novels by religious people are 'meaningless'; why there's no point in criticising your contemporaries ('even C. P. Snow'), why book reviewers are like 'a flea in the hair of the dog ... gnawing ignominiously and futilely at its bottom': echoing and responding to the criticisms he puts into the mouths of the horrible offspring in *Nothing*, he writes:

> We, that is the thin blooded, who have been in two wars, have not much left. We had starvation in the first and bombardment in the second. My generation regards with contempt what one can only describe as the social double meanings of Amis *et al.*
>
> Amis and Wain in their novels often put their young men to rise on the backs of women in the red-brick universities of which there are plenty of buildings in Cambridge as well as Reading. So why should one complain? I don't know, except that they are both really bad writers.[56]

And for all that Green's slippery wartime comments could look disarmingly self-aware ('a mouthbreather with a silver spoon'), his post-war responses are unambiguously grumpy now that 'we are all to be beggared by the Govt. & left destitute because we won the war'.[57]

CHAPTER 5

Evelyn Waugh and the ends of minority culture

> We must forego our freedom to be free. And if proof were needed that we understand this situation, witness the speed with which Parliament on our behalf lately granted the Government full powers of control over all persons and all property ... Not so much 'Socialism in our time', a Labour Member wittily observed, as 'Socialism in no time'.
> 'Magna Carta, 1215–1940', *The Listener*, 13 June 1940.[1]

> What changes of taste this war, and the reactions following it, may produce, no one can foresee. But at least it can hardly give rise to arts unintelligible outside a Bloomsbury drawing-room, and completely at variance with those stoic virtues which the whole nation is now called upon to practise.
> 'Eclipse of the Highbrow', *The Times*, 25 March 1941.[2]

The Emergency Powers (Defence) Act passed in May 1940 made Britain a totalitarian state. 'Today, on your behalf', Clement Attlee began his broadcast to the nation, 'Parliament has given to the Government full power to control all persons and property. There is no distinction between rich and poor, between worker and employer; between man and woman; the services and property of all must be at the disposal of the Government for the common task'.[3] Although 'socialism in no time' is an overstated way of describing the reformed capitalism that followed the war's experiment in the planned economy and expanded welfare state, the passing of this Act marked a clear political turning point in the century: the official rejection of the Liberal tenet at the heart of pre-war parliamentary politics, that government worked negatively rather than actively. Henry Green's lifelong friend and admirer Evelyn Waugh built his notorious late career vociferously protesting, as Green more quietly did, the effects of this change on the British political landscape.

Waugh's career as a second-generation modernist writer and critic had begun much as Green's had, precociously and wholeheartedly on the side of the avant-garde. Aged 14 in 1917, Waugh had published an article on

Cubism in which he wondered 'Should Art be like life?' He answered his own question: 'No ... the resemblance to life does not in the least concern the merits of the picture'.[4] Green was meanwhile a schoolboy in the Eton Society of Arts where, 'with a great sense of settling everything, we said, one after the other, that art was not representation'.[5] When he said so in his memoir *Pack My Bag*, he was obviously ironising his youthful faith in the unquestionable rightness of modernist anti-realism ('with a great sense of settling everything'), suggesting that now in 1940 he could no longer assume the prevalence of his old modernist convictions. He may have been right to worry. Shortly afterwards, and in the spring that followed 'socialism in no time', the *Times* announced the death of modernism in an editorial that provoked three weeks of correspondence on its letters page. Precipitated by the publication of Lord Elton's well-meaning but philistine *Notebook in Wartime*, the *Times* leader 'Eclipse of the Highbrow' exulted that the age of creative deviance might be at an end. It deplored how 'the intellectuals of the nineteen-twenties and thirties' had despised the literate public:

They preferred a hasty brilliance, which degenerated rapidly into a habitual clever triviality, upon which, in turn, the more conscientious performers (for there is conscience even in wrong-doing) laboured to graft a pedantic and deliberate obscurity or perversity. Arts were brought down to the level of esoteric parlour games.[6]

The readers' letters in support of the editorial were predictable enough: letters quoting Dr Johnson on the common reader; letters from self-declared middlebrows; letters about how Shakespeare wrote for everyman and so on.[7] Nor was it surprising that the highbrowed dissenters did a more incisive job: Stephen Spender replied with a ferocious letter in which he suggested that this campaign against degenerate art better befitted the *Volkischer Beobachter* than the *Times*, recalling that while the supposedly irresponsible highbrows of the 1930s were raising the alarm about fascism, Lord Elton and the *Times* were championing appeasement.[8]

Also on the side of the highbrows, the publisher Geoffrey Faber wrote to argue that the editorial drew a false distinction between modernism and the notional common reader. Modernism had become the expectation rather than the exception, and there was now a considerable audience for 'difficult' poetry; the new fifth edition of Michael Roberts's modernist anthology *The Faber Book of Modern Verse* (1936) Faber took as evidence that 'The age you so much dislike is in fact by no means past, and its protagonists are by no means ghosts haunting the ruins of a decadent and mythical Bloomsbury'.⁹ His metaphor is itself haunting. Five days later, the newspaper carried this notice:

We announce with regret that it must now be presumed that MRS LEONARD WOOLF (Virginia Woolf, the novelist and essayist), who has been missing since last Friday, has been drowned in the Sussex Ouse, at Rodmell, near Lewes.¹⁰

A long and generous obituary appeared in the same day's *Times*, although the debate about modernism's eclipse continued for another week without mentioning the Bloomsbury highbrow par excellence. This moment in the spring of 1941 is an important one because it posits different possibilities for the story of how modernism ended: what ultimately became the conventional narrative of generational change (the death of major figures) versus the mainstreaming of modernism ('its protagonists are by no means ghosts'). Evelyn Waugh offers a third account of what happened, and this chapter describes the modernist 'ghosts' – as he also calls them – in his wartime fiction. Although Waugh would later produce an admired novel trilogy about the Second World War, the war is primarily important in *Put Out More Flags* (1942) and *Brideshead Revisited* (1945) as the impetus for these novels' valedictions to the high culture of interwar England.

IF I WERE NOT A COSMOPOLITAN, JEWISH PANSY...

Waugh and Green's shared milieu of 1920s Oxford has often been discussed, and this group of very young men – most famous among them Waugh, Green, Harold Acton, Brian Howard and Anthony Powell – tend be described in semi-mythic terms. What Waugh began in *Brideshead Revisited* was later pursued in Martin Green's *Children of the Sun* and Humphrey Carpenter's *The Brideshead Generation*, and this reverence for a group of virtual schoolboys, however talented, runs uncomfortably close to an uncritical nostalgia for the orgy of whimsy that the privileged world of the boys' private club made possible; in many respects this group embodies interwar England's intersections of economic and cultural privilege. Still, I think Valentine Cunningham was too quick to summarise the versions of the 1930s against which he was writing as a choice between 'the Auden generation' and the Brideshead story of the Eton-and-Oxford aesthetes. Leaving aside the more obviously gifted writers (Green, Waugh, Powell), even Harold Acton and Brian Howard were more than the 'odd couple of Old Etonian aesthetes' that Cunningham calls them: it was Acton, for instance, who brought Gertrude Stein to

Oxford; while Erika Mann (daughter of Thomas, wife of Auden) called Howard 'the first Englishman to recognise the full immensity of the Nazi peril').[11] It is partly true, as Cunningham writes, that they 'became jokes, butts, jibed at by the likes of Evelyn Waugh and Cyril Connolly', but it is also the case that Connolly took Howard's political writing seriously enough to publish it in *Horizon*.[12] Less ephemerally, Waugh made these two the basis of the most significant character in his wartime fiction, 'an aesthetic bugger ... 2/3 Brian 1/3 Harold Acton'.[13] The synopsis may sound dismissive, and typically offensive, but this figure from the 1920s appears in his Second World War novels to enact Waugh's own rebellion against conservative measures of social and cultural value. Representing modernism itself, he offers a challenge to the reactionary Tory insularity that Waugh would come in the end to epitomise.

In *Put Out More Flags*, he is the gay Jewish aesthete Ambrose Silk and one of the 'race of ghosts' Waugh described in the novel's dedication to the soldier-politician Randolph Churchill: 'the survivors of the world we both knew ten years ago, which you have outflown in the empyrean of strenuous politics'.[14] The dedication is double-edged given the distinction the novel then goes on to make between idealistic artistic 'ghosts' and the sheer cynicism of 'strenuous politics'. Structured by the parallel efforts of the apolitical Ambrose Silk and the viciously political Basil Seal to find niches for themselves in wartime, *Put Out More Flags* describes how creative dissidence is victimised by political expediency masquerading as patriotic duty. On the make, Seal advances his career in the Intelligence Services by informing on his artistic friends' activities; while Ambrose rejects the work offered at the Ministry of Information where all the interwar creative people are now busy writing the equivalent of Penguin Specials ('a very nice little series on '"What We Are Fighting For"') or working on propaganda films that recall Humphrey Jennings's work at the Crown Film Unit, 'designed to impress neutral countries with the pastoral beauty of English life' (*POMF*, 76, 243). Instead, and in a libellously close rendering of *Horizon*, Ambrose founds his journal *Ivory Tower*, because 'For years now we've allowed ourselves to think of nothing but concrete mixers and tractors' (*POMF*, 139). The plot contrivance is that the intelligence services are prompted to close down Ambrose's journal for what Basil Seal affects to consider its treacherous politics.

Ambrose's first leading article in his version of *Horizon*, ' "The Minstrel Boys, or *Ivory Tower* v. *Manhattan Skyscraper*" defined once and for all Ambrose's attitude in the great Parsnip-Pimpernell controversy'

(*POMF*, 238). The controversy in question recalls, and not subtly, what Robert Hewison evaluates as 'the most important literary event since Spain':[15] the emigration of W. H. Auden and Christopher Isherwood to the United States (Waugh's Parsnip and Pimpernell are the authors of 'Guernica Revisited' and the 'Christopher Sequence'). The real life model for this first issue of *Ivory Tower* is the overblown editorial of *Horizon*'s second, in which Connolly argued that the departure of Isherwood and Auden meant that they had 'abandoned what they consider to be the sinking ship of European democracy, and by implication the aesthetic doctrine of social realism that has been prevailing there'; in what becomes Ambrose Silk's flight from the aesthetic of 'concrete mixers and tractors' Connolly goes on to argue for an end to the realist backlash and a restoration of modernist modes.[16] Meanwhile, in the effort to further his career in the security services, Seal pretends to take seriously the politics of the 1930s intelligentsia, including such artists as Poppet Green, the bad New-Apocalyptic painter, whose works would have been 'twenty years ago Pierrots and willow trees; now, in 1939, they were bodiless heads, green horses and violet grass, seaweed, shells and funguses' (*POMF*, 31). With an eye on the main chance, he calls her communist bluff, affecting to confuse the political posturing of artists with the fifth-column political activism that the wartime government seeks to monitor:

She pretends to be a painter, but you have only to look at her work to realize it is a cloak for other activities. Her studio is the meeting place for a Communist cell. She has an agent in the United States named Parsnip; he has the alias of Pimpernell; he puts it about that he is a poet, two poets in fact, but there again the work betrays him. (*POMF*, 212)[17]

Ambrose, however, has already become disaffected with Poppet, Parsnip and Pimpernell – as opportunistic as Basil Seal in their own way – and their attempts to turn him proletarian by insisting 'that he should employ himself in some ill-paid, unskilled labour of a mechanical kind': Ambrose, like his name, is 'irredeemably bourgeois. Parsnip often said so' (*POMF*, 37–8, 71).

The novel makes the war a forceful reality check to the 'taking sides' of the 1930s. For all the political grandstanding of the period, Ambrose finds himself alone and trapped between two terrifying totalitarianisms, subject to persecution by either or both of them. He asks his publisher if he might be on the Gestapo blacklist:

'Geoffrey, you were serious when you said that I should be on the black list of Left Wing intellectuals?'

'Quite serious. You're right at the top. You and Parsnip and Pimpernell.' Ambrose winced at the mention of those two familiar names. '*They're* all right', he said. '*They're* in the United States.' (*POMF*, 87–8, emphasis in original)

If the Nazis don't get him, the Communists might. Remembering his time as a fellow traveller, Ambrose Silk realises that 'they do the most brutal things, don't they, to Communists who try to leave the Party?' (*POMF*, 139).

Waugh satirises the polarising effects of the 1930s by suggesting that Ambrose's tolerant liberalism could become untenable in a culture that, refusing to admit positions between left and right, renders effectively 'fascist' anything not explicitly on the left. Ambrose has to flee the country when *Ivory Tower* gets characterised as treasonous propaganda: he has rewritten his gay memoir in response to Basil's pretended complaint about its didactically anti-Nazi conclusion; and in what is nearly an allegorical rendering of the gap between the aesthetic intellectual and the political cynicism of his milieu, what ruins Ambrose Silk is not the invasion that (as the novel's first readership in 1942 knew) never came, but his vulnerability on the home front. After all, Basil Seal is only a recherché instance of a solidly establishment propensity for finding a way to profit from the new opportunities that the war will open up. Unlike all the other characters, Ambrose is capable of thinking seriously – humanely, despairingly – about what the war is supposed to be for:

This is all anyone talks about, thought Ambrose; jobs and the kind of war it is going to be ... I don't care about their war. It's got nothing to do with me. But if, thought Ambrose, I were one of these people, if I were not a cosmopolitan Jewish pansy, if I were not all that the Nazis mean when they talk about 'degenerates', if I were not a single, sane individual, if I were part of a herd, one of these people, normal and responsible for the welfare of a herd, Gawd strike me pink, thought Ambrose, I wouldn't sit around discussing what kind of war it was going to be. I'd make it *my* kind of war. I'd set about killing and stampeding the other herd as fast and as hard as I could. Lord love a duck, thought Ambrose, there wouldn't be any animals nosing about for suitable jobs in *my* herd ... Cor chase my Aunt Fanny round a mulberry bush, thought Ambrose; what a herd. (*POMF*, 87–8)

Shoved to the margins because he's gay, Jewish and an artist ('a cosmopolitan Jewish pansy ... a single, sane individual'), Ambrose knows what the self-appointed representatives of public authority ought to be doing but are not. In this novel, the establishment is an abyss of abused power and sharp practice; even the owner of the novel's inevitable country estate, for instance, is no idealised custodian of the common heritage, only 'gifted with that sly, sharp instinct for self-preservation that passes for wisdom among the rich' (*POMF*, 9). As Ambrose marvels: 'what a herd'.

Against everything Waugh's notorious conservatism should make likely, Ambrose Silk is as close as the novel has to a moral centre. He remembers how the Nazis hated his lover even before they knew he was Jewish 'because in their gross minds they know him to represent something personal and private in a world where only the mob and the hunting pack have the right to live' (*POMF*, 240–1). The Nazi 'mob and the hunting pack' recall the English 'herd' that Ambrose knows at home.

Born after his time, in an age which made a type of him, a figure of farce; like mothers-in-law and kippers, the century's contribution to the national store of comic objects ... and Hans, who at last, after so long a pilgrimage, had seemed to promise rest, Hans, so simple and affectionate, like a sturdy young terrier, Hans lay in the unknown horrors of a concentration camp. (*POMF*, 46–7)

This linking of British homophobia 'in an age which made a type of him' and the Nazi murdering of his lover recalls the Woolfian insight of four years previously; Ambrose, like one of her *Three Guineas*' Outsiders, is gifted political clarity by his position beyond the establishment 'herd' (although Waugh certainly registers a distinction between homophobic derision and 'unknown horrors'). Living in a country that has closed ranks to render difference ridiculous, and whose established social elite sees the war just as an opportunity for self-advancement, Ambrose is the only character in Waugh's novel not locked into his own stupidity, snobbery or self-interest. Oddly, to my mind, the left leaning critics Alan Munton and Alan Sinfield have both independently read this the other way round, as further evidence of Waugh's horrible politics that 'there is no place in the defence of Britain for a homosexual Jew with internationalist cultural sympathies'; 'This stereotyping enacts, virtually, a fascistic centring of 'normal' Englishness by identifying and despising an outgroup.'[18] I think this is Waugh's point.

Because that Waugh is speaking through Ambrose Silk is clear from the camp expression he uses to ridicule those around him: 'Cor chase my Aunt Fanny round a mulberry bush ... what a herd', essentially Waugh's own language for deriding wartime opportunism when he saw it appearing in less expected places. The *Horizon* manifesto 'Why Not War

Writers?' provoked a bracing response from Waugh when it appeared in the autumn of 1941 with such signatories as Connolly, Harrisson, Orwell and Spender.[19] Waugh replied by questioning the basis of their demands for special exemptions for writers in wartime:

But what do your chums propose doing? They would like to form an Official Group; they would go on jaunts to the Americas and Dominions; they would have 'the facilities of journalists' which, as far as I have seen, merely means the privileges of commissioned rank without its obligations – cheap railway tickets, entrance to ward-rooms and officers' messes and investitures; they would 'co-ordinate war-effort emotionally'. *Cor chase my Aunt Nancy round the prickly pair!* The General Staff love initials; they would, I am sure, rejoice to put an armlet D.A.E.C.W.E. on someone's arm and call him Deputy Assistant Emotional Co-ordinator of War Effort ... I am afraid that I do not believe that these young men want to write; they want to be writers ... They have been whimpering for years for a classless society, and now that their own class is threatened with loss of privilege they are aghast. That is the plain meaning of your manifesto.[20]

Here Waugh disparages the readiness of the literary establishment ('chums') to be co-opted by an inefficient jobs-for-the-boys bureaucracy safely distant from, and professionally euphemising ('D.A.E.C.W.E.'), the realities of the war. Waugh uses the camp slang of Ambrose Silk in order to mock what he thought of as the effort among writers to capitalise on the war as they had on the political climate of the 1930s. 'Here is the war, offering a new deal for everyone', Ambrose Silk thinks, 'I alone bear the weight of my singularity (*POMF*, 72).

Waugh, too, saw himself bearing the weight of his singularity: if it seems a ridiculous pose initially, it accrues massive moral significance by the end of the novel. Waugh's narrator steps into Ambrose's place in his subsequent novels about the war in order to remark the imaginative failure of an establishment-on-the-make that only the marginalised Ambrose has been credited with the capacity for recognising. In *Men at Arms* (1952), the first of Waugh's retrospective *Sword of Honour* trilogy, a more conventionally realist narrator makes direct attacks on wartime British stupidity, oblivious to 'the lightless concentration-camp which all Europe had suddenly become', and on 'a public quite indifferent to those trains of locked vans still rolling East and West from Poland and the Baltic, that were to roll on year after year bearing their innocent loads to ghastly unknown destinations'.[21] In the same novel, a reminder of 'those secret forests where the trains were ... while the Halberdiers ... sat bemused by wine and harmony' even interrupts what is, on the face of it, absolutely Waugh's cup of tea: a description of snobbish luxury in the barracks of a socially exclusive old regiment.[22] The omniscient narrator is performing the function of recalling the gap between the war's social opportunities and what the war ought to be about, the function given in the proper war novel to the 'cosmopolitan Jewish pansy'.

'HERE AT THE AGE OF THIRTY-NINE I BEGAN TO BE OLD ...'

Given that only three years separated *Put Out More Flags* and *Brideshead Revisited*, Waugh was suggestively casual about recycling much of the first novel in the second; indeed, Anthony Blanche in *Brideshead* is practically the same character as Ambrose Silk, with the effect that modernism gets turned exuberantly queer in both novels. In a comically compressed who's-who of modernism, Blanche had 'dined with Proust and Gide and was on closer terms with Cocteau and Diaghilev; Firbank sent him his novels with fervent inscriptions; he had aroused three irreconcilable feuds in Capri; he had practised black art in Cefalu; he had been cured of drug-taking in California and of an Oedipus complex in Vienna'.[23] From the gloomy perspective of the war, Ambrose Silk is prompted likewise to reflect that 'It had been a primrose path in the days of Diaghilev ... in Paris he had frequented Jean Cocteau and Gertrude Stein; he had written and published his first book there, a study of Montparnasse Negroes that had been banned in England by Sir William Joynson-Hicks' (*POMF*, 48). By the Second World War, then, modernism can be historicised as a lost golden age of psychoanalytic inquiry, outlawed books (the Home Secretary Joynson-Hicks had declared Radclyffe Hall's *The Well of Loneliness* and Lawrence's *Lady Chatterley's Lover* obscene), and gay creativity (Proust, Gide, Cocteau, Diaghilev, Firbank, Stein). In coding modernism as queer, and mourning its loss as such, Waugh indulges in a sleight of hand that conflates two largely antithetical modern meanings of minority culture: 'minority' as elite and 'minority' as marginalised. Waugh would be no one's first candidate in the search for liberalism's mid-century mouthpiece, but the championing of modernism that he embarks on here rests squarely on the liberal defence of solitary dissidence.

These two war novels are largely novels about modernism and very self-consciously after modernism, and in neither is there anything to compensate for what has been lost, culturally and artistically. Although the art of the New Apocalypse (represented by Poppet Green and her cronies) was an easy target for ridicule, the nostalgic offerings of the ostentatiously pious Künstlerroman *Brideshead Revisited* are less predictably rendered a creative disappointment. An Army Captain who has not been in action yet, the narrator-protagonist Charles Ryder finds himself in the novel's prologue billeted at the derelict Brideshead Castle. Recounting that he 'had been there before ... knew all about it', he narrates his love affairs with Lord Sebastian and Lady Julia Flyte and the career as an architectural painter that began there (*BR*, 17). His painting is the product of nostalgia and class fantasy, the necessary outcome of his belief that the democratic progress of modernity is the destruction of a more whole, more beautiful past:

> The camp stood where, until quite lately, had been pasture and ploughland; the farm-house still stood in a fold of the hill and had served us for battalion offices; ivy still supported what had once been the walls of a fruit garden; half an acre of mutilated old trees behind the wash-houses survived of an orchard. The place had been marked for destruction before the army came to it. Had there been another year of peace, there would have been no farmhouse, no wall, no apple trees. Already half a mile of concrete road lay between bare clay banks, and on either side a chequer of open ditches showed where the municipal contractors had designed a system of draining. Another year of peace would have made the place part of the neighbouring suburb. (*BR*, 3–4)

That, as Waugh wrote elsewhere, 'German bombs have made but a negligible addition to the sum of our own destructiveness' is a familiar refrain in his later work.[24] As in Woolf's *Between the Acts*, and counter to the official strain of anti-conservative and socially reformist rhetoric of the wartime administration, the war here becomes a fight for the preservation of a sanitised past.

Of course, Waugh identified rural England with the aristocracy, with the country estate and its privileged way of life, in a way that Woolf struggled to avoid. Infamously, the problem with *Brideshead Revisited* is that the narrator's veneration of the feudal order is to be taken at face value; Waugh said as much when he retrospectively called the novel a 'panegyric' over the aristocracy's 'empty coffin'.[25] Anticipating a debate that would become very familiar in the years after the war – that more will mean worse – Viscount Esher wrote an article for *Horizon* in 1942 that prefigured the novel's elegiac mood:

> The first effect of a transference of wealth is a levelling down, and not as the optimists hoped, a levelling up. If there is to be only one class on the railways, it is the first-class that disappears, and everybody goes third. As the minimum

standard of life for the poor has been raised by the social services, the burden of taxation from which to create those services has lowered the standard of life for the rich. Under this process the ultimate and perfect expression of English aristocratic culture, the country-house life, has declined, and must disappear.[26]

It would be a stretch to suggest that, since Waugh had likely read this article (as a reader of and regular correspondent to *Horizon*), Viscount Esher's railway analogy is being rendered quite literally when the narrator and Lord Sebastian Flyte travel third-class to Venice on the money intended for Sebastian's first-class journey. The principle is certainly the same one, even if, in an almost predictable Second World War irony, it is Viscount Esher, the aristocrat, who finally concedes that the 'levelling down' is going to be worthwhile – not an argument Waugh was ever likely to advance.

That said, *Brideshead Revisited* makes it hard to ignore the self-hating qualities of Waugh's nostalgia, coded as a ruinous straightness of sexual and artistic ambition on the narrator's part. Not only does the middle-class protagonist contribute to the wrecking of the dynastic and aristocratic dream when he tries to get inside it by marrying Sebastian's sister, but he is simultaneously there as an artist cashing in on the loss by memorialising it. What emerge from this are the inconsistent politics of the self-deluded and the mediocre art of the conservative in retreat from modernity:

The financial slump of the period, which left many painters without employment, served to enhance my success, which was, indeed, itself a symptom of the decline. When the water-holes were dry people sought to drink at the mirage. After my first exhibition I was called to all parts of the country to make portraits of houses that were soon to be deserted or debased; indeed, my arrival seemed often to be only a few paces ahead of the auctioneers, a presage of doom. I published three splendid folios – *Ryder's Country Seats*, *Ryder's English Homes*, and *Ryder's Village and Provincial Architecture*, which each sold its thousand copies at five guineas apiece. (*BR*, 227)

So the would-be modernist artist ends up producing coffee-table books that might be ungenerously described as the visual equivalent of Waugh's own novel, a lucrative and parasitic art predicated on the snobberies of not just the house owners (whose loss was presumably real enough in human terms), but those of a voyeuristic public. In a misfiring metaphor of stunningly appropriate bathos, Ryder likens his first visit to Brideshead Castle to 'a glimpse only, such as might be had from the top of an omnibus into a lighted ballroom', and the aristocratic Sebastian Flyte has no compunction about reminding Charles of his tourist status, and responds to his friend's desire to see more of the glories of Brideshead Castle with the put-down that 'On Queen Alexandra's Day it's all open for a shilling' (*BR*, 38).

Their common friend James Lees-Milne tells an anecdote in his memoir of Henry Green which points unflatteringly to the *Brideshead* demographic – himself an architectural conservator and an arch-snob, Lees-Milne was well placed to recognise social pretensions when he saw them:

I saw *Caught* in Heywood Hill's bookshop where Nancy Mitford was then working. She was amazed that I did not realize Henry Green was really Henry Yorke (indeed, it was a difficult thing to grasp). At a luncheon party Nancy remarked in her languid Mitford voice that if only Henry had spelt the title *Court* and written about royalty and the aristocracy instead of firemen the novel would, in those days of austerity when everyone pounced upon books recalling glamour and glitter, have sold like hot cakes.[27]

The modernist survivor Anthony Blanche gets to point out what an artistically worthless activity this aspirational fluff really is: 'the shade of the cedar tree, the cucumber sandwich, the silver cream-jug, the English girl dressed in whatever English girls do wear for tennis … your art, my dear – is a dean's daughter in flowered muslin' (*BR*, 272). Ryder's (and Waugh's) efforts at tragic grandeur are rendered ridiculous, literally parochial, a middlebrow commercialism in the style of their contemporary John Betjeman, rather than the high tragedy to which the book's refrain of 'quomodo sedet sola civitas' aspires (*BR*, 220, 237, 351). 'I cannot understand this keen zest to be well-bred', Blanche tells Ryder, 'English snobbery is more macabre to me even than English morals' (*BR*, 271). If there's anything to redeem this book from what the heritage industry turned it into, and even what Waugh surely intended it to be, it's the layer of self-criticism provided by this blast from the cosmopolitan modernist past: 'part Gallic, part Yankee, part, perhaps, Jew; wholly exotic'.[28] As if the novel were rebelling against itself, this character turns up periodically in both of Waugh's wartime novels to point out that class-bound and chauvinistic insularity isn't going to be enough.

'PURE, AUTHENTIC 1914'

Although Ambrose Silk and Anthony Blanche form the reminder of insufficient political and creative values in the novels in which they appear, the rewriting that takes place between *Put Out More Flags* and *Brideshead Revisited* is more than suggestive. While *Brideshead* is almost impossibly deferential, Waugh doesn't let his conservative sympathies stand in the way of a good joke in *Put Out More Flags* where he ridicules the crude politics of the upper classes, as when Basil Seal's friends 'spoke of him in terms they normally reserved for the mining community of South Wales, as feckless and unemployable', and when Waugh characterises Seal's modus operandi as 'a system of push, appeasement, agitation and blackmail, which ... ran parallel to Nazi diplomacy' (*POMF*, 53, 56). And, to take an event that appears in both of the novels, the breaking of the General Strike by upper-class volunteers is ridiculed in the earlier novel when Waugh summarises one aristocrat's performance in the Strike with 'he had driven about the poorer quarters of London in a closed van to break up seditious meetings and had clubbed several unoffending citizens' (*POMF*, 51). The irony is directed against the misplaced fervour of the threatened; and, in fact, Waugh elsewhere argued (seriously) that the breakers of the General Strike were the closest thing to real fascists that interwar Britain had produced.[29] This casts useful light on the scene in *Brideshead* when Ryder works against the strike alongside 'a Belgian Futurist, who ... claimed the right to bear arms in any battle anywhere against the lower classes', and who tells Ryder that he 'should have been in Budapest when Horthy marched in' (*BR*, 201, 202). By the time the book was published, Admiral Horthy would evoke only the puppet regimes of Central and Eastern Europe. But the Belgian futurist ends up in hospital after he has 'a pot of ferns dropped on his head by an elderly widow in Camden' (*BR*, 207), and thus the book retreats into noncommittal slapstick and away from its own political implications; strongest among them that (as in *Put Out More Flags*) there's too much common ground between people with official fascist sympathies and the English establishment on the defensive.

The same ambivalence about conservative politics gets played out when in *Brideshead* Waugh takes with the most extravagantly pious reverence the imperialist and militarist historiography that he had taken to pieces in *Put Out More Flags*. The aristocratic sister of Basil Seal, for instance, responds to the declaration of war by fantasising about her vicious brother 'as Siegfried Sassoon ... as T. E. Lawrence and Rupert Brooke' (*POMF*, 13), and a comparable satirical exposure of military mythmaking resurfaces in *Men at Arms*, in which the dorms of a requisitioned prep school are named after the most shattering of the Great War battlefields, as if amplifying the argument Woolf had made when she gave the name of Jacob Flanders to her representative and victim of patriarchal education. Similarly, Basil Seal's mother places him easily into the conservatively imperialist version of English history she has inherited, 'a simple tale of the maintenance of right against the superior forces of evil':

> The steel engravings of her schoolroom lived before her eyes, like tableaux at a charity fête – Sidney at Zutphen, Wolfe at Quebec, Nelson at Trafalgar ... and to this tremendous assembly (not unlike, in Lady Seal's mind, those massed groups of wealth and respectability portrayed on the Squadron Lawn at Cowes and hung with their key plans in lobbies and billiard rooms) was added that morning a single new and rather improbable figure, Basil Seal. (*POMF*, 16–17)

This nostalgic, heroic version of imperial history is imagined as the cause of and pretext for every kind of stupidity; but then, bizarrely, it gets resurrected so that in *Brideshead* Ryder can take as damning evidence of his junior officer's lower-class crassness that he has never learned the properly deferential and romantic version of history, has never 'wept' as Charles has, 'for Henry's speech on St. Crispin's Day, nor for the epitaph at Thermopylae ... Gallipoli, Balaclava, Quebec, Lepanto, Bannockburn ... ' (*BR*, 9).

Rebecca West diagnosed Waugh as suffering from a 'crackbrained confusion between the moral and the aesthetic'.[30] Although she was talking about the tendency among her religious contemporaries to use the trappings of Catholic ritual to turn belief into a private member's club, a comparably 'crackbrained confusion' of artistic and spiritual grace comes into operation when Waugh lavishly describes the lost beauties of Brideshead. Waugh knew that he had fallen into what he subsequently diagnosed as 'the common English confusion of the antiquated with the sublime' and could afford retrospectively to laugh at some of the novel's extravagances, 'written in 1943, at a time of acute scarcity, and in a mood of sentimental delusion'.[31] Still, the political clear-sightedness of Waugh's comic fiction about the war makes the gullible seductions of *Brideshead* all the more perverse. It makes nonsense, for instance, of the wistful elegies in which the aristocrats are still engaged in the 1920s when Lady Marchmain commissions a memorial book for her brothers, 'three legendary heroes' killed in the First World War – it is 'a treasure-house of period gems', Samgrass the history tutor ironically tells Ryder, 'pure authentic 1914' (*BR*, 109, 125).

Mr Samgrass's deft editorship had assembled and arranged a curiously homogeneous little body of writing – poetry, letters, scraps of a journal, an unpublished essay or two – which all exhaled the same high-spirited, serious, chivalrous, other-worldly air; and the letters from their contemporaries, written after their deaths, all in varying degrees of articulateness, told the same tale of men who were, in all the full flood of academic and athletic success, of popularity and the promise of great rewards ahead, seen somehow as set apart from their fellows, garlanded victims, devoted to the sacrifice. These men must die to make a world for Hooper; they were the aborigines, vermin by right of law, to be shot off at leisure so that things might be safe for the travelling salesman, with his polygonal pince-nez, his fat wet hand-shake, his grinning dentures. (*BR*, 139)

The whimsical political argument (the imperialist class as 'aborigines') falls apart in the making since it is perfectly obvious that the heroes of the 1914 war, the fine flower of the nation and so on (the whole set of elitist lost-generation myths Hugh MacDiarmid was denouncing with his 'professional murderers'), are no more real than the grotesquely grinning salesman. Against this 'pure authentic 1914' of the sub-literary snob culture to which Lady Marchmain is contributing, the Great War only appears in the 'very unusual' circumstance of Ryder's mother having been killed working with the Red Cross in Serbia, and in Rex Mottram's observation that an oblivious aristocracy has been going bust since 1914 (*BR*, 40, 174).

The difference between the two wartime books – one debunking, one nostalgic – can at least partly be attributed to the comic effects of ironic prophecy after the fact. Published in 1942, as the war turned in Britain's favour, *Put Out More Flags* is full of historical ironies directed against the un-heroic gerontocracy of the kind that, as I suggested earlier, even Eliot found risibly incompetent. On her way back from France, one of the characters overhears someone praising French toughness while remarking that 'It's a pity they haven't got anyone like old Pétain to command them this time' (*POMF*, 27), while the running joke embodied by one of the novel's most establishment characters, the elderly Sir Joseph Mainwaring, is that he is continually mispredicting the direction of the war:

I'm the last man to prophesy rashly, but I think we can take one thing as axiomatic. There will be no air attack on London. The Germans will never attempt the Maginot Line. The French will hold on forever, if needs be, and the German air bases are too far away for them to be able to attack us. . . . (*POMF*, 20)

The joke is that all of this is recent history, and wrong in every detail. The dominant mood of *Put Out More Flags* is that of the lucky escape, the high spirits of a novel about how the British got off more lightly than their political leadership merited. The gloomy *Brideshead Revisited*, in contrast, is about what happens next, about what, domestically, winning the war is going to mean for artists and for private individuals.

'THE NEW RULING CLASS'

Between writing *Put Out More Flags* and *Brideshead Revisited* Waugh recorded in his diary a mid-war realisation that the 'chief use' of the war 'would be to cure artists of the illusion that they were men of action ... I don't want to be of service to anyone or anything. I simply want to do my work as an artist'.[32] His fiction had made the same point – albeit in the equivalent of ironic inverted commas – when he had Ambrose Silk argue that 'European culture has become convental; we must make it coenobitic' (*POMF*, 225). If this initially seems too affected a way of saying that art should be solitary rather than corporate to be taken seriously, it is endorsed at the end of the novel when another character thinks that he is safer alone on the battlefield than in his platoon because a solitary soldier is not a worthwhile target for enemy fire: 'there's danger in numbers; divided we stand, united we fall ... He did not know it but he was thinking exactly what Ambrose had thought when he announced that culture must cease to be conventual and become coenobitic' (*POMF*, 268). He, like Ambrose, is entirely wrong to believe that 'No one had anything against the individual'; trusting in his solitary safety, he is killed in action as surely as Ambrose is outlawed for his defence of ivory tower privacy.

If Waugh's diary epiphany – his stand for a 'coenobitic' art – marked a turn away from the 1930s belief in the capacity of the creative writer to change the world, he certainly had more than most to recant: 'It was fun being pro-Italian when it was an unpopular and (I thought) losing cause', he wrote to Katherine Asquith, 'I have little sympathy with these exultant fascists now.'[33] It sounds as though his fascism was largely a childish pose; in his autobiography, he recalled that he had oscillated as a teenager among professing socialism and 'the restoration of the Stuarts, anarchism and the rule of a hereditary caste'.[34] Whatever Waugh's motivations, however, his posturing meant that his was one of the few responses to the *Left Review* survey on Spain that could be printed on the pro-Franco side:

I know Spain only as a tourist and a reader of the newspapers. I am no more impressed by the 'legality' of the Valencia Government than are English

Communists by the legality of the Crown, Lords and Commons. I believe it was a bad Government, rapidly deteriorating. If I were a Spaniard I should be fighting for General Franco. As an Englishman I am not in the predicament of choosing between two evils. I am not a Fascist nor shall I become one unless it were the only alternative to Marxism. It is mischievous to suggest that such a choice is imminent.[35]

Given how close this is to the pamphlet's middle sequence of neutral (or 'Neutral?') answers, it is likely that Waugh was placed on the pro-Franco side of the pamphlet on the basis of the position he had taken earlier on the Italian invasion of Abyssinia. Like the writers identified as 'Neutral?' Waugh felt by the end of the 1930s that 'the distinctions of Left and Right ... are now becoming as meaningless and mischievous as the circus colours of the Byzantine Empire'.[36]

It is worth pausing one last time on that *Left Review* pamphlet, since the Spanish Civil War created an influential version of the end of modernism: a climbing down from the ivory tower of the 1920s in response to the new pressure from international political events. All the same, some of the pamphlet's most memorable responses, appearing in the wayward neutral section of the pamphlet, refuse to do precisely that: 'To hell with sides', Norman Douglas declared, 'Everything that ends in "ism" is just b . . . s, so far as I am concerned'; Sean O'Faolain wrote: 'If you want to know, I do think Fascism is lousy. So is your Communism, only more so'; Vita Sackville-West's more conventionally eloquent reply elaborated on the rhetorical omissions that gave the pamphlet its apparently unquestionable moral authority:

I dislike Communism and Fascism equally; and, in fact, cannot see any difference between them, except in their names. It seems to me that each bully and oppress the individual; and, through the individual, Society at large. That is chiefly why I cannot make up my mind to take either side in the Spanish quarrel, which is really a quarrel between Communism and Fascism in Europe, not only in Spain.

One point in your questionnaire strikes me as ambiguous. You stress "the *legal* Government" of Spain, as the Government you wish to support. Is this because it is the *legal* Government, or because it is a Communist Government? If it is because it is the *legal* Government, then you ought also to be prepared to support Hitler or Mussolini in the event of a rebellion against them. Yet I do not think you would do so?

Therefore what you really mean is that you want to see Communism established in Spain as well as in Russia, and you do not care a snap of the fingers whether a Government is "legal" or not. If so, why not have said so frankly?[37]

These 'Neutrals?' based their position on their hostility to the communism that the pamphleteers did not once mention. The official alternatives that the questionnaire had posited meant choosing between fascism and legality, and insofar as there was an alternative to taking sides at all it was the discredited old ivory tower of the high modernists, but 'the equivocal attitude, the Ivory Tower, the paradoxical, the ironic detachment, will no longer do'.[38]

A characteristic tag used in the 1930s of the 1920s, most impartially 'the ivory tower' is an attack on rarefied literary specialisation; more insidiously, it seems to have been a way of attacking writers without orthodox left sympathies. The modernists of the 1920s, Cyril Connolly wrote in 1938, 'believed in the importance of their art, in the sanctity of the artist and his sense of vocation. They were inmates of the Ivory Tower'; 'What he will not be', Connolly wrote of the ivory tower modernist, 'is a Fighter or a Helper'.[39] Of course there is a very real sense in which the ivory tower was, to swap metaphors, a straw man, because the narrow class and metropolitan base of literary and political culture in interwar Britain made it virtually impossible for writers not to have social and familial connections with the political establishment. It was never, in other words, a simple matter of artistic versus political life. Married to a diplomat, politician and writer, and herself a prize-winning poet and a famous gardener, Vita Sackville-West might be seen as exemplary of a dilettante culture that only produced modernism against the grain of an unselfconscious polymathy encouraged by independent wealth.

Sean Latham has recently used Woolf's homage to Sackville-West to suggest some of the ways in which high modernism's lofty aspirations were implicated in more banal forms of social climbing. Describing how Woolf in *Orlando* 'clings to an explicitly romantic ideal of the English aristocracy' as the protectors of high cultural values, Latham writes: 'Already at the very top of the social ladder and thus freed from art's antieconomy economy, they [the aristocracy] alone possess both the material means to sustain their artistic pursuits and the self-confidence to reject either the acclaim or the dismay of the reading public.'[40] If Latham is right, it should not be altogether surprising that late modernist survivors finally produced panegyrics over aristocratic coffins; and, if *Brideshead Revisited* does so more stridently than most – 'I piled it on rather', Waugh confessed[41] – it only represents a more widespread fear that, as Ambrose Silk privately thinks, 'every creed promises a paradise which will be absolutely uninhabitable for anyone of civilized taste' (*POMF*, 70). The post-war mourning implicated even the most studiously apolitical of

Waugh's generation. Henry Green's dystopian *Concluding* (1948) – the title tells its own story – is set in a country house that has been taken over by a government so highly bureaucratised as to be totalitarian. Unlike Orwell's infinitely better known dystopia of the same period, Green's novel represents a deliberately banal, faceless, unappealing but not especially malevolent kind of totalitarianism, perhaps the variety that the Tories invoked when as an unsuccessful (not to say tasteless) tactic in the 1945 election campaign they described Labour's levelling intentions as 'reeking of totalitarianism'.[42] That ancestral estates within Green's family had to be given up after the war offers some context to *Concluding*'s bitter asides about how the State has dealt with the old order: the dispossessed aristocrat is known as the 'life tenant ... which was their way of referring to the private owner of this estate, from whom the State had lifted everything'.[43] Like the Tory true-blue, Evelyn Waugh would also have recourse to the language of despotism each time he referred to this first post-war administration as 'the Cripps-Attlee terror', 'the Attlee-Cripps regime when the kingdom seemed to be under enemy occupation', or just, clownishly, 'the Occupation'.[44]

Late modernism in Britain represents with increasing anxiety its sense of being superseded by a world that it had helped make possible, its consciousness of being displaced from its old position near the centres of political authority. After all, modernism had always been operating close to the domestic structures that became known in the 1950s as the Establishment. Evelyn Waugh (whose ancestors included Holman Hunt and Edmund Gosse), like Virginia Woolf and 'Rebecca West' (likewise Stephen Spender and John Lehmann), were the offspring of eminent men of letters. All these writers belonged to a world in which cultural wealth, like an unearned income of £500 a year (because it was never just a room of one's own) was a hereditary privilege, and they all knew it. 'An intricate web of kinship linked the traditional lineages which produced scholars and thinkers to each other and to their common social group', Perry Anderson wrote in a late-1960s essay on the subject of the pre-war national culture, 'Intellectuals were related by family to their class, not by profession to their estate.'[45] 'There was the Macaulay-Cripps-Hobhouse-Babington-Booth-Beatrice Webb clan', Noel Annan began his catalogue of the British intellectual aristocracy:

There was the Arnold-Trevelyan-Huxley-Darwin-Wedgwood clan, which contained members of the Keynes, Vaughan-Williams, Sidgwick, Cornford and Barlow families. Or the Fry-Hodgkin-Haldane-Mitchison-Butler-Faber-Adam

Smith connection. Or the Stephen-Venn-Elliot-Strachey-Barnes-Shuckburgh strain, and so on.[46]

Woolf belonged to the last of these, of course, and in the scrap of memoir she wrote at the same time as public events were forcing her to look unblinkingly at her inheritance, she described her origins in terms that would do service for most English modernists: 'born into a large connection, born not of rich parents, but of well-to-do parents, born into a very communicative, literate, letter writing, visiting, articulate, late nineteenth century world'.[47] This, though Woolf never lived to see it disappear, was the *rentier* class that the first post-war administration had determined entirely to dissolve. This was also 'socialism in no time' and the 'break up' that Angus Wilson thought had eventually 'done for' Henry Green, when the balance of electoral power was turned on its head within a decade. Whereas the middle and upper classes had been the addressees and beneficiaries of interwar parliamentary politics, their interests now felt secondary: this, after all, was a government willing to use class hatred – quite literally – as an instrument of policy.[48]

Only a little younger than the writers I have discussed so far, Angus Wilson had known the dissolving *rentier* world from the inside, and between Woolf's sketch of the past and his sketch of a 1954 present lies a small revolution. In another essay on the mid-century chestnut of 'The Future of the English Novel', Wilson described how 'the better novelists of today belong to [a] vanished world':

The new ruling class – that strange mixture of business experts, bureaucrats, social scientists, and the rest of the Welfare set-up – are firmly in the saddle ... It is a world which cannot inform the creations of those of us who were born before it came into being. If we attempt to use it for creative inspiration we shall inevitably be too conscious of its outlines ... But a new generation is arising from the new ruling class who will accept the world they dominate, for whom it will be so much a background that it shapes their art as it does their morality without their being conscious of it.[49]

Mutatis mutandis, this is the argument that Woolf had made in 'The Leaning Tower' about the need for writers to be productively unconscious of the society in which they live; according to her reading of the 1930s, the Auden generation had ruined their art by being too much aware of the economic privilege that made it possible. What Wilson is describing is the ascendancy of social specialisation ('intellectuals') that gave Henry Green such anxiety, and there's a straight line from the

Webbs (Mrs Ramsay's 'what with her untrained mind she greatly admired, an investigator, elucidating the social problem'), through the political activism and domestic anthropology of the 1930s, to 'the Welfare set-up ... firmly in the saddle' after the war. Professionally suspicious of dramatic watersheds, historians routinely point out that the Beveridge Report had its origins in a minority report by Beatrice Webb from decades earlier, and that the welfare state had been on the cards since the Liberal government of 1906–11: it was 'as if the country had been sitting in committee on the matter for half a century', as Noel Annan put it.[50] Social modernisation and literary modernism have the same timeframe and trajectory; both proved casualties of their liberal foundations.

To describe the resentment and unease that the welfare state provoked among the writers who began their careers around the Great War makes the end of modernism sound a wholesale conservative retrenchment, and it would be easy to play the new icon-bashing game of 'Familiar Fascism' in which modernist writers with notoriously repellent politics are identified by their unconscionable pronouncements.[51] Of course, there is plenty of transparently self-protective snobbery around the middle of the century, as when T. S. Eliot in *Notes Towards the Definition of Culture* (1948) mounted a panicky defence of what he called 'a graded society' on the tautological grounds that 'it is an essential condition of the preservation of the quality of the culture of the minority, that it should continue to be a minority culture'.[52] But in a belated consequence of the polemical division of left and right which dominated the 1930s, politicised modernist criticism has not always coped well with ideological impurity, and English modernism was always politically impure, had never been a simple matter of progressive virtue and reactionary villainy impermeably divided. This is the point Evelyn Waugh made most aggressively in *Put Out More Flags*:

'Ambrose has turned fascist,' she said.
'Not really?'
'He's working for the Government in the Ministry of Information and they've bribed him to start a new paper.'
'Is it a fascist paper?'
'You bet it is.'
'I heard it was to be called the *Ivory Tower*.'
'That's fascist if you like.' (*POMF*, 147)

Beneath the left–right dichotomy is what George Dangerfield famously and prematurely called 'the strange death of liberal England'; and liberalism had always been a contradictory formation of progressive social views against authoritarian ones and laissez-faire economics against protectionism. It is a historical cliché that the Great War destroyed Liberalism as a party-political force, so less has been said about its survival well beyond. Even putting aside the fact that the three most important figures of mid-century British history – Churchill, Keynes and Beveridge – had been or were members of the Liberal Party, interwar politicians of all three major parties were 'heirs to and, in politics, practitioners of the liberal tradition ... Liberalism informed all British political thought and practice'.[53] In part the fear of 'socialism in no time' has its roots on both sides of old Liberal territory: to a suspicion about the incursions of the state on the aspirations of the private citizen; and to an anxiety about the fate of high culture under the welfare state, 'an essay in utilitarianism', Annan fearfully called the welfare state – and he was in favour of it.[54]

Discussing the universalising and democratic idea of 'citizenship' enshrined in the post-war programme of reform, Beveridge's biographer Jose Harris has argued that, although much has been said about the ways in which the Second World War was a landmark in the cultural acceptance of the interventionist state, historians overlook 'widespread evidence of sentiments of the opposite kind: of continuing scepticism of state authority, dislike of personal contact with officialdom and tenacious attachment to old notions of privacy and personal liberty – all of which were not weakened but reinforced by the experience of mass mobilisation'.[55] Harris is talking about a broader demographic than mine (she takes her evidence from popular humour and public opinion surveys), but her conclusions certainly hold for the upper-middle-class writers that I have discussed here. It goes almost without saying that dissent from welfare capitalism can be both socially elitist and economically self-interested, but it is also perhaps more historically specific than this. This is the product of a generation that had grown up with social responsibility as a private choice rather than a state compulsion, but also one that had witnessed the planned economies and centralised 'high' cultures of Germany and Russia work out catastrophically all round.

Given that the late modernists looked at the welfare state and saw an oppressive and anti-individualist flattening out of legitimate cultural differences, it seems richly ironic that post mortem accounts of the failures of 1945–51, tinged by all colours of political feeling, have suggested that the main figures of the Labour administration failed to implement the necessary changes because they were themselves far too much like old-fashioned liberals experiencing 'queasy ambivalence when it came to harnessing the power of the state'.[56] Clement Attlee's boast that the British were 'able to put new wine into old bottles without bursting them' was prophetic of that failure.[57] In the end, the war marked neither the golden dawn nor the end of a gilded age. Keynesian intervention, the mixed economy and the welfare compromise would last till the mid-1970s, when hardcore monetarism and the free market principle surfaced alongside the right-leaning social policy that policed the consequences of a Darwinian economy. The efforts of welfare capitalism to mitigate capitalism's worst social effects only worked while the system remained productive enough to pay for it, and, by the time it collapsed thirty years on, neither right nor left would speak with affection of what is thought of as the age of consensus politics.

Alan Sinfield, writing in the late 1980s, lamented that 'the failure of the postwar settlement has allowed the initiative to pass to the New Right, and we experience a return to the conditions that the settlement was designed originally to avoid: unemployment, poverty, social rupture and authoritarian government'.[58] Writing from the left in the second term of the Thatcher administration, Patrick Wright had made a similar argument when in *On Living in an Old Country* he summarised the results of 'that long drawn-out betrayal known in more polite circles as the postwar settlement':

While the post-war years have indeed seen some realisation of egalitarian and democratic ideas, an overwhelming greyness has also crept over the picture – the bureaucracy, the waiting lists, the destruction of communities and traditional forms of self-understanding, the reduction of ideas of change, social responsibility, emancipation and development to the pallid state practices of 'nationalisation' and 'planning', the political principles of democracy caricatured in the pragmatic bargaining which has gone on between the most powerful partners in the corporatist arrangement. If an earlier time saw the making of the working class, the events of the post-war years have lent great strength to those interests which now benefit from its unmaking.[59]

What strikes this reader, twenty years on, is that Wright's critique sounds as socially and aesthetically nostalgic as if it came from the wartime centre: mourning the 'destruction of communities and traditional forms of self-understanding' and 'an overwhelming greyness' represent the structures of feeling on which the *rentier* modernists seemed to have a monopoly. It is fitting that the end of the post-war settlement should have resurrected *Brideshead Revisited*, a book that just keeps turning up in contemporary fiction. I want to finish by describing its rewritings in estate novels published in the three decades since the collapse of a post-war settlement it violently, if not accurately, prophesied. Retrospective fiction about the Second World War presents an embarrassment of riches: the following speculations on national historiography after modernism are more coda than conclusion.

Coda: National historiography after the post-war settlement

> In their own fashion they cared deeply about politics, though not as politicians would have us care; they desired that public life should mirror whatever is good in the life within.
> E. M. Forster, *Howards End* (1910)[1]

> Our Vision of Life Rejected.
> Title of Noel Annan's chapter on Thatcherism in *Our Age* (1990)[2]

Reviewing Angus Wilson's final novel in the *New Statesman*, David Lodge made the telling reproach that 'art, in this novel, is so closely associated with hereditary wealth and privilege' and that 'the author's delight in high art and high civilisation has led him to be over-indulgent' to his aristocratic main characters.[3] Margaret Drabble expressed similar concerns in her review of the novel a week earlier when she warned her *Listener* readers that 'it is risky, in 1980, to choose a titled family and a great house as one's subject, especially when one's message is essentially democratic'.[4] These reviews speak revealingly of their moment at the end of the post-war settlement. In *1980*, high culture and high society should be off-limits to any serious writer because of their old liability to get mixed up in one another.

Wilson's estate novel *Setting the World on Fire* marked the end of a career that had begun in the twilight years of *Horizon* and spanned the thirty years of the post-war settlement. Published in the year Wilson controversially accepted a knighthood for his contributions to literature from the new Thatcher government that, as a Labour supporter and a gay rights activist, he had plenty of reasons to dislike, *Setting the World on Fire* revisits the modernist form of the Künstlerroman at the same time as it reviews the after-modernist society of the post-war decades. Told in vignettes from 1948, 1956 and 1969, the novel tells of how the successful theatre director Piers Mosson comes into his artistic and aristocratic inheritance in an invented stately home behind Westminster Abbey. Tothill House is the work of the neoclassical Roger Pratt with baroque additions by Vanbrugh and Verrio, whose *trompe l'oeil* rendering of Phaeton falling from the sky forms the centrepiece of Piers's appropriately high-risk artistic triumph when he stages Lully's opera *Phaeton* in the great hall of the house. Exemplifying the intertwining of economic and creative privilege that gave reviewers cause for concern, this long-planned production of *Phaeton* has to be deferred until Piers comes into his familial inheritance, the stately home.

'LONG AGO IN 1945 ALL THE NICE PEOPLE IN ENGLAND WERE POOR'

The war casts a long shadow over post-war high culture, but not quite as mid-century writers such as Green and Waugh bemoaned. In Wilson's version of the estate novel, post-war life at Tothill House picks up where pre-war life had opulently left off, even if Uncle Hubert complains about the efforts of Hugh Dalton, the Labour Chancellor, to get aristocrats to open their homes to the public and 'let anyone in who chooses to produce his ration book'.[5] That the consequences of the war are suspiciously amenable to denial is suggested when the hero's American grandmother, a Christian Scientist, dismisses as 'Error' a catalogue of threats to her sublime order that includes sex, pain, death and 'that old Adam dream of war' (*STWOF*, 31). The war is so forgettable that her son Hubert is on the verge of marrying a friend of Mussolini's son-in-law and foreign minister, Ciano. The widow of an assassinated fascist industrialist, Marina Luzzi is herself an unreconstructed fascist implicated in the terrorist attack that brings the novel to its strange and operatic end. Provocatively aligned with creative energy, this persisting fascism is the opposite term to the attempted democracy of the drab post-war years; for Piers, artistic form offers an escape from what he dismisses as 'tedious Suezes' (*STWOF*, 38). The Suez crisis of 1956, when the United States forced Britain to climb down from its gung-ho military response to Nasser's nationalising of the Suez Canal, was widely seen as a massive final blow to Britain's international prestige, and it forms the backdrop to the novel's middle section: 'Socialist Britain', scorns Marina the fascist, 'No surprise you were beaten down at Suez'; she is filled with horror when *Phaeton* is described as 'of all Lully's work the people's opera': 'No, we can't 'ave *that* nonsense. People's Operas. My God!' (*STWOF*, 56, 85, emphasis in original).

Marina Luzzi is the characterological equivalent of the unexploded bomb that brings to its climax Muriel Spark's retrospective novel about the war, *The Girls of Slender Means* (1963). Set in a genteel girls's hostel between VE and VJ Days, Spark's novel ridicules the comforting 'people's war' mythology through her ironic repetition of variants of the novel's opening line that 'long ago in 1945 all the nice people in England were poor'.[6] In Spark's version, there is nothing to be consoled by, not least because, aside from the UXB left over from the Blitz, there is a newer and even worse bomb in the garden by the time the war concludes in Japan. Voting Conservative solely because it 'was associated with a desirable order of life that none of the members was old enough to remember from direct experience', the girls in the hostel listen to Churchill's election speeches on the wireless making their 'Sinaitic predictions of what fate should befall the freedom-loving electorate should it vote for Labour in the forthcoming elections' (*TGOSM*, 12, 86):

> The wirelesses suddenly started to reason humbly:
> We shall have Civil Servants ...
> The wirelesses changed their tones, they roared:
> No longer civil ...
> Then they were sad and slow:
> No longer ...
>   *servants*. (*TGOSM*, 87, emphasis in original)

There is a more famous part of this speech that Spark doesn't quote: what the historian Peter Hennessy calls 'Churchill's howler', when the Prime Minister proposed that a socialist Labour government 'would have to fall back on some form of Gestapo'; a ludicrous proposition, but not a million miles away from the inflated late modernist anxiety about the supposedly 'totalitarian' impulses of Labour policy.[7] The old bomb explodes on the day of the Labour victory and kills some of hostel's residents, among them the poetry-loving Joanna Childe. The daughter of a vicar, Joanna recites Day 27 in the Anglican Order as the hostel burns around her:

Except the Lord build the house: their labour is but lost that build it.
Except the Lord keep the city: the watchman waketh but in vain.
It is but lost labour that ye haste to rise up early, and so late take rest, and eat the bread of carefulness: for so he giveth his beloved sleep.
Lo, children ...
Any Day's liturgy would have been equally mesmeric. But the words for the right day was Joanna's habit. (*TGOSM*, 128)

Insofar as these are 'the words for the right day' – the day of the Labour victory when the Blitz promise of the New Jerusalem looked about to be realised – they are clearly a warning against the illusory security of the secular. So much for the niceness encouraged by shared poverty: as the hostel collapses, one beautiful resident slithers through a window too narrow to allow the less slender girls an escape in order to rescue a Schiaparelli dress, a desirable commodity in these austere times. The event provokes a religious conversion in one horrified bystander, who has initially believed that the slinky object retrieved in Selina's arms was a rescued friend: he turns Catholic because 'a vision of evil may be as effective to conversion as a vision of good' (*TGOSM*, 140). Spark's novel is emblematic of the refusal to use the war in wholly consolatory ways: the enforced communitarianism of shared hardship scarcely made a difference to the squalid selfishness of human motive.

That post-war fiction has predominantly historiographic preoccupations is a familiar idea, but although they are to different degrees marginal to current accounts of post-war British fiction, writers like Spark and Wilson have much to say to the substantial body of recent work on modern British cultural identity that details the post-imperial nostalgia of its retrospective fictions.[8] Spark's savage ironising of comforting national mythology can be explained and domesticated by the religious principles underlying her scepticism about a secular version of the New Jerusalem; sardonic and clear-eyed, she was a favourite author of Evelyn Waugh. On the other hand, the completely unreligious Angus Wilson points to a far more knowing account of historical retrospection than criticism is currently equipped for. There is a standard methodology for a novel like *Setting the World on Fire*: fictions with stately homes at their centre invariably get read alongside the 'heritage' industries that emerged in the early 1980s, when 'the past' had become, in David Lowenthal's contemporary comments, 'a foreign country with a booming tourist trade'.[9] The next critical step is to use the heritage industries as the bridge between these novels and the loss of empire; the novels then become melancholic elegies for a time when Britain was bigger, revelatory of 'agonistic yearnings', 'a powerful yearning for lost national glory', 'Britain's dominant cultural narratives of loss and mourning', 'the surviving fragment of the lost object of desire'.[10]

Though no one would want to deny the presence of uncritical, chauvinistic and downright vicious nativism in post-imperial British culture ('there ain't no black in the Union Jack' and so on), there may well be something dubious about an unacknowledged psychoanalytic methodology that assumes the unknowingness of the cultural products whose pathological denials it purports to be diagnosing. At the other end of the century, modernism's estate novels – work by Ford, Lawrence, Forster and Woolf – were already implicated in a narrative of decline insofar as they worried that the traditional custodians could no longer perform their old roles; but by no stretch of the imagination were they mourning the British Empire, a live enterprise that most of these writers heartily despised (Forster's Wilcoxes and Turtons?). To make the estate novel 'an opportunity to covertly mourn the loss of empire' implies that this kind of fiction emerged ex nihilo some time around the Falklands War.[11] What Robert Hewison termed 'the heritage industry' in his attack on culture under Margaret Thatcher's government is as old as modernism itself (Hewison's own book records that the National Trust was founded in 1895, the snobbish and conservative *Country Life* in 1897).[12] Even its most recognisably Thatcherite manifestation, the obsession with stately homes, goes back half a century, as Waugh recognised when he wrote in his sheepish 1959 preface to *Brideshead Revisited* of 'the present cult of the English country house'.[13]

The psychoanalytic paradigm speaks as resonantly of the not-always-discriminately traumatic 1990s as of the period it tries to describe. 'Postimperial melancholy' is certainly one way of describing 'the fetish' of the country house in post-war English fiction (the terms are Ian Baucom's), but many of these texts are so self-conscious about the genre's provenance that they undertake fundamentally materialist and historicist critiques of its potential for the smug escapism offered by the backward glance at more luxurious times.[14] Even the most obviously elegiac of the lot, the sixty-year-old *Brideshead Revisited*, satirises the cultural-historical capital of the country house, and Waugh does not for a second mistake his surrogate's saleable coffee-table books of threatened English heritage (*Ryder's Country Seats, Ryder's English Homes, Ryder's Village and Provincial Architecture*) for anything more regenerative than warm baths of social nostalgia taken at a high cultural cost. I described earlier how Anthony Blanche is the character who draws the line between meaningful creativity and middlebrow heritage, but he is also Waugh's mouthpiece for articulating the alternative cultural history of Ryder's dynastic dream: if the stately home articulates a powerful fantasy of organic community, it has simultaneously been the *locus classicus* of less respectable genres. That the Marchmains are a barren family occupying a doomed castle with a decrepit retainer in the attic speaks to a repressed literary history of the Gothic which Waugh has Anthony Blanche detail at length in

Coda: National Historiography   147

cataloguing Lord Sebastian Flyte's *'very sinister'* and 'quite, quite *gruesome*' family (*BR*, 53, emphasis in original). Sebastian's brother is like 'something archaic, out of a cave that's been sealed for centuries'; 'There ought to be an Inquisition especially set up to burn [his sister]', 'Nothing is known of [the younger sister] *yet* except that her governess went mad and drowned herself'; Lord Marchmain is 'a magnifico, a voluptuary, Byronic, bored, infectiously slothful'; Lady Marchmain 'keeps a small gang of enslaved and emaciated prisoners for her exclusive enjoyment. *She sucks their blood*' (*BR*, 54–6, emphasis in original). Evoking its long literary history, Waugh shows the seeming idyll of the English country house to have an old dark secret of cruelty and abused power.

That the 'dark' secret is the imperial money on which these houses have been built is taken as a given in Wilson's *Setting the World on Fire*, in which characters blandly and repeatedly allude to the origins of the family fortune in what Wilson in the novel's fake historical preface calls 'the West India trade': the slave trade and sugar plantations. It is no coincidence that the book opens in 1948, the year when the arrival of the *Empire Windrush* with five hundred passengers from Jamaica symbolically initiated the Caribbean diaspora in Britain. What is more, the novel registers how the imperial project bleeds into the post-war period: although the 1950s and 1960s saw extensive African decolonisation (Harold Macmillan's famous 'wind of change' speech in Cape Town was made early in 1960), the hero's scatterbrained mother emigrates to Rhodesia (Zimbabwe) under the white minority government of Ian Smith. Among Smith's backers were many British nationals who had emigrated there in revulsion or in tax exile from post-war 'Socialist Britain', and Wilson deploys a blunt historical irony when he has his character write home in 1969 about 'how content and friendly the blacks are, quite a lesson to us over-sophisticated whites' (*STWOF*, 243).

The gothic grotesque that binds the imperial history of the estate novel to a history of high style is delineated in Wilson's catalogue of the curiosities in Tothill House:

The winter light in the great patches of five equal breadths was the embodiment of Sir Roger's great art, as were the shadowed white panels that separated the five windows – miracles of proportion and delicate strength. But what of the objects, the curiosities for which Sir Thomas Tothill had asked Sir Roger to design the original Cabinet Room – the mummified marmoset, the petrified lava from Etna shaped like a negro's thick lips, the caul taken from a Berber baby, 'sent home to me by my deare Brother from among the Moors', a sea-serpent turned to rock as it rose in spirals to strike, a mouse taken from the belly of a Chinaman, an anal fistula bottled in spirits, the skeleton of a great bat ('such as did abound in these parts during the late civil disturbances') found in the Woodwork at Tothill, the webbed, eight-fingered hand of a baby born at Tewkesbury in 1620. (*STWOF*, 76)

The cabinet room designed by the impeccably classical Sir Roger Pratt is an effort at containment; foreign and freakish bodies are held in check by the disciplinary architecture of the imperial centre, but the project of containment is rendered monstrous by the artefacts Wilson has it contain (an anal fistula bottled in spirits?). Excessive and bizarre, these imperial souvenirs spill out of the architectural and narrative frame that gets built to house them. Aesthetic conservatism is fighting a losing battle to manage its own peculiar provenance.

Noel Annan claimed that 'the country had always been bored with the Empire: on this matter a gulf yawned between the mass of the population and the ruling class'.[15] Though it's certainly possible to overstate the importance of the loss of empire in contemporary British self-imagining, going the whole hog with Annan potentially advances questionable exculpatory ends. I would just point out here that it is far easier to see British culture right across the twentieth century as inward to the point of parochialism than to find evidence of its nostalgic hankerings for lost global space. In the same year as Wilson published this final novel, an elderly Q. D. Leavis endeavoured to define 'The Englishness of the English Novel' in terms that were every bit as chauvinistic as the title of her paper suggests. The realist golden age of fiction was, no real surprise here, the product of 'The traditional English life of the countryside, one of great house, parsonage, chapel, schoolhouse, farm and cottage united in a local culture and centring economically on the market-town and spiritually on the cathedral close, [which] made for mutual knowledge and accommodation.'[16] Much as Leavis would have hated to occupy any common ground with her, Woolf had indulged in the same nostalgic little-Englandish fantasy fifty years earlier when she pictured the world in which Sophocles had written:

Even nowadays such villages are to be found in the wilder parts of England, and as we enter them we can scarcely help feeling that here, in this cluster of cottages, cut off from rail or city, are all the elements of a perfect existence. Here is the Rectory; here the Manor house, the farm and the cottages; the church for worship, the club for meeting, the cricket field for play. Here life is simply sorted out into its main elements.[17]

If Leavis was ostensibly talking about the nineteenth-century novel (and Woolf, rather more oddly, about Sophocles), her own values had a famously eighteenth-century pedigree in their identification of the rural estate with the model of the good society. But even then there were equally well-known efforts to tone down the high cultural excesses of stately home wealth. In a text that Angus Wilson's novel can't help evoking, Alexander Pope derided conspicuous displays of wealth in his Epistle to Burlington: 'On painted ceilings you devoutly stare, / Where sprawl the saints of *Verrio*, or *Laguerre*'.[18] The stately home of literature was never exclusively a smug rewriting of economic power as spiritual wealth; this fear of the glossy surface – culture without roots; high style without high seriousness – runs alongside it.

So if the stately home offered a model and centre for the well-ordered society it was simultaneously an object lesson in the depthless and deathly beauty of aristocracy. This is one reason why Wilson in his essay 'Evil in the English Novel' quoted with such contempt the famous passage in Jane Austen's *Northanger Abbey* where Henry Tilney tells Catherine Morland that her readings in Gothic sensationalism have led her madly astray:

'If I understand you rightly, you had formed a surmise of such horror as I have hardly words to – Dear Miss Morland, consider the dreadful nature of the suspicions you have entertained. What have you been judging from? Remember that we are English: that we are Christians. Consult your own understanding, your own sense of the probable, your own observation of what is passing around you. Does our education prepare us for such atrocities? Do our laws connive at them? Dearest Miss Morland, what ideas have you been admitting?'[19]

For Wilson, this is further damning evidence of the parochialism of the English novel's values; its belief that Englishness alone acts as a guarantor of good behaviour.[20] I would add a little more to this: alongside 'that we are English: that we are Christians', another reason Catherine Morland's fancies of a clandestine murder are misplaced is that 'we' are not quite aristocratic enough to have these skeletons in the closet. And Wilson himself participates, with knowing jokes about the gothic legacy, in this middle-class fantasy that the aristocracy has all the sinister fun; the Tothill-Mosson dynasty of *Setting the World on Fire* has a long pedigree of sexual weirdness, from the naked concubines and numbered pageboys of the ancestors to the death in a brothel of Uncle Hubert, flagellant. Like another under-read modern example of the genre, Henry Green's *Loving*, which absolutely refuses to mourn the end of colonial power in Ireland, Wilson's *Setting the World on Fire* suggests that the twentieth-century estate novel can be more than a whited sepulchre for imperial cruelties or a lugubrious dirge for fading imperial grandeur.

'A NEW DRAFT, AN ATONEMENT ...'[21]

A former student of Wilson, Ian McEwan used the same passage from *Northanger Abbey* as the epigraph to his novel *Atonement* (2001). Set, in the manner of *Brideshead Revisited*, in a country house in a hot summer prior to the Second World War, the novel participates wholeheartedly in the habitual modernist structuring patterns of having the English country house stand for Englishness and having a domestic betrayal represent a national one. It describes the impact of a lie told by an imaginative young girl who turns out in the end to be the narrator and a successful elderly novelist. She destroys the life of her sister's working-class lover when she falsely accuses him of rape and the novel both narrates and embodies her attempts to 'atone' for the sixty-year-old crime. As the trick ending indicates, the novel is highly self-conscious, and in affecting to be realism, and withholding its status as a narrative shaped by an individual subjective consciousness implicated in the events she recounts, *Atonement* offers a commentary on the procedures of modern fictionalising.

That this is a novel about modernism as well as the war is signalled when Robbie, prior to his unjust indictment, has poems rejected by the *Criterion* ('initialled by Mr Eliot himself' [*A*, 77]), and when Briony submits a manuscript to *Horizon* that Cyril Connolly rejects for being plotless and inconclusive, too derivative of Woolf. In the novel's closing section, the reader finds out that Briony is the book's 'author' in a section dated 1999, which describes the celebration of her seventy-seventh birthday – which is to say that she is a child of 1922, the *annus mirabilis* of literary modernism. McEwan in an interview called his novel 'a conversation with modernism and its dereliction of duty in relation to what I have Cyril Connolly call the backbone of the plot',[22] but in fact McEwan puts into Connolly's mouth a more profound indictment of modernism than this when Connolly asks if Briony's impressionistic vignette might be imbued with more significance than its author has so far allowed it: '*If this girl has so fully misunderstood or been so wholly baffled by the strange little scene that has unfolded before her, how might it affect the lives of the two adults? Might she come between them in some disastrous fashion?*' (*A*, 295, italics in original). By this point, the reader already knows that Briony has intervened in the situation between her sister and Robbie, and that the appalling consequences of her actions are incommensurate with the dreamy and lyrical rendering of a hot summer afternoon she has offered to *Horizon*. Briony will survive to create a new version of events, and the working-class Robbie, another might-have-been-modernist, will not.

Coda: National Historiography 151

In Briony's retrospective and 'atoning' version of events, the body of the novel itself, the victimised Robbie survives Dunkirk and is reunited with Briony's sister who has survived the Blitz. The closing section of the novel has Briony come clean about her authorial role:

All the preceding drafts were pitiless. But now I can no longer think what purpose would be served if, say, I tried to persuade my reader, by direct or indirect means, that Robbie Turner died of septicemia at Bray Dunes on 1 June 1940, or that Cecilia was killed in September of the same year by the bomb that destroyed Balham Underground station. (*A*, 350)

But does this first person narrative in disguise amount to atonement or exculpation? 'I like to think', Briony writes of her happy ending, 'that it isn't weakness or evasion, but a final act of kindness, a stand against oblivion and despair, to let my lovers live and to unite them at the end' (*A*, 351). Briony ends her book liberated from self-blame by the wishful thinking that postulates retrospective fictions as compensation for a devastating crime. Learning to forgive yourself becomes the important thing, despite the fact that – or, really, because – your crimes are so awful that their consequences cannot be reversed. Given that Briony's crime stands for the national crime of Dunkirk – an avoidable military catastrophe swiftly rewritten as a triumph of British courage – this postulates the historical fiction of the century's end as atonement, as a remedial national historiography.

But the ease with which self-incrimination can be turned into self-forgiveness is demonstrated by Kazuo Ishiguro's *The Remains of the Day* (1989), which intervenes chronologically between Wilson and McEwan's novels. The parallels between it and *Atonement* are easily drawn; an unreliable narrator retrospectively tells a story of British guilt that uses a devastating private betrayal to allegorise a well-known instance of national failure around the Second World War (appeasement for Ishiguro, Dunkirk for McEwan). Set in the year of the Suez Crisis, *The Remains of the Day* is narrated by a butler who has been employed in an aristocratic interwar establishment along the lines of the Astors' Cliveden, and in the course of the novel he comes to realise his complicity in his employer's pro-appeasement guilt. As in *Atonement*, appeasable guilt becomes the benchmark of moral growth, although Ishiguro does not destabilise his quasi-modernist first person narration, whereas the trick ending of *Atonement* recalls quite jarringly the disparity between the seriousness of the crime and the inadequacy of the attempt to redress it.

Historical victims become collateral damage: a liberal humanist novel of the individual conscience, very much in the manner of Forster, makes Ishiguro's Quisling narrator more complexly damaged than the housemaids whom he sacks, at his employer's behest, for being Jewish.

The book follows the self-congratulatory although scarcely believable A. J. P. Taylor line of argument that Munich was the apotheosis of liberalism, and 'a triumph for all that was best and most enlightened in British life; a triumph for those who had preached equal justice between peoples; a triumph for those who had courageously denounced the harshness and short-sightedness of Versailles ... With skill and persistence, Chamberlain brought first the French, and then the Czechs, to follow the moral line.'[23] In Ishiguro's novel, even Lord Darlington's political antagonists believe that he is motivated by idealism:

'His lordship is a gentleman. That's what's at the root of it. He's a gentleman, and he fought a war with the Germans, and it's his instinct to offer generosity and friendship to a defeated foe. It's his instinct. Because he's a gentleman, a true old English gentleman ... How could you not have seen it? The way they've [the Germans] used it, manipulated it, turned something fine and noble into something else – something they can use for their own foul ends'.[24]

At the beginning of his journey west, the butler discounts the possibility that Lord Darlington was 'motivated by egotism or arrogance'; on the contrary, he was driven by 'a deep sense of moral duty' (*TROTD*, 61). Darlington has been motivated by his friendship with a German officer from the time they met on the Front ('He was my enemy ... but he always behaved like a gentleman' [*TROTD*, 73]) to his suicide in ruined Germany.

Appeasement and Munich follow from how the Treaty of Versailles has outraged Lord Darlington's sense of honour, because 'It does us great discredit to treat a defeated foe like this. A complete break with the traditions of the country' (*TROTD*, 71). If this is treated ironically, what is presented as an alternative system of values is downright sinister, as when the scheming American senator denounces the behind-the-scenes conference aiming at the revision of Versailles:

'Let's take our good host here. What is he? He is a gentleman. No one here, I trust, would care to disagree. A classic English gentleman. Decent, honest, well-meaning. But his lordship here is *an amateur* ... He is an amateur and international affairs today are no longer for gentlemen amateurs. The sooner you here in Europe realize that the better. All you decent, well-meaning gentleman, let me ask you, have you any idea what sort of place the world is becoming around you? ... You here in Europe need professionals to run your affairs ... Let me make a toast. To professionalism.' (*TROTD*, 102)

To uproarious applause, Lord Darlington replies that what Lewis calls amateurism 'is what I think most of us here still prefer to call "honour"', and that professionalism means 'getting one's way by cheating and manipulating ... serving the dictates of greed and advantage rather than those of goodness and the desire to see justice prevail' (*TROTD*, 103).

Of course, historical fiction is as revealing of its own time as of the era it describes, and the novel's denunciation of amoral and philistine professionalism, and its at least partly nostalgic (and not simply satirical) treatment of interwar idealism, speak directly to its late-1980s present. The one-nation Tory Lord Darlington may seem a period piece in the light of the appeasement policy that sees his downfall, but even in the 1980s he was recognisable enough as one of Margaret Thatcher's 'Wets', the cultured amateurs, paternalist or corporatist, whom she ridiculed and replaced with a more ruthless professionalism. 'Professionalism' becomes an excuse for philistinism, vulgarity and amoral self-interest in this novel.[25] It matters, in this contemporary context, that the villainous senator is an American, and that Darlington Hall is in American hands at the end of the novel. Again, there's a danger of exceptionalism here – *The Good Soldier* ends with the English country estate in American hands as well – but it may be telling that Ishiguro follows suit in years when, as Arthur Marwick summarises it, 'an important part of the Thatcherite spirit was a welcoming into Britain of all things thought to pertain to American culture'.[26] He later adds that 'both the spirit and the end product of the heritage idea are very American'.[27] Since Marwick never explains these observations, they could probably be bracketed as a familiar anti-American reflex of the British left – except that Ishiguro clearly agrees with them. When Mr Farraday, the new American proprietor of Ishiguro's country estate, wants staff 'worthy of a grand old English house' (*TROTD*, 6), he expostulates with the butler about Stevens' reticence about his and the house's pedigree:

'I mean to say, Stevens, this *is* a genuine grand old English house, isn't it? That's what I paid for. And you're a genuine old-fashioned English butler, not just some waiter pretending to be one. You're the real thing, aren't you? That's what I wanted, isn't that what I have?' (*TROTD*, 124, emphasis in original)

That Stevens knows that he has been bought as 'part of the package' (*TROTD*, 242) underscores the novel's suggestion that national self-imaginings are not exclusively for domestic consumption, but need to be seen projected outwards as well as inwards. Whatever the cultural needs they fulfil, the transatlantic popularity of books like *The Remains of the Day* and *Atonement* shows that these needs are not exclusively British. As if it were still 1940, British culture is selling to the United States the most saleable version of Englishness: if Englishness is gratifyingly compromised by its failures – and it is hardly damning to say that a culture is too gentlemanly for its own good – it is no less seductively scenic for all that.

But however easy it would be to identify *The Remains of the Day* with the commercial aesthetics of the English tourist board, its domestic context gives reason to hesitate. Ishiguro was not alone in deciding to revisit the motivations underpinning appeasement during the 1980s; British rightwing historians, too, were committed to producing revisionist accounts of the war, with (I think here of David Irving) varying degrees of plausibility and influence. One credible rightwing maverick was Correlli Barnett, whose masochistic reckonings *The Audit of War* (1986) and *The Lost Victory* (1995) demonstrated how the Second World War destroyed 'great' Britain. The rot set in at an early stage; the opening sentence of *The Audit of War* makes that – and the tenor of Barnett's argument – plain:

While Winston Churchill and the nation at large were fighting for sheer survival in the face of Nazi Germany's then victorious power, members of the British cultural élite had begun to busy themselves with design studies for a 'New Jerusalem' to be built in Britain after the war was won.[28]

In other words, the desire for social justice was unrealistic and irresponsible, and a minority interest out of touch with 'the nation at large'. Chapter 1 of Barnett's book elaborates on the foolish idealism of the postwar settlement's originators, and on the project that 'they proceeded successfully *to press on the British people* between 1940 and 1945, with far-reaching effects on Britain's postwar chances as an industrial power struggling for survival and prosperity'.[29]

This was, as the liberal novelist and critic Malcolm Bradbury put it, 'the age of Sado-Monetarism'.[30] It does not take much political savvy to identify the agenda that Barnett's rethinking of the war advances, and none at all when he reaches his satirical closing denunciation of the post-war New Jerusalem as 'a dream turned to a dank reality of a segregated, subliterate, unskilled, unhealthy and institutionalised proletariat hanging on the nipple of state maternalism'.[31] The culprits Barnett held

Coda: National Historiography

responsible for decline are, like Ishiguro's quixotic aristocrat, 'the British small-'l' liberal Establishment ... tender-hearted and highminded', ridiculed for, among many other things, privileging high culture and liberal education.[32] The derisive attack on the humane liberalism of 'the British cultural elite', the intellectual aristocracy of late modernism, found its political corollary in Thatcherite ideology, which welcomed with open arms both its philistinism and its apportioning of blame for industrial decline to the idiocies of the progressively minded. The narrative of 'decline' with all its attendant fault-finding could scarcely be more reactionary: the years of the post-war settlement brought vast leaps in the standard of living for women and the working class; they saw the abolition of capital punishment, the decriminalising of homosexuality and the legalisation of abortion; and brought the first steps towards devolved government in Wales and Scotland as well as the end of colonisation abroad. To buy into 'decline' is to buy into the equation of strength with domestic and imperial stratification; it is a way of showing that the social democracy of the post-war settlement proved a catastrophic mistake. And the most tenacious critical cliché accuses post-war fiction in Britain of believing the same thing, of being a plaintive whine of where-did-it-all-go-wrong? In the words of one professional book reviewer, 'If the post-war English novel has a public theme, that theme is decline.'[33]

But when is a decline not a decline? Halfway through the century, Robert Graves and Alan Hodge revisited their *The Long Weekend: A Social History of Great Britain 1918–1939*, a 500-page farewell to the interwar period completed 'about the time of the Dunkirk invasion ... when there was a grave risk that German might soon be spoken in Whitehall'.[34] Writing their new preface in 1950, they measured the cultural excitement of the interwar decades against the drab first phase of the post-war, conceding how seductive it had become retrospectively to mourn the end of a 'legendary golden age when everyone could go where he pleased and do as he pleased when he got there, and income-tax was only a shilling or two in the £'; these were the glorious years when 'Britain (then called England) was still a first-class power':

Re-reading *The Long Week-end* is a little embarrassing ... It is also a salutary reminder that the years between the two wars were not at all so golden and that, whatever you may say of the dullness and restrictiveness of the present, Britain is at any rate well rid of its nastier internal dissentions and its neurotic sense of imminent catastrophe. You feel that the worst has now happened, that it was deserved, that the British as a whole have behaved better than at any period of their history, and that though it is hard to decide whether one should view the cutting-away of so much national top-hamper with admiration or resentment, they may, even, after all, have a future.[35]

I suggested in the introduction to this book that late modernism saw diminution as an aspiration rather than a form of political retreat, but I have been trying to describe the cultural anxiety that came between the aspiration and its realisation, as modernism reached middle age in a world that it anticipated and helped to make possible, but which became decreasingly kind to it. Diminution rather than decline may well be too consoling a conclusion: Forsterian, anachronistic, soppy. It is almost certainly an alternative way of suggesting, as a character in Ishiguro's novel does, 'that for a great many people, the evening was the best part of the day ... of course, the man had been speaking figuratively' (*TROTD*, 240). And so he had.

Notes

INTRODUCTION: MODERNISM BEYOND THE BLITZ

1 T. S. Eliot, *Little Gidding, Collected Poems, 1909–1962* (New York, San Diego, CA, and London: Harcourt Brace, 1991), 207.
2 Eliot, *Little Gidding*, 201.
3 Lucy Noakes, *War and the British: Gender, Memory and National Identity* (London and New York: IB Tauris, 1998), 3.
4 'The New Europe', *The Times*, 1 July 1940, 5.
5 Sir F. Fremantle, quoted by Tony Mason in 'Hunger ... is a very good thing: Britain in the 1930s', Nick Tiratsoo (ed.), *From Blitz to Blair: A New History of Britain since 1939* (London: Weidenfeld & Nicolson, 1997), 7.
6 T. S. Eliot, *East Coker, Collected Poems, 1909–1962*, 185.
7 The last decade has seen some useful attempts to address the critical neglect of the literature of the Second World War, among them: Adam Piette, *The Imagination at War: British Fiction and Poetry 1939–1945* (Basingstoke: Macmillan, 1995); Gill Plain, *Women's Fiction of the Second World War: Gender, Power and Resistance* (Edinburgh: Edinburgh University Press, 1996); Jenny Hartley, *Millions Like Us: British Women's Fiction of the Second World War* (London: Virago, 1997); Karen Schneider, *Loving Arms: British Women Writing the Second World War* (Lexington, KY: The University Press of Kentucky, 1997); Phyllis Lassner, *British Women Writers of WWII: Battlegrounds of their Own* (Basingstoke: Macmillan, 1998); Mark Rawlinson, *British Writing of the Second World War* (Oxford: Oxford University Press, 2000).
8 Quoted in Paul Fussell, *Wartime: Understanding and Behavior in the Second World War* (New York and Oxford: Oxford University Press, 1989), 133.
9 Cyril Connolly, 'Comment', *Horizon* 2 (Aug–Dec 1940), 5.
10 Keith Douglas, 'Desert Flowers', *Collected Poems*, John Waller, G. S. Fraser and J. C. Hall (eds.) (London: Faber, 1966), 129.
11 Richard M. Titmuss, *Problems of Social Policy* (London: HMSO, 1950), 335–6.
12 Tony Judt, *Postwar: A History of Europe since 1945* (New York: Penguin, 2005), 18.
13 Randall Stevenson, *The British Novel since the Thirties: An Introduction* (Athens, Ga: University of Georgia Press, 1986), 119.

14 Katherine Mansfield in a letter to John Middleton Murry dated 10 November 1919, in *The Collected Letters of Katherine Mansfield*, 5 vols., Vincent O'Sullivan and Margaret Scott (eds.) (Oxford: Clarendon, 1993), Vol. 3, 82.
15 Rebecca West, *The Return of the Soldier* (London: Virago, 1996), 133.
16 T. S. Eliot, *The Waste Land*, *Collected Poems, 1909–1962*, 57.
17 Margaret R. Higonnet and Patrice L-R. Higonnet, 'The Double Helix', Margaret Randolph Higonnet, Jane Jenson, Sonya Michel and Margaret Collins Weitz (eds.), *Behind the Lines: Gender and the Two World Wars* (New Haven, CT, and London: Yale University Press, 1987), 46.
18 This was Woolf describing the narrative construction of *The Waves*. *The Diary of Virginia Woolf*, 5 vols., Anne Olivier Bell and Andrew McNeillie (eds.), (London: Hogarth, 1984), Vol. 3, 209, 230.
19 Lawrence Rainey, *Institutions of Modernism: Literary Elites and Public Culture* (New Haven, CT, and London: Yale University Press, 1998), 4.
20 Paul Fussell, *The Great War and Modern Memory* (London, Oxford and New York: Oxford University Press, 1977), 75.
21 C. Day Lewis, 'Where are the War Poets?' *Word Over All* (London: Jonathan Cape, 1946), 30.
22 George Orwell, 'Spilling the Spanish Beans', *The Collected Essays, Journalism and Letters of George Orwell*, 4 vols., Sonia Orwell and Ian Angus (eds.) (London: Secker & Warburg, 1968), Vol. 1, 274.
23 E. M. Forster, 'George Orwell', *Two Cheers for Democracy* (London: Edward Arnold, 1951), 73.
24 Virginia Woolf, *The Diary of Virginia Woolf*, Vol. 5, 297.
25 'Adversary Proceedings' is the title of the chapter on the polarising effects of the war's conduct. Fussell, *The Great War and Modern Memory*, 75–113.
26 Rebecca West, 'Notes on the Way', *Time and Tide* 23 (1942), 853.
27 C. E. M. Joad, *For Civilization* (London: Macmillan, 1940), 24.
28 Harold Nicolson, *Why Britain is at War* (Harmondsworth: Penguin, 1939), 150–1.
29 Cyril Connolly, 'Comment', *Horizon* 1 (Jan–July 1940), 313.
30 Wyndham Lewis, *Blasting and Bombardiering* (Berkeley and Los Angeles, CA: University of California Press, 1967), 50–1, 191, 219, 234.
31 Vincent Sherry, *The Great War and the Language of Modernism* (Oxford and New York: Oxford University Press, 2003), 19.
32 T. J. Clark, *Farewell to an Idea: Episodes from a History of Modernism* (New Haven, CT, and London: Yale University Press, 1999), 21.
33 According to North, what emerged in the separation of modernism from its contexts was 'the preservation of something called "modernism" in intellectual amber, something whose purported insulation from the cultural world into which it was introduced is now retrospectively accomplished by critical consensus'. Michael North, *Reading 1922: A Return to the Scene of the Modern* (Oxford and New York: Oxford University Press, 1999), 11.
34 John Lehmann, *New Writing in Europe* (Harmondsworth: Penguin, 1940), 18–19.
35 Tyrus Miller, *Late Modernism: Fiction, Politics, and the Arts Between the World Wars* (Berkeley, CA: University of California Press, 1999), 5.

Notes to pages 16–26   159

36 Fredric Jameson, *A Singular Modernity: Essay on the Ontology of the Present* (London: Verso, 2002), 165.
37 Fredric Jameson, *The Seeds of Time* (New York: Columbia University Press, 1994), 118–19.
38 Jed Esty, *A Shrinking Island: Modernism and National Culture in England* (Princeton, NJ, and Oxford: Princeton University Press, 2003), 1.
39 Marianna Torgovnick, *The War Complex: World War II in Our Time* (Chicago, IL: Chicago University Press, 2005).
40 Henry Green, 'Unloving', *Surviving: The Uncollected Writings of Henry Green*, Matthew Yorke (ed.), (New York: Viking, 1993a), 283.
41 Raymond Williams, *Marxism and Literature* (Oxford and New York: Oxford University Press, 1977), 121, 123.

I   VIRGINIA WOOLF AND THE PASTORAL PATRIA

1 Edward R. Murrow, *This Is London*, Elmer Davis (ed.) (New York: Simon & Schuster, 1941), 146.
2 Virginia Woolf, *The Letters of Virginia Woolf*, 6 vols., Nigel Nicolson (ed.) (London: Hogarth, 1980), Vol. 6, 434–5.
3 On the reception of *Britain Can Take It*, see Anthony Aldgate and Jeffrey Richards, *Britain Can Take It: British Cinema in the Second World War* (Oxford and New York: Blackwell, 1986), 120–2; and James Chapman, *The British at War: Cinema, State and Propaganda* (London and New York: IB Tauris, 1998), 98–9.
4 Raymond Williams, *The Country and the City* (New York: Oxford University Press, 1973), 248.
5 That Williams was not thinking about modernism when he discussed the persistence of the rural ideal is evident in his account of institutionalised modernism in the essays posthumously collected in *The Politics of Modernism*, which assumes (in order to critique) the fundamentally metropolitan basis of modernist writing. See *The Politics of Modernism: Against the New Conformists*, Tony Pinkney (ed.) (London: Verso, 1989).
6 Laura Marcus, *Virginia Woolf* (Tavistock: Northcote House, 1997), 166.
7 C. F. G. Masterman, *The Condition of England* (London: Methuen, 1960), 148. On the importance of pastoral in the First World War, see the chapter 'Arcadian Recourses', in Paul Fussell's *The Great War and Modern Memory* (Oxford, New York and London: Oxford University Press, 1975), 230–69.
8 Samuel Chamberlain and Donald Moffatt, *This Realm, This England ... The Citadel of a Valiant Race Portrayed by Its Greatest Etchers* (New York: Hastings House, 1941), 5.
9 Chamberlain and Moffatt, *This Realm, This England*, 5.
10 Virginia Woolf, 'Thoughts on Peace in an Air Raid', *The Death of the Moth and Other Essays* (New York: Harcourt Brace, 1942), 244.
11 Mollie Panter-Downes, *London War Notes: 1939–1945*, William Shawn (ed.) (New York: Farrar, Straus & Giroux, 1971), 5, 11.

12 Virginia Woolf, *Between the Acts* (San Diego, CA, New York and London: Harcourt, 1969), 181–2. Hereafter cited parenthetically.
13 See Alex Zwerdling, *Virginia Woolf and the Real World* (Berkeley and Los Angeles, CA, and London: University of California Press, 1986), 283, 292–3. Wayne Chapman and Janet Manson speculate that Woolf took a more active role in her husband's political deliberations. They describe a draft paper in manuscript called 'In'l Re'ns' (which they suggest became 'The Enforcement of International Law') as a 'Leonard and Virginia Woolf collaboration'. Wayne K. Chapman and Janet M. Manson, 'Carte and Tierce: Leonard, Virginia Woolf, and the War for Peace', *Virginia Woolf and War: Fiction, Reality, and Myth*, Mark Hussey (ed.) (Syracuse, NY: Syracuse University Press, 1991), 64.
14 Gillian Beer, '*Between the Acts*: Resisting the End', *Virginia Woolf: The Common Ground* (Edinburgh: Edinburgh University Press, 1996), 137.
15 Virginia Woolf, *Jacob's Room* (New York: Harcourt Brace, 1923), 208.
16 Virginia Woolf, *Three Guineas* (San Diego, CA, New York and London: Harcourt, 1966), 102.
17 Woolf, *Three Guineas*, 10–11.
18 Woolf, *Three Guineas*, 103, 141.
19 When 'The Duchess and the Jeweller' was rejected because its anti-Semitism would be likely to offend an American readership, Woolf eliminated the direct references to the jeweller's Jewishness; still, the story remains fairly objectionable:

> he was the richest jeweller in England; but his nose, which was long and flexible, like an elephant's trunk, seemed to say by its curious quiver at the nostrils (but it seemed as if the whole nose quivered, not only the nostrils) that he was not satisfied yet; still smelt something under the ground a little further off. Imagine a giant hog in a pasture rich with truffles; after unearthing this truffle and that, still it smells a bigger, a blacker truffle under the ground further off. So Oliver snuffed always in the rich earth of Mayfair another truffle, a blacker, a bigger further off. ('The Duchess and the Jeweller', *The Complete Shorter Fiction of Virginia Woolf*, Susan Dick [ed.] [San Diego, CA, New York and London: Harcourt Brace Jovanovich, 1985], 243).

Woolf described in a letter to Vanessa Bell how her New York agent 'wants to shuffle out of the Jew and the Duchess, as well he may. But I shall be as hard as flint' (Woolf, *Letters*, Vol. 6, 173).

To draw attention to the historically specific aspects of *Three Guineas*, and to some questionable assumptions that underpin it, is only to suggest that Woolf's anti-fascism is less trans-historically relevant than some recent scholarship claims. Merry M. Pawlowski's edited collection *Virginia Woolf and Fascism: Resisting the Dictators' Seduction* (Basingstoke and New York: Palgrave, 2001) is sometimes compromised by this mood of reverent celebration. In Pawlowski's introduction, for example, she cites Barbara Ehrenreich's argument that gendered approaches to fascism have to proceed cautiously:

> It would be a mistake, however, Ehrenreich warns, to conclude simplistically that all men are fascists and thereby court the danger of trivializing Nazi genocide by

forgetting that real Jewish, Catholic, gypsy, and communist women and men were murdered. *Woolf herself* acknowledges that Jewish men were *as much at risk* from the tyranny of dictators as women had been for centuries. (3, emphasis added).

It seems to me that this is almost exactly the wrong way round. I think Phyllis Lassner has done very useful work to situate *Three Guineas* in a more substantial context of women's war writing. Lassner argues that 'Claims for Woolf's unique courage situate her on the margins not only of male-dominated debates about war, but as the only credible feminist position on war. Such an approach ignores the vibrancy of a more historically accurate and complex set of responses to World War II'. *British Women Writers of WWII: Battlegrounds of their Own* (Basingstoke: Macmillan, 1998), 29.

20 Virginia Woolf, *The Diary of Virginia Woolf,* 5 vols., Anne Olivier Bell and Andrew McNeillie (eds.) (London: Hogarth, 1984), Vol. 5, 147.
21 Woolf, *Diary*, Vol. 5, 166, 170, 174.
22 Woolf, *Diary*, Vol. 5, 297.
23 Woolf, *Diary*, Vol. 5, 289, 295, 297, 317, 318.
24 The first quotation is from Anna Snaith, *Virginia Woolf: Public and Private Negotiations* (New York: St Martin's, 2000), 144; the second is from Alex Zwerdling, *Virginia Woolf and the Real World*, 307–8. Zwerdling is usually so measured that his overstated account of Giles is a little surprising: 'His aggressive masculinity and Nordic looks remind one of the Master Race ... He is a good indigenous example of the ethos Woolf had seen in the first days of Italian Fascism' (308).
25 Philip Larkin, 'An Arundel Tomb', *Collected Poems* (London: The Marvell Press and Faber & Faber, 1989), 111.
26 See, for instance, the description of Jacob's library at Cambridge: 'Lives of the Duke of Wellington ... a *Manual of the Diseases of the Horse*'. Woolf, *Jacob's Room*, 60.
27 Snaith, *Virginia Woolf*, 145. Karen Schneider more tentatively argues that the Second World War 'forced [Woolf] to reexamine both her espousal of pacifism and eschewal of patriotism', but she concludes that 'Woolf did not, ultimately, soften her critique or abandon her radical views'. *Loving Arms: British Women Writing the Second World War* (Lexington, KY: The University Press of Kentucky, 1997), 111.
28 Leonard Woolf, *The War For Peace* (London: Routledge, 1940), 216.
29 Herbert Read, 'Art in an Electric Atmosphere', *Horizon* 3 (Jan–June 1941), 309.
30 'Bestseller' sounds a little theatrical, but the Beveridge Report sold astonishingly well – 635,000 copies – for a government publication, and its proposals for reform quickly became well known. The political historian Peter Hennessy gives a useful summary of the report's popular reception in *Never Again: Britain, 1945–1951* (New York: Pantheon, 1993), 75–8.
31 Mark Rawlinson, *British Writing of the Second World War* (Oxford: Oxford University Press, 2000), 29, 143–4.

32 Janet Montefiore, *Men and Women Writers of the 1930s: The Dangerous Flood of History* (London and New York: Routledge, 1996), 13.
33 John Mepham, *Virginia Woolf: A Literary Life* (New York: St Martin's, 1991), 191. But no wonder Woolf's declarations of solidarity fail to convince: '200 betwixt and betweens' is how she summed up her audience in a letter the following day to Vita Sackville-West (*Letters*, Vol. 6, 394).
34 Virginia Woolf, *To the Lighthouse* (New York and London: Harcourt Brace Jovanovich, 1981), 8–9.
35 Woolf, *To the Lighthouse*, 95, 58–9.
36 Woolf, *To the Lighthouse*, 28.
37 Woolf, *To the Lighthouse*, 60.
38 E. M. Forster, 'Does Culture Matter?' *Two Cheers for Democracy*, 112.
39 'A Pageant Play: "England's Pleasant Land"', *The Times*, 11 July 1938, 12.
40 Tom Harrisson, *Living through the Blitz* (London: Collins, 1976), 231.
41 Forster, 'The Challenge of our Time', *Two Cheers for Democracy*, 70.
42 Louise Blakeney Williams, *Modernism and the Ideology of History* (Cambridge: Cambridge University Press, 2002), 59. She later summarises:

> The conclusion that all the Modernists came to by the beginning of 1914 was that modern problems began when a way of life dominated by a superior aristocracy, who provided control and direction for the masses, and who respected great art, ended. What replaced it was the chaos of a government and society that guaranteed freedom to the selfish and ignorant middle classes and 'mob'. The world would be a better place, the Modernists concluded, if the values and structures of an aristocratic age of the past were returned. (74–5)

43 Williams, *The Country and the City*, 50.
44 Aneurin Bevan, *In Place of Fear* (Melbourne, London and Toronto, ON: Heinemann, 1952), 64.
45 D. H. Lawrence, *Lady Chatterley's Lover* (New York: Modern Library, 2001), 168.
46 Lord Macmillan, *Recording Britain* (London: Oxford University Press in association with the Pilgrim Trust, 1946), v.
47 C. E. M. Joad, 'The Face of England: How It Is Ravaged and How It May Be Preserved', *Horizon* 5 (Jan-June 1942), 335.
48 Joad, 'The Face of England', 335.
49 Woolf, 'The Duchess and the Jeweller', *The Complete Shorter Fiction of Virginia Woolf*, 242.
50 Harrisson, *Living through the Blitz*, 11.
51 Mrs Miniver's debt to Woolf was suggested in the 1950s by the novelist Angus Wilson when he created Mrs Green, a devastating parodic composite of Woolf's heroines: 'Was it not, with extra emphasis upon courage and nostalgia, the same Mrs Green who emerged so opportunely as Mrs Miniver?' Angus Wilson, 'The View from the 1950s', *Diversity and Depth in Fiction: Selected Critical Writings of Angus Wilson*, Kerry McSweeney (ed.) (London: Secker & Warburg, 1983), 122.

Notes to pages 39–46   163

52 Jed Esty, *A Shrinking Island: Modernism and National Culture in England* (Princeton, NJ, and Oxford: Princeton University Press, 2004), 58.
53 George Orwell, 'Films: This England', *Time and Tide* 22 (Jan–Dec 1941), 463.
54 Woolf, *Diary*, Vol. 5, 353.
55 Aptly enough, this was also a return to Woolf's own origins as a novelist. See Mark A. Wollaeger's reading of Woolf's Conradian debut *The Voyage Out* (1915) in 'The Woolfs in the Jungle: Intertextuality, Sexuality, and the Emergence of Female Modernism in *The Voyage Out*, *The Village in the Jungle*, and *Heart of Darkness*' *Modern Language Quarterly* 64 (2003), 33–69.
56 Joseph Conrad, *Heart of Darkness* (New York and London: Norton, 2006), 5. Evelyn Waugh, *The Sword of Honour Trilogy* (New York: Knopf, 1994), 20.
57 Woolf, *To the Lighthouse*, 137.
58 Virginia Woolf, 'The Death of the Moth', *The Death of the Moth and Other Essays*, 6.
59 Zwerdling, *Virginia Woolf and the Real World*, 279.
60 Woolf, *Three Guineas*, 109.

2   REBECCA WEST'S ANTI-BLOOMSBURY GROUP

1 Hilary Mantel, 'No Passes or Documents Are Needed: The Writer at Home in Europe', *On Modern British Fiction*, Zachary Leader (ed.) (Oxford: Oxford University Press, 2002), 99.
2 This is quoted from the text of the broadcast published as Neville Chamberlain, 'The Crisis: National Broadcast', *In Search of Peace* (New York: Putnam, 1939), 174.
3 'Circles of Perdition', *Time* 50 (July–Dec 1947), 116.
4 For an account of her relationship with Ford, see Victoria Glendinning, *Rebecca West: A Life* (New York: Knopf, 1987), 39–41.
5 Rebecca West, *The Meaning of Treason* (New York: Viking, 1949), 111–12.
6 William Shakespeare, *Henry V*, T. W. Craik (ed.) (London and New York: Routledge, 1995), 311–12.
7 See, for instance, Paul Fussell, *Abroad: British Literary Traveling Between the Wars* (New York and Oxford: Oxford University Press, 1980) and Bernard Schweizer, *Radicals on the Road: The Politics of English Travel Writing in the 1930s* (Charlottesville, VA, and London: University Press of Virginia, 2001).
8 Rebecca West, *Black Lamb and Grey Falcon: A Journey Through Yugoslavia* (Edinburgh: Canongate, 1993), 826–7. Hereafter cited parenthetically.
9 See, for example, the title essay of *For Lancelot Andrewes* (1928), in which Eliot argued that 'a Church is to be judged by its intellectual fruits, by its influence on the sensibility of the most sensitive and on the intellect of the most intelligent'. T. S. Eliot, *For Lancelot Andrewes* (London: Faber, 1970), 13. Twenty years later he was proclaiming that 'the convert of the intellectual or sensitive type is drawn towards the more Catholic type of worship and doctrine' in T. S. Eliot, *Notes Towards the Definition of Culture* (London: Faber, 1948), 80. The famous declaration that he was classicist in literature, royalist in politics

and Anglo-Catholic in religion comes from the preface to *For Lancelot Andrewes* (7). George Orwell's accusation is made in 'Inside the Whale', *The Collected Essays, Journalism and Letters of George Orwell*, 4 vols., Sonia Orwell and Ian Angus (eds.) (London: Secker & Warburg, 1968), Vol. 1, 509.
10 T. S. Eliot, 'Religion and Literature', *Selected Prose of T. S. Eliot*, Frank Kermode (ed.) (San Diego, CA, New York and London: Harcourt, 1975), 104.
11 Cyril Connolly, *Enemies of Promise* (London: Routledge, 1938), 143–4.
12 Rebecca West, 'The Labour Party's Treachery: What is Lloyd George?' *The Young Rebecca: Writings of Rebecca West*, Jane Marcus (ed.) (London and Basingstoke: Macmillan, in association with Virago, 1982), 110.
13 *Authors Take Sides on the Spanish War* (London: Left Review, 1937), unpaginated.
14 'Rebecca West', *Authors Take Sides*, unpaginated.
15 This is in a letter from West to Stoyan Pribicevic dated 5 June 1945. *Selected Letters of Rebecca West*, Bonnie Kime Scott (ed.) (New Haven, CT, and London: Yale University Press, 2000), 189.
16 Naomi Mitchison, *Vienna Diary* (New York: Harrison Smith and Robert Hass, 1934), 74.
17 E. M. Forster, 'What I Believe', *Two Cheers for Democracy* (London: Edward Arnold, 1951), 78; Virginia Woolf, *Three Guineas* (San Diego, CA, New York and London: Harcourt, 1966), 78.
18 Virginia Woolf, *The Diary of Virginia Woolf*, 5 vols., Anne Olivier Bell and Andrew McNeillie (eds.) (London: Hogarth, 1984), Vol. 5, 173.
19 Virginia Woolf, *Three Guineas*, 109.
20 John Maynard Keynes, *The Economic Consequences of the Peace* (New York: Penguin, 1988), 133.
21 Keynes, *Economic Consequences*, 5.
22 Keynes, *Economic Consequences*, 36.
23 Keynes, *Economic Consequences*, 266, 291.
24 Keynes, *Economic Consequences*, 146.
25 Etienne Mantoux, *The Carthaginian Peace, or The Economic Consequences of Mr. Keynes* (New York: Scribner, 1952), 61.
26 E. H. Carr was also the author of the *Times* editorial 'The New Europe' discussed in the introduction.
27 Rebecca West, 'Notes on the Way', *Time and Tide* 23 (1942), 401–2.
28 A. J. P. Taylor, *The Origins of the Second World War* (London: Hamish Hamilton, 1961), 25.
29 Mantoux, *The Carthaginian Peace*, 4.
30 Mantoux, *The Carthaginian Peace*, 3.
31 Mantoux, *The Carthaginian Peace*, 17.
32 Harold Nicolson, 'Introduction, 1943', *Peacemaking 1919* (London: Constable, 1945), ix.
33 'Onlooker', 'Two Germanies?' *The Listener* 23 (Jan–June 1940), 478. The question mark is rhetorical; the article describes how the secrecy and violence

Notes to pages 57–60   165

with which dictatorships work make it vital to distinguish between the Nazi leadership and the German people.

34 Noël Coward, 'Don't Let's Be Beastly to the Germans', *The Complete Lyrics*, Barry Day (ed.) (Woodstock and New York: The Overlook Press, 1998), 207.
35 Coward, 'Don't Let's Be Beastly to the Germans', 207.
36 Coward tells of West's postcard in his memoir, *Future Indefinite* (London: Heinemann, 1954), 113. He and West met in 1918 and remained close friends until his death in 1973. See, for instance, his diary entry for 16 October 1962 – full of praise for 'Rebecca ... gay and considerate, and, oh, how gloriously intelligent' (*The Noël Coward Diaries*, Graham Payn and Sheridan Morley [eds.] [London: Weidenfeld & Nicolson, 1982], 515). Vansittart and Coward knew each other through their association with the theatre in the 1920s: Vansittart loved Coward's writing and thought he had 'more sense of politics than is usual in the profession' (Lord Vansittart, *The Mist Profession* [London: Hutchinson, 1958], 346); Coward's line on the war was a much oversimplified Vansittartism: 'I have little respect or admiration for a race, however cultured, sensitive and civilised, that willingly allows itself time and time again to be stampeded into the same state of neurotic bestiality and arrogance' (Noël Coward, *Middle East Diary* [London: Heinemann, 1944], 85).
37 Lord Vansittart, *The Roots of the Trouble and The Black Record of Germany, Past, Present and Future?* (New York: Avon, 1944), 67.
38 This is the context: 'The flag-waving and Hun-hating is absolutely nothing to what it was in 1914–1918, but it is growing ... Vansittart's hate-Germany pamphlet, Black Record, sold like hot cakes'. George Orwell, 'London Letter to Partisan Review', *The Collected Essays, Journalism and Letters*, 114.
39 The admitted domestic casualties of German bombs were 14,300 British killed and 20,500 seriously injured. I have taken this from *The Times*, 6 November 1940, 5; it probably goes without saying that wartime statistics are not necessarily reliable. The point here is how dangerous the Germans would have been perceived to be while Vansittart was at the centre of this controversy.
40 Benny Morris, *The Roots of Appeasement: The British Weekly Press and Nazi Germany during the 1930s* (London: Frank Cass, 1991), 25.
41 Hamilton Fyfe, *The Illusion of National Character* (London: Watts & Co, 1940), 92, 94–5.
42 Fyfe, *The Illusion of National Character*, 270. The Communist advocacy seems to be at the heart of his anti-Semitism: the Jewish ingratitude ('even when they are well treated ... ') refers to complaints from Jewish citizens about their status in the Soviet Union.
43 Adam Fox, *Dean Inge* (London: John Murray, 1960), 243–4.
44 Malcolm Muggeridge, *The Thirties: 1930–1940 in Great Britain* (London: Collins, 1967), 175–6.
45 Quoted in Glendinning, *Rebecca West*, 161.
46 Vansittart, *The Mist Procession*, 503.
47 Chamberlain's memo is quoted in Norman Rose, *Vansittart: Study of a Diplomat* (London: Heinemann, 1978), 207. A recent reappraisal of

Chamberlain has suggested that Vansittart 'stood, perhaps second only to Churchill, as a consistent opponent of Nazi Germany, a man who had repeatedly warned of the looming menace of Adolf Hitler' (David Dutton, *Neville Chamberlain* [London: Arnold, 2001], 93).
48 'Evil Propaganda', *The New Statesman and Nation* 21 (Jan–June 1941), 76.
49 Rebecca West, 'Notes on the Way', *Time and Tide* 23 (1942), 853.
50 Lord Vansittart, *The Roots of the Trouble*, 91.
51 W. H. Auden, 'September 1, 1939', *Selected Poems*, Edward Mendelson (ed.) (London: Faber, 1979), 86.
52 Lloyd George, *The Truth about the Peace Treaty*, 2 vols. (London: Gollancz, 1938) was published the following year in the United States as the less inflammatory *Memoirs of the Peace Conference*, 2 vols., (New Haven, CT: Yale University Press, 1939).
53 Vansittart, *The Mist Procession*, 224.
54 Vansittart, *Black Record*, 25, 58.
55 Orwell, 'London Letter to Partisan Review', 175. Bad writing throughout, but a delicious account of Teutonic heroism: 'Siegfried, the German hero of heroes, the usual mixture of force and fraud'; 'the Tarnhelm, a helmet which ... enabled one to take any shape one liked, particularly a shady one'; 'Brunhild ... hard as nails ... An impossible woman I should say'; 'Now the Nibelunglied is interesting precisely because it is not immediately apparent to anyone but a German where Loyalty and Straightforwardness come in' (Vansittart, *Black Record*, 60–2).
56 Orwell, 'Looking Back on the Spanish War', 253.
57 Rebecca West, 'Confessions of Lord Vansittart', *The Sunday Times*, 4 May 1958, 6.
58 Vansittart, *Black Record*, 37 (emphasis in original).
59 John Maynard Keynes, 'To the Editor of *The New Statesman*, 14 October 1939', *The Collected Writings of John Maynard Keynes*, 30 vols., Donald Moggridge (ed.) (London: Macmillan and Cambridge University Press for the Royal Economic Society, 1978), Vol. 22, 37.
60 J. B. Priestley, 'The War – and After', *Horizon* 1 (Jan–July 1940), 15.
61 Rebecca West, 'Introduction' to Emma Goldman, *My Disillusionment in Russia* (Gloucester, MA: Peter Smith, 1983), ix.
62 Rebecca West, *The New Meaning of Treason* (New York: Viking, 1964), 158.
63 'Land of Sacrifice: Beauty and Terror in Serbia, an English Writer's Explorations', *Times Literary Supplement* 85 (1942), 102.
64 Rebecca West, 'A Training in Truculence: The Working Women's College', *The Young Rebecca*, 155.
65 The speech was delivered 4 June 1940, and is quoted here from 'Wars Are Not Won by Evacuations', *Blood, Toil, Tears and Sweat: The Speeches of Winston Churchill*, David Cannadine (ed.) (Boston, MA: Houghton Mifflin, 1989), 165.
66 T. S. Eliot, '*Ulysses*, Order, and Myth', *Selected Prose of T. S. Eliot*, 177–8.
67 Letters to the Editor: The War and the Left, *Time and Tide* 20 (1939), 1651.

68 The phrase is from Auden's poem 'In Praise of Limestone'. This 1948 poem celebrates the humanistic impermanence of limestone ('chiefly / Because it dissolves in water'), advancing the poet's 'antimythological myth' against the bogus stability of imperialist and totalitarian dogma. (W. H. Auden, 'In Praise of Limestone', *Selected Poems*, 186).
69 John Maynard Keynes, 'My Early Beliefs', in *The Bloomsbury Group: A Collection of Memoirs and Commentary*, S. P Rosenbaum (ed.) (Toronto, ON, Buffalo, NY, and London: University of Toronto Press, 1995), 96.
70 John Maynard Keynes, 'My Early Beliefs', 95.
71 Mantoux, *The Carthaginian Peace*, 180.
72 Keynes, 'My Early Beliefs', 96.
73 Steven Connor, 'Modernity and Myth', *The Cambridge History of Twentieth-Century English Literature*, Laura Marcus and Peter Nicholls (eds.) (Cambridge: Cambridge University Press, 2004), 262.
74 Perry Anderson, 'Origins of the Present Crisis', *English Questions* (London and New York: Verso, 1992), 35.
75 Virginia Woolf, 'Modern Fiction', *The Common Reader: First Series* (Harvest: San Diego, CA, New York and London, 1994), 148.
76 Keynes, 'My Early Beliefs', 96.
77 Mantoux, *The Carthaginian Peace*, 43.
78 Benedict Anderson, *Imagined Communities: Reflections on the Origin and Spread of Nationalism* (London and New York: Verso, 1991), 53. Emphasis in original.
79 Anderson, *Imagined Communities*, 10.
80 Angus Calder, *The Myth of the Blitz* (London: Jonathan Cape, 1991), 43.
81 Hugh MacDiarmid, 'Another Epitaph on an Army of Mercenaries', *Complete Poems 1920–1976*, 2 vols., Michael Grieve and W. R. Aitken (eds.) (London: Martin Brian & O'Keefe, 1978), Vol. 1, 551.
82 Hugh MacDiarmid, 'To Those of My Old School Who Fell in the Second World War', *Complete Poems 1920–1976* Vol. 2, 1121. Only minor changes (for instance, 'rightly' is taken out of parenthesis; 'in this War' replaces 'in Spain') separate this passage from its precursor in 'The International Brigade' (971).

3 THE SITUATIONAL POLITICS OF FOUR QUARTETS

1 Wyndham Lewis, *Blasting and Bombardiering* (Berkeley and Los Angeles, CA: University of California Press, 1967), 4.
2 T. S. Eliot, 'A Note on War Poetry', *Collected Poems 1909–1962* (New York, San Diego, CA, and London: Harcourt Brace, 1991), 215.
3 T. S. Eliot, 'A Dedication to My Wife', *Collected Poems 1909–1962*, 221.
4 T. S. Eliot, 'Defense of the Islands', *Collected Poems 1909–1962*, 213.
5 Eliot, 'Defense of the Islands', *Collected Poems 1909–1962*, 213–14.
6 Eliot, 'A Note on War Poetry', *Collected Poems 1909–1962*, 215.
7 Eliot, 'A Note on War Poetry', *Collected Poems 1909–1962*, 216.

Notes to pages 73–79

8 Michael Levenson, 'Does *The Waste Land* Have a Politics?' *Modernism/Modernity* 6, 3 (September 1999), 1–13.
9 Vincent Sherry, *The Great War and the Language of Modernism* (Oxford and New York: Oxford University Press, 2003), 3; T. S. Eliot, 'Gerontion', *Collected Poems 1909–1962*, 30.
10 Eliot, 'Gerontion', *Collected Poems 1909–1962*, 29; Sherry, *The Great War*, 191. Sherry puts the poem to powerful use in his captions to the book's illustrations, such as 'Bitten by flies, fought' beneath the photograph of a rotten corpse hardly distinguishable from the mud in which it lies face down (209).
11 T. S. Eliot, *East Coker*, *Collected Poems 1909–1962*, 185. Subsequent references to *Four Quartets* refer to this edition, and are cited parenthetically as *BN* (*Burnt Norton*), *EC* (*East Coker*), *DS* (*The Dry Salvages*) and *LG* (*Little Gidding*), followed by page numbers.
12 Eliot, 'Gerontion', *Collected Poems 1909–1962*, 29.
13 Eliot, 'A Note on War Poetry', *Collected Poems 1909–1962*, 215.
14 'Cato', *Guilty Men* (New York: Frederick Stokes, 1940), 63.
15 George Orwell, *The Lion and the Unicorn: Socialism and the English Genius*, reprinted in *The Collected Essays, Journalism and Letters of George Orwell*, 4 vols., Sonia Orwell and Ian Angus (eds.) (London: Secker & Warburg, 1968), Vol. 2, 67, 84, 86.
16 Malcolm Muggeridge, *The Thirties: 1930–1940 in Great Britain* (London: Collins, 1967), 317.
17 Evelyn Waugh, in a letter to *The Spectator* dated 13 October 1961, reprinted in *The Letters of Evelyn Waugh*, Mark Amory (ed.) (London: Weidenfeld and Nicolson, 1980), 574.
18 See Lyndall Gordon, *T. S. Eliot: An Imperfect Life* (London: Norton, 1999), 377–8.
19 Lord Vansittart, *The Mist Procession: The Autobiography of Lord Vansittart* (London: Hutchinson, 1958), 430.
20 'T. S. Eliot', *Authors Take Sides on the Spanish War* (London: Left Review, 1937), unpaginated.
21 T. S. Eliot, 'The Art of Poetry', *Paris Review* 21 (1959), 57, 59.
22 John Xiros Cooper, *T. S. Eliot and the Ideology of* Four Quartets (Cambridge: Cambridge University Press, 1995), 167. Cooper is especially unforgiving on the poem-as-music rhetoric that still pervades readings of *Four Quartets*: 'Music, in these accounts, stands for a certain cognitively satisfying complexity and the clean sequestration of the artefact from external contexts, which are seen at every turn as threatening to plunge the work into the confusing domains of history and ideology' (169).
23 Sebastian D. G. Knowles, *A Purgatorial Flame: Seven British Writers in the Second World War* (Philadelphia, PA: University of Pennsylvania Press, 1990), 101.
24 Steve Ellis, *The English Eliot: Design, Language and Landscape in* Four Quartets (London and New York: Routledge, 1991), 24, 91; Jed Esty, *A Shrinking Island: Modernism and National Culture in England* (Princeton, NJ, and Oxford: Princeton University Press, 2004), 155.

25 T. S. Eliot, *The Idea of a Christian Society* (New York: Harcourt Brace, 1940), 5–6.
26 Eliot, *The Idea of a Christian Society*, 58–9.
27 Gerard de Groot, *Blighty: British Society in the Era of the Great War* (London and New York: Longman, 1996), 9.
28 George Orwell, 'Inside the Whale', *The Collected Essays, Journalism and Letters of George Orwell*, Vol. 1, 515.
29 Katherine Mansfield, 'The Daughters of the Late Colonel', *Selected Stories*, Vincent O'Sullivan (ed.) (New York and London: Norton, 2006), 216; Virginia Woolf, *The Voyage Out* (New York: Modern Library, 2001), 66.
30 'Colonel Blimp in Low's *Evening Standard* cartoons was a bald, fat, walrus-moustached old man, usually depicted emerging from Turkish bath with a towel round his middle, and preluding some fatuous Diehard remark with "Gad, sir, Chamberlain – or Baldwin or Hitler or Mussolini – is right!"' (Robert Graves and Alan Hodge, *The Long Weekend: A Social History of Great Britain 1918–1939* [London: Faber, 1950], 390). In Michael Powell and Emeric Pressburger's 1943 film *The Life and Death of Colonel Blimp*, Colonel Blimp is the aristocratic Clive Winn-Candy, a distinguished and well-meaning dinosaur, a decorated veteran of the Boer War and the Great War but superannuated by the Second World War, though doing his best by his own comically antiquated standards.
31 Stephen Spender, 'How Shall We Be Saved?' *Horizon* 1 (Jan–July 1940), 55.
32 Esty, *A Shrinking Island*, 124.
33 Virginia Woolf, *Between the Acts* (San Diego, CA, New York and London: Harcourt, 1969), 78.
34 Woolf, *Between the Acts*, 76.
35 Virginia Woolf, 'Anon', in Brenda R. Silver, '"Anon" and "The Reader": Virginia Woolf's Last Essays', *Twentieth-Century Literature* 25 (1979), 384.
36 Kingsley Amis, *Lucky Jim* (Harmondsworth: Penguin, 1992), 223, 227.
37 T. S. Eliot, '*Ulysses*, Order and Myth', *Selected Prose of T. S. Eliot*, Frank Kermode (ed.) (San Diego, CA, New York and London: Harcourt, 1975), 177.
38 T. S. Eliot, 'The Love Song of J. Alfred Prufrock', *Collected Poems 1909–1962*, 3.
39 W. H. Auden, *The Orators: An English Study* (London: Faber, 1966), 14.
40 Cyril Connolly, 'Comment', *Horizon* 1 (Jan–July 1940), 5.
41 J. F. Hendry, 'Midnight Air-Raid', *The Bombed Happiness* (London: Routledge, 1942), 15.
42 Henry Treece, 'Growing Up in War-Time', *How I See Apocalypse* (London: Lindsay Drummond, 1946), 5. The rhetoric of surgery lands Treece in discomforting places when he finishes with 'we may yet live to thank God for Hitler, symptom of social disease, who has made us purge ourselves, and, in overcoming his assaults, step forward to a cleaner, more equitable and saner way of life' (12).
43 Henry Treece, 'Towards a Personal Armageddon – A Sequence', *Invitation and Warning* (London: Faber, 1942), 75.

44 The New Apocalyptic credo is summarised from Linda M. Shires, *British Poetry of the Second World War* (New York: St. Martin's, 1985), 30.
45 Stefan Schimanski and Henry Treece, 'Introduction: The Personalist View of Romanticism', *A New Romantic Anthology* (London: The Grey Walls Press, 1949), 19–20.
46 Tom Harrisson and Charles Madge (eds.), *War Begins at Home* (London: Chatto & Windus, 1940), 131, 134.
47 T. S. Eliot, 'Defense of the Islands', *Collected Poems 1909–1962*, 213.
48 T. S. Eliot, 'To the Indians Who Died in Africa', *Collected Poems 1909–1962*, 217.
49 Eliot, 'To the Indians Who Died in Africa', *Collected Poems 1909–1962*, 217.
50 See Angus Calder, *T. S. Eliot* (Brighton: Harvester, 1987) on the publication of *Little Gidding*.
51 John Donne, 'A Nocturnal upon S. Lucy's Day, Being the Shortest Day', *The Complete English Poems*, A. J. Smith (ed.) (Harmondsworth: Penguin, 1986), 72.
52 Ronald Schuchard, '"If I Think, Again, of This Place": Eliot, Herbert and the Way to "Little Gidding"', in *Words in Time: New Essays on Eliot's Four Quartets* Edward Lobb (ed.) (Ann Arbor, MI: University of Michigan Press, 1993), 77.
53 See also Peter Middleton's marvellous recent account of masculinity in *Four Quartets*, which reads the poems' ghosts alongside the habitual hauntings of Great War writing (Woolf's Septimus Smith, Wilfred Owen's 'Strange Meeting', and so on). Peter Middleton, 'The Masculinity behind the Ghosts of Modernism in Eliot's *Four Quartets*', *Gender, Desire, and Sexuality in T. S. Eliot*, Cassandra Laity and Nancy K. Gish (eds.) (Cambridge: Cambridge University Press, 2004), 83–104.
54 Samuel Hynes, *A War Imagined: The First World War and English Culture* (New York: Atheneum, 1991), xii.

4 THE NEUTRALITY OF HENRY GREEN

1 Virginia Woolf, 'The Leaning Tower', *The Moment and Other Essays* (London: Hogarth, 1947), 122.
2 Henry Green, *Pack My Bag* (London: Hogarth, 1952a), 68. Hereafter cited parenthetically as *PMB*, followed by page numbers.
3 Woolf, 'The Leaning Tower', *The Moment and Other Essays*, 118.
4 Jeremy Treglown, *Romancing: The Life and Work of Henry Green* (London: Faber, 2000), 2–3. The effort to describe Green and make claims for his significance by likening him to canonical modernists is a common tactic. Andrew Gibson suggests that 'his name seems best linked with Kafka's' ('Henry Green as Experimental Novelist', *Studies in the Novel* 16 [1984], 211), John Russell notes affinities with and echoes of Joyce ('Limbo States: The Short Stories of Henry Green', *Twentieth Century Literature* 29 [1983], 447–54) and Andrzej Gąsiorek writes, more generally, of 'a persistent tension between Imagism ... and Symbolism' in Green's work (*Post-War British*

Fiction: Realism and After [London: Edward Arnold, 1995], 34). The most interesting account of Green and the 1930s canon is Carol Wipf-Miller's 'Fictions of "Going Over": Henry Green and the New Realism', *Twentieth-Century Literature* 44 (1998), 135–54. She uses *Pack My Bag* to argue that Green is stuck with a foot in two camps, those of the modernists and the reconstructed bourgeois of the Auden group.

5 Keynes's summary is quoted in Robert Skidelsky, *John Maynard Keynes, 1883–1946: Economist, Philosopher, Statesman* (London: Macmillan, 2003), 595. Keynes's plan was to fund the war while simultaneously keeping down inflation and raising standards of living for the poor (John Maynard Keynes, *How to Pay for the War: A Radical Plan for the Chancellor of the Exchequer* [London: Macmillan, 1940]).

6 Rod Mengham, *The Idiom of the Time: The Writings of Henry Green* (Cambridge: Cambridge University Press, 1982), 57.

7 William Harrison's 'A Hogarth "Ghost" of Sorts: Henry Green's *Living* (1929)', *ANQ* 16 (2003), 51–4, describes bibliographic references to a non-existent Hogarth edition of Green's second novel; *Party Going* was the first Henry Green novel to be published by Hogarth.

8 Leonard Woolf, *The Journey Not the Arrival Matters* (London: Hogarth, 1969), 10.

9 Henry Green, *Party Going, Loving/Living/Party Going* (Harmondsworth: Penguin, 1993c), 466. Hereafter cited parenthetically as *PG* followed by page numbers.

10 Wyndham Lewis, *The Art of Being Ruled* (New York and London: Harper & Brothers, 1926), 140.

11 Wyndham Lewis, *Men without Art* (London: Cassell, 1934), 18, 40.

12 Quoted in A. J. P. Taylor, *The Origins of the Second World War* (London: Hamish Hamilton, 1961), 116.

13 Tom Harrisson, *Living through the Blitz* (London: Collins, 1976), 24.

14 W. H. Auden, 'Consider This and In Our Time', *Selected Poems*, Edward Mendelson (ed.) (London: Faber, 1979), 15.

15 Henry Green, 'A Novelist to his Readers: I', *Surviving: The Uncollected Writings of Henry Green*, Matthew Yorke (ed.) (New York: Viking, 1993), 139.

16 Michael Gorra, *The English Novel at Mid-Century: From the Leaning Tower* (New York: St. Martin's, 1990), 39–40.

17 Nigel Dennis, 'The Double Life of Henry Green', *Life*, 4 August 1952, 94.

18 Bronislaw Malinowski, *Argonauts of the Western Pacific: An Account of Native Enterprise and Adventure in the Archipelagoes of Melanesian New Guinea* (London: Routledge, 1922), xv.

19 Henry Green, *Caught* (New York: Viking, 1952), 43. Hereafter cited parenthetically as *C* followed by page numbers.

20 Thomas C. Foster, 'Henry Green', *Review of Contemporary Fiction* 20 (2000), 22.

21 Quoted in Virginia Woolf, 'Thoughts on Peace in an Air Raid', *The Death of the Moth and Other Essays* (New York: Harcourt Brace, 1942), 245.

22 Lyndsey Stonebridge, 'Bombs and Roses: The Writing of Anxiety in Henry Green's *Caught*,' *Diacritics* 28 (1998), 25–43.
23 Gąsiorek, *Post-War British Fiction*, 36.
24 Keith C. Odom, 'An Interview with John Lehmann about Henry Green', *Twentieth-Century Literature* 29 (1983), 399.
25 Michael North, *Henry Green and the Writing of his Generation* (Charlottesville, VA: University Press of Virginia, 1984), 144.
26 Henry Green, *Loving, Loving/Living/Party Going* (Harmondsworth: Penguin, 1993), 18. Hereafter cited parenthetically as *L* followed by page numbers.
27 Kate O'Brien, *The Last of Summer* (London: Heinemann, 1943), 50.
28 O'Brien, *The Last of Summer*, 85, 187.
29 Henry Green, 'Before the Great Fire', *Surviving*, 265.
30 David Low, *Low on the War: A Cartoon Commentary of the Years 1939–1941* (New York: Simon & Schuster, 1941), 114.
31 'Mr. de Valera and Defence of Eire: A Disputed Passage', *The Times*, 28 December 1940, 3.
32 Cyril Connolly, 'Comment', *Horizon* 5 (Jan–June 1942), 11.
33 M. J. Macmanus, 'Eire and the World Crisis', *Horizon* 5 (Jan–June 1942), 18.
34 Green, 'The Art of Fiction', *Surviving: The Uncollected Writings of Henry Green*, 249.
35 Mengham, *The Idiom of the Time*, 144. And Mengham also notes that Nanny Swift suffers, as Jonathan Swift did, from deafness (127).
36 Henry Green, *Back* (New York: Viking, 1950), 90. Hereafter cited parenthetically as *B* followed by page numbers.
37 Mengham, *The Idiom of the Time*, 158. The prevalence of incomprehensible acronyms before and after the war seems to have had a basis in historical fact: see Paul Fussell's *Wartime: Understanding and Behavior in the Second World War* (New York and Oxford: Oxford University Press, 1989), 258–60.
38 Gerard Barrett, 'Souvenirs from France: Textual Traumatism in Henry Green's *Back*', *The Fiction of the 1940s: Stories of Survival*, Rod Mengham and N. H. Reeve (eds.) (Basingstoke: Palgrave, 2001), 171.
39 Tom Harrisson, 'War Books', *Horizon* 4 (July–Dec 1941), 417.
40 Harrisson, 'War Books', 432.
41 Barrett, 'Souvenirs from France', *The Fiction of the 1940s* 169; Kristine Miller, 'The Wars of the Roses: Sexual Politics in Henry Green's *Back*', *Modern Fiction Studies* 49 (2003), 241.
42 Paul Fussell, *The Great War and Modern Memory* (Oxford, New York and London: Oxford University Press, 1975), 244–5.
43 Mollie Panter-Downes, *London War Notes 1939–1945*, William Shawn (ed.) (New York: Farrar, Straus & Giroux, 1971), 62.
44 Bernard Wasserstein, *Britain and the Jews of Europe 1939–1945*, 2nd edn (London and New York: Leicester University Press in association with the Institute for Jewish Policy Research, 1999), 8, 148, 315.

45 George Orwell, 'Looking Back on the Spanish War,' *The Collected Essays, Journalism and Letters of George Orwell*, 4 vols., Sonia Orwell and Ian Angus (ed.) (London: Secker & Warburg, 1968), Vol. I, 252–3.
46 Henry Green, *Nothing/Doting/Blindness* (Harmondsworth: Penguin, 1993), 254.
47 Virginia Woolf, *The Diary of Virginia Woolf*, 5 vols., Anne Olivier Bell and Andrew McNeillie (eds.) (London: Hogarth, 1984), Vol. 5, 135.
48 Angus Wilson, 'Henry Green', *Diversity and Depth in Fiction: Selected Critical Writings of Angus Wilson*, Kerry McSweeney (ed.) (New York: Viking, 1983), 218.
49 Wilson, 'Henry Green', *Diversity and Depth in Fiction*, 218.
50 Dennis, 'The Double Life of Henry Green', 86.
51 Dennis, 'The Double Life of Henry Green', 83.
52 E. M. Forster, 'The New Disorder', *London Calling: A Salute to America*, Storm Jameson (ed.) (New York and London: Harper & Brothers, 1942), 110–11.
53 Forster, 'The New Disorder', *London Calling: A Salute to America* 112–13.
54 Steven Fielding, 'The Good War: 1939–1945', *From Blitz to Blair: A New History of Britain since 1939*, Nick Tiratsoo (ed.) (London: Weidenfeld & Nicolson, 1997), 52.
55 Henry Green, *Nothing/Doting/Blindness*, 54.
56 Henry Green, 'Unloving', *Surviving*, 281–83.
57 Quoted in Treglown, *Romancing*, 197.

5 EVELYN WAUGH AND THE ENDS OF MINORITY CULTURE

1 'Magna Carta, 1215–1940', *The Listener* 23 (Jan–June 1940), 1120.
2 'Eclipse of the Highbrow', *The Times*, 25 March 1941, 5.
3 C. R. Atlee, 'Each Must Make His Contribution', broadcast on 22 May 1940, quoted from the transcript published in *The Listener* 23 (Jan–June 1940), 1036.
4 Evelyn Waugh, 'In Defence of Cubism', *The Essays, Articles and Reviews of Evelyn Waugh*, Donat Gallagher (ed.) (London: Methuen, 1983), 7.
5 Henry Green, *Pack My Bag* (London: Hogarth, 1952), 171–2.
6 'Eclipse of the Highbrow', *The Times*, 25 March 1941, 5.
7 On Dr Johnson, see Letters: 'Eclipse of the Highbrow' *The Times*, 2 April 1941, 5; on Middlebrows, see Letters: 'Eclipse of the Highbrow' *The Times*, 29 March 1941, 5; on Shakespeare, see Letters: 'Eclipse of the Highbrow' *The Times*, 2 April 1941, 5.
8 See Letters: 'Eclipse of the Highbrow', *The Times*, 27 March 1941, 5.
9 See Letters: 'Eclipse of the Highbrow', *The Times*, 28 March 1941, 5.
10 'Obituary: Mrs. Leonard Woolf and Lord Rockley', *The Times*, 3 April 1941, 4. The full obituary appears on page 7 of that day's newspaper.
11 Valentine Cunningham, *British Writers of the Thirties* (Oxford: Oxford University Press, 1988), 17. Erika Mann is quoted in Martin Green, *Children*

of the Sun: A Narrative of 'Decadence' in England after 1918 (New York: Wideview, 1980), 266.
12 Cunningham, *British Writers of the Thirties*, 17.
13 Quoted in Selina Hastings, *Evelyn Waugh: A Biography* (London: Sinclair-Stevenson, 1994), 485. In Waugh's autobiography, he disavows the identification of the aesthete character with Harold Acton but reinforces the connection with Brian Howard (Evelyn Waugh, *A Little Learning: An Autobiography by Evelyn Waugh, The Early Years* [Boston, MA: Little, Brown, 1964], 204).
14 Evelyn Waugh, *Put Out More Flags* (Boston, MA: Little, Brown, 1970), no page number. Subsequent references cited parenthetically as *POMF* followed by page numbers.
15 Robert Hewison, *Under Siege: Literary Life in London* (Weidenfeld & Nicolson: London, 1977), 8.
16 Cyril Connolly, 'Comment', *Horizon* 1 (Jan–July 1940), 69.
17 Waugh had reviewed Auden and Isherwood's collaborative *Journey to a War* (1939) as 'this pantomime appearance as hind and front legs of a monster'. Although Waugh admired Isherwood, he was savage about the veneration of Auden: 'His work is awkward and dull, but it is no fault of his that he has become a public bore' (Evelyn Waugh, 'Mr Isherwood and Friend', *The Essays, Articles and Reviews of Evelyn Waugh*, Donat Gallagher [ed.] [London: Methuen, 1983], 251–2.).
18 Alan Munton, *English Fiction of the Second World War* (London: Faber, 1989), 37; Alan Sinfield, *Literature, Politics and Culture in Postwar Britain*, 2nd edn (London and Atlantic Highlands, NJ: Athlone, 1997), 57.
19 'Why Not War Writers: A Manifesto', *Horizon* 4 (July–Dec 1941), 236–9.
20 'Combatant', 'Letter: Why Not War Writers', *Horizon* 4 (July–Dec 1941), 438 (my emphasis). I am indebted to Selina Hastings's biography of Waugh for the identification of 'Combatant'.
21 Evelyn Waugh, *The Sword of Honour Trilogy* (New York: Knopf, 1994), 118, 204.
22 Waugh, *Sword of Honour*, 70.
23 Evelyn Waugh, *Brideshead Revisited: The Sacred and Profane Memories of Captain Charles Ryder* (Boston, MA: Little, Brown, 1973), 46. Subsequent references are cited parenthetically as *BR* followed by page numbers.
24 Evelyn Waugh, 'What To Do with the Upper Classes', *The Essays, Articles and Reviews of Evelyn Waugh*, 314.
25 Evelyn Waugh, 'Preface', *Brideshead Revisited: The Sacred and Profane Memories of Captain Charles Ryder* (Harmondsworth: Penguin, 1959), 8.
26 Viscount Esher, 'Freedom from Want', *Horizon* 5 (Jan–Jun 1942), 238–9.
27 James Lees-Milne, 'Henry Yorke and Henry Green 1905–1973', *Fourteen Friends* (London: John Murray, 1996), 123.
28 This summary appears only in the later editions of the novel, and is cited here from Evelyn Waugh, *Brideshead Revisited: The Sacred and Profane Memories of Captain Charles Ryder* (Harmondsworth: Penguin, 1964), 34. This is the 1959 revision of the novel.

Notes to pages 130–136   175

29 A letter that he wrote to the *New Statesman* (5 March 1938) protested sloppy uses of the 'fascist' label:

> Only once was there anything like a Fascist movement in England; that was [during the General Strike] in 1926 when the middle class took over the public services; it does now not exist at all except as a form of anti-Semitism in the slums. Those of us who can afford to think without proclaiming ourselves 'intellectuals' do not want or expect a Fascist regime. But there is a highly nervous and highly vocal party who are busy creating a bogy; if they persist in throwing the epithet about it may begin to stick. They may one day find that there is a Fascist party which they have provoked ... it is because I believe we shall all lose by such a development that I am addressing this through your columns. (Evelyn Waugh, 'Fascist', *The Essays, Articles and Reviews of Evelyn Waugh*, 223)

30 Rebecca West, *The Meaning of Treason* (New York: Viking, 1947).
31 Waugh, *A Little Learning*, 44, 191.
32 Diary entry dated 29 August 1943. Evelyn Waugh, *The Diaries of Evelyn Waugh*, Michael Davie (ed.) (London: Weidenfeld & Nicolson, 1976), 548.
33 Quoted in Hastings, *Evelyn Waugh*, 341.
34 Waugh, *A Little Learning*, 122.
35 'Evelyn Waugh', *Authors Take Sides on the Spanish War* (London: *Left Review*, 1937), unpaginated.
36 The brisk dismissal of the left/right distinction comes from a review of a book by Mass-Observation in which Waugh regretted the drably didactic epilogue by Malinowski: 'no more funny footnotes ... no further pleasure ... Was Mass-Observation perhaps too independent for an age that can only digest propaganda?' (Waugh, 'The Habits of the English', *The Essays, Articles and Reviews of Evelyn Waugh*, 227–8).
37 'Norman Douglas', 'Sean O'Faolain', 'Vita Sackville West', *Authors Take Sides on the Spanish War*, Emphasis in original.
38 *Authors Take Sides on the Spanish War*, unpaginated.
39 Cyril Connolly, *Enemies of Promise* (London: Routledge, 1938), 35, 36.
40 Sean Latham, *Am I a Snob? Modernism and the Novel* (Ithaca, NY, and London: Cornell University Press, 2003), 106.
41 'I piled it on rather, with passionate sincerity'. Waugh, 'Preface', *Brideshead Revisited*, 8.
42 Quoted in Malcolm Smith, *Britain and 1940: History, Myth, and Popular Memory* (London and New York: Routledge, 2000), 113.
43 Henry Green, *Concluding* (Normal, IL: Dalkey Archive Press, 2000), 13.
44 Evelyn Waugh, 'Manners and Morals – I', *The Essays, Articles and Reviews of Evelyn Waugh*, 589; Waugh, 'Aspirations of a Mugwump', *The Essays, Articles and Reviews* of Evelyn Waugh, 537; Waugh, 'The Scandinavian Capitals: Contrasted Post-War Moods', *The Essays, Articles and Reviews* of Evelyn Waugh, 339.
45 Perry Anderson, 'Components of the National Culture', *English Questions* (London and New York: Verso, 1992), 59–60.

46 Noel Annan, *Our Age: English Intellectuals Between the World Wars – A Group Portrait* (New York: Random House, 1990), 7.
47 Virginia Woolf, 'A Sketch of the Past', *Moments of Being*, 2nd edn, Jeanne Schulkind (ed.) (San Diego, CA, New York and London: Harcourt, 1985), 65.
48 The political historian Richard Whiting tells of John Maynard Keynes's efforts to mitigate what he called an 'element of hate' in the Chancellor of the Exchequer's attempt to get at the rich through estate duty: '"Hate"', Whiting suggests, 'was what Dalton was interested in'. See Richard Whiting, *The Labour Party and Taxation: Party Identity and Political Purpose in Twentieth-Century Britain* (Cambridge: Cambridge University Press, 2000), 73.
49 Angus Wilson, 'The Future of the English Novel', *Diversity and Depth in Fiction: Selected Critical Writings of Angus Wilson*, Kerry McSweeney (ed.) (New York: Viking, 1983), 127.
50 Annan, *Our Age*, 338.
51 'Familiar Fascism' is the quiz that opens Molly Abel Travis's essay 'Eternal Haunts and its 'Home Haunts' in the Leavises' Attacks on Bloomsbury and Woolf', *Virginia Woolf and Fascism: Resisting the Dictators' Seduction*, Merry M. Pawlowski (ed.) (Basingstoke: Palgrave, 2001), 165–77. The game is a list of crypto- or proto-fascist statements from Lawrence, Eliot, Pound and others, to be identified for 'ten points apiece' (165).
52 T. S. Eliot, *Notes Towards the Definition of Culture* (London: Faber, 1948), 48, 107.
53 Benny Morris, *The Roots of Appeasement: The British Weekly Press and Nazi Germany during the 1930s* (London: Frank Cass, 1991), 2.
54 Annan, *Our Age*, 305.
55 Jose Harris, "Contract' and 'Citizenship', *The Ideas that Shaped Post-War Britain*, David Marquard and Anthony Seldon (eds.) (London: Fontana, 1996), 135.
56 Peter Hennessy, *Never Again: Britain, 1945–1951* (New York: Pantheon, 1993), 430. The rightwing historian Correlli Barnett likewise describes a 'temperamental aversion to the exercise of will' (*The Lost Victory: British Dreams, British Realities 1945–1950* [London: Macmillan, 1995], 189). The economist Thomas Balogh had hinted at this failure as early as 1959 when he wrote that:

> The lesson of 1945–1951 seems unmistakeable. Mr. Attlee had immense advantages. He had a Parliamentary majority unparalleled since 1906, and a clear mandate for far-reaching reforms. He had, what was not ever enjoyed by any Socialist Government anywhere, a fully working war economic system of direct controls at his disposal, built up in the teeth of the vested interests and the bureaucracy. In five years he went far in divesting himself of this power. The repeated failures in economic planning, despite grandiloquent promises, did the rest. Though his reforms, within the rather narrow limits set, were admirable, he wasted his majority by 1951, without achieving a new social order or even economic stability.

(Thomas Balogh, 'The Apotheosis of the Dilettante: The Establishment of Mandarins', *The Establishment*, Hugh Thomas [ed.] [London: Anthony Blond, 1959], 117.)
57 Quoted in Becky Conekin, Frank Mort and Chris Waters, *Moments of Modernity: Reconstructing Britain 1945–64* (London and New York: Rivers Oram Press, 1999), xiii.
58 Sinfield, *Literature, Politics and Culture*, 3.
59 Patrick Wright, *On Living in an Old Country: The National Past in Contemporary Britain* (London: Verso, 1985), 45, 153.

CODA: NATIONAL HISTORIOGRAPHY AFTER THE POST-WAR SETTLEMENT

1 E. M. Forster, *Howards End* (Harmondsworth: Penguin, 2000), 24.
2 Noel Annan, *Our Age: English Intellectuals Between the World Wars – A Group Portrait* (New York: Random House, 1990), 424–46.
3 David Lodge, 'Pratt & Van', *The New Statesman*, 100 (1980), 26.
4 Margaret Drabble, 'Are the Social Graces Suspect? Is Art Itself Suspect?' *The Listener*, 104 (1980), 52.
5 Angus Wilson, *Setting the World on Fire* (London: Secker & Warburg, 1980), 19. Hereafter cited parenthetically as *STWOF*.
6 Muriel Spark, *The Girls of Slender Means* (Harmondsworth: Penguin, 1966), 7. Hereafter cited parenthetically as *TGOSM*.
7 Peter Hennessy, *Never Again: Britain, 1945–1951* (New York: Pantheon, 1993), 84. Hennessy quotes the notorious passage in full on page 82.
8 On the linking of the historical turn to 'Post-imperial conditions', see for example Suzanne Keen, *Romances of the Archives in Contemporary British Fiction* (Toronto, ON: University of Toronto Press, 2001), 3–27. Less inclined to see the contemporary historical emphasis as a consolatory manoeuvre, Margaret Scanlan notices that when British (imperial) history is described in post-war fiction, 'the particular moments chosen are mostly inglorious or violent; the novels are more likely to evoke defeats than victories, stupidity and arrogance than heroism' (*Traces of Another Time: History and Politics in Postwar British Fiction* [Princeton, NJ: Princeton University Press, 1990], 6).
9 David Lowenthal, *The Past Is a Foreign Country* (Cambridge: Cambridge University Press, 1985), xvii.
10 Ian Baucom, *Out of Place: Englishness, Empire, and the Locations of Identity* (Princeton, NJ: Princeton University Press, 1999), 165, 173; John J. Su, 'Refiguring National Character: The Remains of the British Estate Novel', *Modern Fiction Studies* 48 (2002), 552; Alistair Davies, 'Faltering at the Line: Auden and Postwar British Culture', *British Culture of the Postwar: An Introduction to Literature and Society 1945–1999*, Alistair Davies and Alan Sinfield (eds.) (London and New York: Routledge, 2000), 137.
11 Baucom, *Out of Place*, 165.

12 Robert Hewison, *The Heritage Industry: Britain in a Climate of Decline* (London: Methuen, 1987), 26, 57.
13 Evelyn Waugh, 'Preface', *Brideshead Revisited: The Sacred and Profane Memories of Captain Charles Ryder* (Harmondsworth: Penguin, 1959), 8.
14 Baucom, *Out of Place*, 165.
15 Annan, *Our Age*, 32. The intellectuals' flight into 'internal exile' and the 'alienation of organised intelligence from a state with apparently philistine values'.
16 Q. D Leavis, 'The Englishness of the English Novel', *Collected Essays*, 3 vols., G. Singh (ed.) (Cambridge and London: Cambridge University Press, 1983), Vol. 1, 321.
17 Virginia Woolf, 'On Not Knowing Greek', *The Common Reader First Series* (San Diego, CA, New York and London: Harvest, 1994), 24.
18 Alexander Pope, 'An Epistle to Richard Boyle, Earl of Burlington', *Alexander Pope*, The Oxford Authors, Pat Rogers (ed.) (Oxford and New York: Oxford University Press, 1993), 248.
19 Jane Austen, *Northanger Abbey* (Harmondsworth: Penguin, 1985), 199–200.
20 Angus Wilson, 'Evil in the English Novel', *Diversity and Depth in Fiction: Selected Critical Writings of Angus Wilson*, Kerry McSweeney (ed.) (New York: Viking, 1983), 3–24.
21 Ian McEwan, *Atonement* (New York: Anchor, 2003), 330. Hereafter cited parenthetically as *A* followed by page numbers.
22 Quoted in Brian Finney, 'Briony's Stand against Oblivion: The Making of Fiction in Ian McEwan's *Atonement*', *Journal of Modern Literature* 27 (2004), 71.
23 A. J. P. Taylor, *The Origins of the Second World War* (London: Hamish Hamilton, 1961), 189.
24 Kazuo Ishiguro, *The Remains of the Day* (New York: Vintage, 1993), 223. Hereafter cited parenthetically as *TROTD*.
25 On the 'philistinism' of the Thatcher government, see Hewison's *The Heritage Industry*, which quotes the *Times Higher Education Supplement* on the intellectuals' flight into 'internal exile ... alienation of organised intelligence from a state with apparently philistine values' (121); at the very end of the book, Hewison identifies the heritage industry with 'a philistine government' (145).
26 Arthur Marwick, *Culture in Britain since 1945* (Oxford: Blackwell, 1991), 141–2.
27 Marwick, *Culture in Britain*, 167.
28 Correlli Barnett, *The Audit of War: The Illusion and Reality of Britain as a Great Nation* (London: Macmillan, 1986), 11.
29 Barnett, *The Audit of War*, 19.
30 Malcolm Bradbury, *Rates of Exchange* (New York: Knopf, 1983), 20.
31 Barnett, *The Audit of War*, 304.
32 Correlli Barnett, *The Lost Victory: British Dreams, British Realities 1945–1950* (London: Macmillan, 1995), 125.
33 D. J. Taylor, *After the War: The Novel and English Society since 1945* (London: Chatto & Windus, 1993), xxii.
34 Robert Graves and Alan Hodge, *The Long Weekend: A Social History of Great Britain 1918–1939* (London: Faber, 1950), 6.
35 Graves and Hodge, *The Long Weekend*, 7.

Bibliography

Addison, Paul, *The Road to 1945: British Politics and the Second World War* (London: Jonathan Cape, 1975).
Aldgate, Anthony, and Jeffrey Richards, *Britain Can Take It: British Cinema in the Second World War* (Oxford and New York: Blackwell, 1986).
Amis, Kingsley, *Lucky Jim* (Harmondsworth: Penguin, 1992).
Anderson, Benedict, *Imagined Communities: Reflections on the Origin and Spread of Nationalism* (London and New York: Verso, 1991).
Anderson, Perry, *English Questions* (London and New York: Verso, 1992).
Annan, Noel, *Our Age: English Intellectuals Between the World Wars – A Group Portrait* (New York: Random House, 1990).
Attlee, C. R., 'Each Must Make His Contribution', *The Listener* 23 (Jan–June 1940), 1036.
Auden, W. H., *Selected Poems*, ed. Edward Mendelson (London: Faber, 1979).
The Orators: An English Study (London: Faber, 1966).
Auden, W. H. et al. *Authors Take Sides on the Spanish War*, London: Left Review, 1937.
Austen, Jane, *Northanger Abbey* (Harmondsworth: Penguin, 1985).
Barnett, Correlli, *The Lost Victory: British Dreams, British Realities 1945–1950* (London: Macmillan, 1995).
The Audit of War: The Illusion and Reality of Britain As a Great Nation (London: Macmillan, 1986).
Barrett, Gerard, 'Souvenirs from France: Textual Traumatism in Henry Green's *Back*', in *The Fiction of the 1940s: Stories of Survival*, eds. Rod Mengham and N. H. Reeve (Basingstoke: Palgrave, 2001), 169–84.
Baucom, Ian, *Out of Place: Englishness, Empire, and the Locations of Identity* (Princeton, NJ: Princeton University Press, 1999).
Beer, Gillian, '*Between the Acts*: Resisting the End', *Virginia Woolf: The Common Ground* (Edinburgh: Edinburgh University Press, 1996), 125–48.
Bevan, Aneurin, *In Place of Fear* (Melbourne, London and Toronto, ON: Heinemann, 1952).
Bowen, Elizabeth, *Bowen's Court* (New York: Knopf, 1942).
The Last September (New York: Knopf, 1952).
Bradbury, Malcolm, *Rates of Exchange* (New York: Knopf, 1983).

Calder, Angus, *The Myth of the Blitz* (London: Jonathan Cape, 1991).
The People's War (London: Jonathan Cape, 1969).
Calder, Angus, and Dorothy Sheridan, eds., *Speak For Yourself: A Mass Observation Anthology, 1937–1949* (London: Jonathan Cape, 1984).
Calder, Robert, *Beware the British Serpent: The Role of Writers in British Propaganda in the United States 1939–1945* (Montreal, ON, and Ithaca, NY: McGill-Queen's University Press, 2004).
Calvocoressi, Peter, Guy Wint and John Pritchard, *The Penguin History of the Second World War* (London: Penguin, 1999).
Carey, John. *The Intellectuals and the Masses: Pride and Prejudice among the Literary Intelligentsia 1880–1940* (London: Faber, 1992).
Carpenter, Humphrey, *The Brideshead Generation: Evelyn Waugh and his Friends* (Boston, MA: Houghton Mifflin, 1990).
Cato [pseud.], *Guilty Men* (New York: Frederick Stokes, 1940).
Chamberlain, Neville, *In Search of Peace* (New York: Putnam, 1939).
Chamberlain, Samuel, and Donald Moffatt, *This Realm, This England . . . The Citadel of a Valiant Race Portrayed by Its Greatest Etchers* (New York: Hastings House, 1941).
Chapman, James, *The British at War: Cinema, State and Propaganda* (London and New York: IB Tauris, 1998).
Chapman, Wayne K. and Janet M. Manson, 'Carte and Tierce: Leonard, Virginia Woolf, and the War for Peace', in *Virginia Woolf and War: Fiction, Reality, and Myth*, ed. Mark Hussey (Syracuse, NY: Syracuse University Press, 1991), 58–78.
Churchill, Winston, *Blood, Toil, Tears and Sweat: The Speeches of Winston Churchill*, ed. David Cannadine (Boston, MA: Houghton Mifflin, 1989).
Clark, T. J., *Farewell to an Idea: Episodes from a History of Modernism* (New Haven, CT, and London: Yale University Press, 1999).
Conekin, Becky, Frank Mort and Chris Waters, eds., *Moments of Modernity: Reconstructing Britain 1945–64* (London and New York: Rivers Oram Press, 1999).
Connolly, Cyril, *Enemies of Promise* (London: Routledge, 1938).
Conrad, Joseph, *Heart of Darkness* (New York and London: Norton, 2006).
The Shadow-Line (London: Penguin, 1993).
Cooper, John Xiros, *T. S. Eliot and the Ideology of Four Quartets* (Cambridge: Cambridge University Press, 1995).
Coward, Noël, *The Complete Lyrics*, ed. Barry Day (Woodstock and New York: The Overlook Press, 1998).
The Noël Coward Diaries, eds. Graham Payn and Sheridan Morley (London: Weidenfeld & Nicolson, 1982).
Future Indefinite (London: Heinemann, 1954).
Middle East Diary (London: Heinemann, 1944).
Cunningham, Valentine, *British Writers of the Thirties* (Oxford: Oxford University Press, 1988).

Davies, Alistair, and Alan Sinfield, eds., *British Culture of the Postwar: An Introduction to Literature and Society 1945–1999* (London and New York: Routledge, 2000).
Day Lewis, C., *Word Over All* (London: Jonathan Cape, 1946).
De Groot, Gerard, *Blighty: British Society in the Era of the Great War* (London and New York: Longman, 1996).
Douglas, Keith, *Collected Poems*, eds., John Waller, G. S. Fraser and J. C. Hall (London: Faber, 1966).
Dutton, David, *Neville Chamberlain* (London: Arnold, 2001).
Eliot, T. S., *Collected Poems, 1909–1962* (New York, San Diego, CA, and London: Harcourt Brace, 1991).
  Selected Prose of T. S. Eliot, ed. Frank Kermode (San Diego, CA, New York and London: Harcourt, 1975).
  For Lancelot Andrewes (London: Faber, 1970).
  'The Art of Poetry', *Paris Review* 21 (1959), 47–70.
  Notes Towards the Definition of Culture (London: Faber, 1948).
  The Idea of a Christian Society (New York: Harcourt Brace, 1940).
Ellis, Steve, *The English Eliot: Design, Language and Landscape in* Four Quartets (London and New York: Routledge, 1991).
VISCOUNT Esher, 'Freedom from Want', *Horizon* 5 (Jan–June 1942), 237–42.
Esty, Jed, *A Shrinking Island: Modernism and National Culture in England* (Princeton, NJ, and Oxford: Princeton University Press, 2004).
Finney, Brian, 'Briony's Stand Against Oblivion: The Making of Fiction in Ian McEwan's *Atonement*', *Journal of Modern Literature* 27 (2004), 68–82.
Fitz Gibbon, Constantine, *The Blitz* (London: Alan Wingate, 1957).
Ford, Ford Madox, *The Good Soldier* (Oxford: Oxford University Press, 1999).
Forster, E. M., *Howards End* (Harmondsworth: Penguin, 2000).
  Two Cheers for Democracy (London: Edward Arnold, 1951).
Foster, Thomas C., 'Henry Green', *Review of Contemporary Fiction* 20 (2000), 7–40.
Fox, Adam, *Dean Inge* (London: John Murray, 1960).
Freedman, Jean R., *Whistling in the Dark: Memory and Culture in Wartime London* (Lexington, KY: University Press of Kentucky, 1999).
Fussell, Paul, *Wartime: Understanding and Behavior in the Second World War* (New York and Oxford: Oxford University Press, 1989).
  Abroad: British Literary Traveling Between the Wars (New York and Oxford: Oxford University Press, 1980).
  The Great War and Modern Memory (London, Oxford and New York: Oxford University Press, 1977).
Gąsiorek, Andrzej, *Post-War British Fiction: Realism and After* (London: Edward Arnold, 1995).
Gibson, Andrew, 'Henry Green as Experimental Novelist', *Studies in the Novel* 16 (1984), 197–214.
Gilbert, Martin, *The Second World War* (New York: Holt, 1989).
Glendinning, Victoria, *Rebecca West: A Life* (New York: Knopf, 1987).

Gordon, Lyndall, *T. S. Eliot: An Imperfect Life* (London: Norton, 1999).
Gorra, Michael, *The English Novel at Mid-Century: From the Leaning Tower* (New York: St. Martin's, 1990).
Graves, Robert, and Alan Hodge, *The Long Weekend: A Social History of Great Britain 1918–1939* (London: Faber, 1950).
Green, Henry, *Concluding* (Normal, IL: Dalkey Archive Press, 2000).
  Surviving: The Uncollected Writings of Henry Green, ed. Matthew Yorke (New York: Viking, 1993a).
  Nothing/Doting/Blindness (Harmondsworth: Penguin, 1993b).
  Loving/Living/Party Going (Harmondsworth: Penguin, 1993c).
  Pack My Bag (London: Hogarth, 1952a).
  Caught (New York: Viking, 1952b).
  Back (New York: Viking, 1950).
Green, Martin, *Children of the Sun: A Narrative of 'Decadence' in England after 1918* (New York: Wideview, 1980).
Hamilton, Fyfe, *The Illusion of National Character* (London: Watts & Co., 1940).
Harris, Jose, ' "Contract" and "Citizenship" ', *The Ideas that Shaped Post-War Britain*, eds. David Marquand and Anthony Seldon (London: Fontana, 1996), 135.
Harrisson, Tom, *Living through the Blitz* (London: Collins, 1976).
  'War Books', *Horizon* 4 (July–Dec 1941), 416–37.
Harrisson, Tom, and Charles Madge, eds., *War Begins at Home* (London: Chatto & Windus, 1940).
Harrison, William, 'A Hogarth "Ghost" of Sorts: Henry Green's *Living* (1929)', *ANQ* 16 (2003), 51–4.
Hartley, Jenny, *Millions Like Us: British Women's Fiction of the Second World War* (London: Virago, 1997).
Hastings, Selina, *Evelyn Waugh: A Biography* (London: Sinclair-Stevenson, 1994).
Hendry, J. F., *The Bombed Happiness* (London: Routledge, 1942).
Hennessy, Peter, *Never Again: Britain, 1945–1951* (New York: Pantheon, 1993).
Hewison, Robert, *The Heritage Industry: Britain in a Climate of Decline* (London: Methuen, 1987).
  Under Siege: Literary Life in London (London: Weidenfeld & Nicolson, 1977).
Higonnet, Margaret R., Jane Jenson, Sonya Michel and Margaret Collins Weitz, eds., *Behind the Lines: Gender and the Two World Wars* (New Haven, CT, and London: Yale University Press, 1987).
Holsinger, M. Paul, and Mary Anne Schofield, eds., *Visions of War: World War II in Popular Literature and Culture* (Bowling Green, OH: Bowling Green State University Popular Press, 1992).
Hussey, Mark, ed., *Virginia Woolf and War: Fiction, Reality, and Myth* (Syracuse, NY: Syracuse University Press, 1991).
Hynes, Samuel, *A War Imagined: The First World War and English Culture* (New York: Atheneum, 1991).
Ishiguro, Kazuo, *The Remains of the Day* (New York: Vintage, 1993).

Jameson, Fredric, *A Singular Modernity: Essay on the Ontology of the Present* (London: Verso, 2002).
The Seeds of Time (New York: Columbia University Press, 1994).
Jameson, Storm, *London Calling: A Salute to America* (New York and London: Harper & Brothers, 1942).
Joad, C. E. M., 'The Face of England: How It Is Ravaged and How It May Be Preserved', *Horizon* 5 (Jan–June 1942), 335–48.
For Civilization (London: Macmillan, 1940).
Judt, Tony, *Postwar: A History of Europe since 1945* (New York: Penguin, 2005).
Keegan, John, *The Second World War* (London: Hutchinson, 1989).
Keen, Suzanne, *Romances of the Archives in Contemporary British Fiction* (Toronto, ON: University of Toronto Press, 2001).
Keynes, John Maynard, 'My Early Beliefs', in *The Bloomsbury Group: A Collection of Memoirs and Commentary* ed. S.P Rosenbaum, (Toronto, ON, Buffalo, NY, and London: University of Toronto Press, 1995), 82–97.
The Economic Consequences of the Peace (New York: Penguin, 1988).
How to Pay for the War: A Radical Plan for the Chancellor of the Exchequer (London: Macmillan, 1940).
Knowles, Sebastian D. G., *A Purgatorial Flame: Seven British Writers in the Second World War* (Philadelphia, PA: University of Pennsylvania Press, 1990).
Larkin, Philip, *Collected Poems* (London: The Marvell Press and Faber & Faber, 1989).
Lassner, Phyllis, *British Women Writers of WWII: Battlegrounds of Their Own* (Basingstoke: Macmillan, 1998).
Latham, Sean, *Am I a Snob? Modernism and the Novel* (Ithaca, NY, and London: Cornell University Press, 2003).
Lawrence, D. H., *Lady Chatterley's Lover* (New York: Modern Library, 2001).
Leader, Zachary, ed., *On Modern British Fiction* (Oxford: Oxford University Press, 2002).
Leavis, Q. D., 'The Englishness of the English Novel', *Collected Essays*, 3 vols. Vol. 1, ed. G. Singh (Cambridge and London: Cambridge University Press, 1983), 303–27.
Lees-Milne, James, 'Henry Yorke and Henry Green 1905–1973', *Fourteen Friends* (London: John Murray, 1996), 122–31.
Lehmann, John, *New Writing in Europe* (Harmondsworth: Penguin, 1940).
Levenson, Michael. 'Does *The Waste Land* Have a Politics?' *Modernism/Modernity* 6, 3 (September 1999), 1–13.
Lewis, Wyndham, *Blasting and Bombardiering* (Berkeley and Los Angeles, CA: University of California Press, 1967).
Men without Art (London: Cassell, 1934).
The Art of Being Ruled (New York and London: Harper & Brothers, 1926).
Lobb, Edward, ed., *Words in Time: New Essays on Eliot's Four Quartets* (Ann Arbor, MI: University of Michigan Press, 1993).

Lloyd George, David, *The Truth about the Peace Treaty*, 2 vols. (London: Gollancz, 1938).
Lodge, David, 'Pratt & Van', *The New Statesman* 100 (1980), 26.
Low, David, *Low on the War: A Cartoon Commentary of the Years 1939–1941* (New York: Simon & Schuster, 1941).
Lowenthal, David, *The Past Is a Foreign Country* (Cambridge: Cambridge University Press, 1985).
MacDiarmid, Hugh, *Complete Poems 1920–1976*, 2 vols., eds. Michael Grieve and W. R. Aitken (London: Martin Brian & O'Keefe, 1978).
McEwan, Ian, *Atonement* (New York: Anchor, 2003).
Macmanus, M. J., 'Eire and the World Crisis', *Horizon* 5 (Jan–June 1942), 18–22.
LORD Macmillan, *Recording Britain* (London: Oxford University Press in association with the Pilgrim Trust, 1946).
Malinowski, Bronislaw, *Argonauts of the Western Pacific: An Account of Native Enterprise and Adventure in the Archipelagoes of Melanesian New Guinea* (London: Routledge, 1922).
Mansfield, Katherine, 'The Daughters of the Late Colonel', *Selected Stories*, ed. Vincent O'Sullivan (New York and London: Norton, 2006), 213–29.
The Collected Letters of Katherine Mansfield, Volume Three, 5 vols., eds. Vincent O'Sullivan and Margaret Scott (Oxford: Clarendon, 1993).
Mantel, Hilary, 'No Passes or Documents Are Needed: The Writer at Home in Europe', in *On Modern British Fiction*, ed. Zachary Leader (Oxford: Oxford University Press, 2002), 93–106.
Mantoux, Etienne, *The Carthaginian Peace, or The Economic Consequences of Mr. Keynes* (New York: Scribner, 1952).
Marcus, Laura, *Virginia Woolf* (Plymouth: Northcote House, 1997).
Marcus, Laura, and Peter Nicholls, eds., *The Cambridge History of Twentieth-Century English Literature*. (Cambridge: Cambridge University Press, 2004).
Marwick, Arthur, *Culture in Britain since 1945* (Oxford: Blackwell, 1991).
Masterman, C. F. G., *The Condition of England* (London: Methuen, 1960).
Mengham, Rod, *The Idiom of the Time: The Writings of Henry Green* (Cambridge: Cambridge University Press, 1982).
Mengham, Rod and N. H. Reeve, eds., *The Fiction of the 1940s: Stories of Survival*, (Basingstoke: Palgrave, 2001),
Mepham, John, *Virginia Woolf: A Literary Life* (New York: St. Martin's, 1991).
Middleton, Peter, 'The Masculinity behind the Ghosts of Modernism in Eliot's *Four Quartets*', in *Gender, Desire, and Sexuality in T. S. Eliot*, eds. Cassandra Laity and Nancy K. Gish, (Cambridge: Cambridge University Press, 2004), 83–104.
Miller, Kristine, 'The Wars of the Roses: Sexual Politics in Henry Green's *Back*', *Modern Fiction Studies* 49 (2003), 228–45.
Miller, Tyrus, *Late Modernism: Fiction, Politics, and the Arts Between the World Wars* (Berkeley, CA: University of California Press, 1999).
Mitchison, Naomi, Letter to the Editor, *Time and Tide* 20 (1939), 1651.

Bibliography 185

Vienna Diary (New York: Harrison Smith and Robert Hass, 1934).
Montefiore, Janet, *Men and Women Writers of the 1930s: The Dangerous Flood of History* (London and New York: Routledge, 1996).
Morris, Benny, *The Roots of Appeasement: The British Weekly Press and Nazi Germany during the 1930s* (London: Frank Cass, 1991).
Muggeridge, Malcolm, *The Thirties: 1930–1940 in Great Britain* (London: Collins, 1967).
Munton, Alan, *English Fiction of the Second World War* (London: Faber, 1989).
Murrow, Edward R., *This Is London*, ed. Elmer Davis (New York: Simon & Schuster, 1941).
Nicolson, Harold, *Peacemaking 1919* (London: Constable, 1945).
Why Britain Is at War (Harmondsworth: Penguin, 1939).
Noakes, Lucy, *War and the British: Gender, Memory and National Identity* (London and New York: IB Tauris, 1998).
North, Michael, *Reading 1922: A Return to the Scene of the Modern* (Oxford and New York: Oxford University Press, 1999).
Henry Green and the Writing of His Generation (Charlottesville, VA: University Press of Virginia, 1984).
O'Brien, Kate, *The Last of Summer* (London: Heinemann, 1943).
Odom, Keith C., 'An Interview with John Lehmann about Henry Green', *Twentieth-Century Literature* 29 (1983), 395–402.
Onlooker [pseud.], 'Two Germanies?' *The Listener* 23 (Jan–June 1940), 478.
Orwell, George, *The Collected Essays, Journalism and Letters of George Orwell*, 4 vols., vol. 1, eds. Sonia Orwell and Ian Angus (London: Secker & Warburg, 1968), 274.
Homage to Catalonia (New York: Harcourt, 1952).
Panter-Downes, Mollie, *London War Notes: 1939–1945*, ed. William Shawn (New York: Farrar, Straus & Giroux, 1971).
Pawlowski, Merry M., ed., *Virginia Woolf and Fascism: Resisting the Dictators' Seduction* (Basingstoke and New York: Palgrave, 2001).
Piette, Adam, *The Imagination at War: British Fiction and Poetry 1939–1945* (Basingstoke: Macmillan, 1995).
Plain, Gill, *Women's Fiction of the Second World War: Gender, Power and Resistance* (Edinburgh: Edinburgh University Press, 1996).
Ponting, Clive, *1940: Myth and Reality* (London: Hamish Hamilton, 1990).
Pope-Hennessy, James, and Cecil Beaton, *History Under Fire: 52 Photographs of Air Raid Damage to London Buildings, 1940–41* (London: B. T. Batsford, 1941).
Priestley, J. B., 'The War – and After', *Horizon* 1 (Jan–July 1940), 15–19.
Rainey, Lawrence, *Institutions of Modernism: Literary Elites and Public Culture* (New Haven, CT and London: Yale University Press, 1998).
Rawlinson, Mark, *British Writing of the Second World War* (Oxford: Oxford University Press, 2000).
Read, Herbert, 'Art in an Electric Atmosphere', *Horizon* 3 (Jan–June 1941), 308–13.
Rose, Norman, *Vansittart: Study of a Diplomat* (London: Heinemann, 1978).
Russell, John, 'Limbo States: The Short Stories of Henry Green', *Twentieth-Century Literature* 29 (1983), 447–54.

Sansom, William, *Westminster in War* (London: Faber, 1947).
Scanlan, Margaret, *Traces of Another Time: History and Politics in Postwar British Fiction* (Princeton, NJ: Princeton University Press, 1990).
Schimanski Stefan, and Henry Treece, eds., *A New Romantic Anthology* (London: The Grey Walls Press, 1949).
Schneider, Karen, *Loving Arms: British Women Writing the Second World War* (Lexington, KY: The University Press of Kentucky, 1997).
Schuchard, Ronald, '"If I Think, Again, of This Place": Eliot, Herbert and the Way to "Little Gidding,"', in *Words in Time: New Essays on Eliot's Four Quartets*, ed. Edward Lobb (Ann Arbor, MI: University of Michigan Press, 1993).
Schweizer, Bernard, *Radicals on the Road: The Politics of English Travel Writing in the 1930s* (Charlottesville, VA, and London: University Press of Virginia, 2001).
Sherry, Vincent, *The Great War and the Language of Modernism* (Oxford and New York: Oxford University Press, 2003).
Shires, Linda M., *British Poetry of the Second World War* (New York: St. Martin's, 1985).
Sinfield, Alan, *Literature, Politics and Culture in Postwar Britain*, 2nd ed (London and Atlantic Highlands, NJ: Athlone, 1997).
Skidelsky, Robert, *John Maynard Keynes, 1883–1946: Economist, Philosopher, Statesman* (London: Macmillan, 2003).
Smith, Malcolm, *Britain and 1940: History, Myth, and Popular Memory* (London and New York: Routledge, 2000).
Snaith, Anna, *Virginia Woolf: Public and Private Negotiations* (New York: St. Martin's, 2000).
Spark, Muriel, *The Girls of Slender Means* (Harmondsworth: Penguin, 1966).
Spender, Stephen, *World within World* (New York: Random House, 2001).
  'How Shall We Be Saved?' *Horizon* 1 (Jan–July 1940), 51–6.
Stevenson, Randall, *The British Novel since the Thirties: An Introduction* (Athens, GA: University of Georgia Press, 1986).
Stonebridge, Lyndsey, 'Bombs and Roses: The Writing of Anxiety in Henry Green's *Caught*,' *Diacritics* 28 (1998), 25–43.
Stout, Janis P., *Coming Out of War: Poetry, Grieving, and the Culture of the World Wars* (Tuscaloosa, AL: University of Alabama Press, 2005).
Su, John J., 'Refiguring National Character: The Remains of the British Estate Novel', *Modern Fiction Studies* 48 (2002), 552–80.
Suleiman, Susan Rubin, *Crises of Memory and the Second World War* (Cambridge, MA, and London: Harvard University Press, 2006).
Taylor, A. J. P., *The Origins of the Second World War* (London: Hamish Hamilton, 1961).
Taylor, D. J., *After the War: The Novel and English Society since 1945* (London: Chatto & Windus, 1993).
Thirkell, Angela, *Cheerfulness Breaks In* (New York: Knopf, 1941).
Thomas, Hugh, ed., *The Establishment* (London: Anthony Blond, 1959).

Tiratsoo, Nick, ed., *From Blitz to Blair: A New History of Britain since 1939* (London: Weidenfeld & Nicolson, 1997).
Titmuss, Richard M., *Problems of Social Policy* (London: HMSO, 1950).
Torgovnick, Marianna, *The War Complex: World War II in Our Time* (Chicago, IL: Chicago University Press, 2005).
Treece, Henry, *How I See Apocalypse* (London: Lindsay Drummond, 1946).
Invitation and Warning (London: Faber, 1942).
Treglown, Jeremy, *Romancing: The Life and Work of Henry Green* (London: Faber, 2000).
LORD Vansittart, *The Mist Profession: The Autobiography of lord Vansittart* (London: Hutchinson, 1958).
The Roots of the Trouble and The Black Record of Germany, Past, Present and Future? (New York: Avon, 1944).
Wasserstein, Bernard, *Britain and the Jews of Europe 1939–1945*, 2nd edn (London and New York: Leicester University Press in association with the Institute for Jewish Policy Research, 1999).
Waugh, Evelyn, *The Sword of Honour Trilogy* (New York: Knopf, 1994).
The Essays, Articles and Reviews of Evelyn Waugh, ed. Donat Gallagher (London: Methuen, 1983).
The Letters of Evelyn Waugh, ed. Mark Amory (London: Weidenfeld & Nicolson, 1980).
The Diaries of Evelyn Waugh, ed. Michael Davie (London: Weidenfeld & Nicolson, 1976).
Brideshead Revisited: The Sacred and Profane Memories of Captain Charles Ryder (Boston, MA: Little, Brown, 1973).
Put Out More Flags (Boston, MA: Little, Brown, 1970).
A Little Learning: An Autobiography by Evelyn Waugh, The Early Years (Boston, MA: Little, Brown, 1964).
'Preface', *Brideshead Revisited: The Sacred and Profane Memories of Captain Charles Ryder* (Harmondsworth: Penguin, 1959), 7–8.
[as 'Combatant', pseud.] 'Letter: Why Not War Writers', *Horizon* 4 (July– Dec 1941), 437–8.
West, Rebecca, *Selected Letters of Rebecca West*, ed. Bonnie Kime Scott, (New Haven, CI, and London: Yale University Press, 2000).
The Return of the Soldier (London: Virago, 1996).
Black Lamb and Grey Falcon: A Journey Through Yugoslavia (Edinburgh: Canongate, 1993).
'Introduction', Emma Goldman, *My Disillusionment in Russia* (Gloucester, MA: Peter Smith, 1983), ix.
The Young Rebecca: Writings of Rebecca West, ed. Jane Marcus (London and Basingstoke: Macmillan, in association with Virago, 1982).
The New Meaning of Treason (New York: Viking, 1964).
'Confessions of Lord Vansittart', *The Sunday Times* 4 May 1958, 6.
The Meaning of Treason (New York: Viking, 1949).
'Notes on the Way', *Time and Tide* 23 (June–Dec 1942), 401–3, 853–5.

Whiting, Richard, *The Labour Party and Taxation: Party Identity and Political Purpose in Twentieth-Century Britain* (Cambridge: Cambridge University Press, 2000).
Williams, Louise Blakeney, *Modernism and the Ideology of History* (Cambridge: Cambridge University Press, 2002).
Williams, Raymond, *The Politics of Modernism: Against the New Conformists*, ed. Tony Pinkney (London: Verso, 1989).
  Marxism and Literature (Oxford and New York: Oxford University Press, 1977).
  The Country and the City (New York: Oxford University Press, 1973).
Wilson, Angus, *Diversity and Depth in Fiction: Selected Critical Writings of Angus Wilson*, ed. Kerry McSweeney (London: Secker & Warburg, 1983).
  Setting the World on Fire (London: Secker & Warburg, 1980).
  The Old Men at the Zoo (London: Secker & Warburg, 1961).
Wipf-Miller, Carol, 'Fictions of "Going Over": Henry Green and the New Realism', *Twentieth-Century Literature* 44 (1998), 135–54.
Wollaeger, Mark A., 'The Woolfs in the Jungle: Intertextuality, Sexuality, and the Emergence of Female Modernism in *The Voyage Out*, *The Village in the Jungle*, and *Heart of Darkness*', *Modern Language Quarterly* 64 (2003), 33–69.
Woolf, Leonard, *The Journey Not the Arrival Matters* (London: Hogarth, 1969).
  The War For Peace (London: Routledge, 1940).
Woolf, Virginia, *The Voyage Out* (New York: Modern Library, 2001).
  The Common Reader: First Series (Harvest: San Diego, CA, New York and London, 1994).
  The Complete Shorter Fiction of Virginia Woolf, ed. Susan Dick (San Diego, CA, New York and London: Harcourt Brace Jovanovich, 1985).
  'A Sketch of the Past', *Moments of Being*, 2nd edn, ed. Jeanne Schulkind (San Diego, New York and London: Harcourt, 1985), 64–159.
  The Diary of Virginia Woolf, 5 vols., eds. Anne Olivier Bell and Andrew McNeillie (London: Hogarth, 1984).
  The Letters of Virginia Woolf, 6 vols., ed. Nigel Nicolson (London: Hogarth, 1980).
  To the Lighthouse (New York and London: Harcourt Brace Jovanovich, 1981).
  'Anon', in Brenda R. Silver, '"Anon" and "The Reader": Virginia Woolf's Last Essays', *Twentieth-Century Literature* 25 (1979), 356–441.
  Between the Acts (San Diego, CA, New York and London: Harcourt, 1969).
  Three Guineas (San Diego, CA, New York and London: Harcourt, 1966).
  The Moment and Other Essays (London: Hogarth, 1947).
  The Death of the Moth and Other Essays (New York: Harcourt Brace, 1942).
  Jacob's Room (New York: Harcourt Brace, 1923).
Wright, Patrick, *On Living in an Old Country: The National Past in Contemporary Britain* (London: Verso, 1985).
Zwerdling, Alex, *Virginia Woolf and the Real World* (Berkeley and Los Angeles, CA, and London: University of California Press, 1986).

Index

Acton, Harold 120—1
Amis, Kingsley
    Lucky Jim 82
Anderson, Benedict 69
Anderson, Perry 67—8, 136
Annan, Noel 136—7, 138, 139, 142, 148
anti-Semitism 38—9, 59, 160
appeasement 53, 66, 74, 75, 77—8, 152—3
    see also Chamberlain, Neville
Astor, Nancy 100
Attlee, Clement 118, 140, 176
'Auden generation' 91—2
Auden, W. H 67
    emigration with Christopher Isherwood 121—3
    'Consider this and in our time' 95
    'September 1, 1939' 60
    The Orators 84
Austen, Jane
    Northanger Abbey 149, 150
Austria
    Austro-Hungarian Empire, Habsburgs 48, 49—50, 51

Baldwin, Stanley 84, 95
    Baldwin-MacDonald coalition 84
Barnett, Correlli 154—5
Barrett, Gerard 110, 111
Baucom, Ian 146
BBC 57—8
Betjeman, John 129
Bevan, Aneurin 36
Beveridge, Sir William 139
    Social Insurance and Allied Services ('Beveridge Report') 4, 32, 138
blackout 40—1, 101
Blake, William
    'Jerusalem' 26, 34
Blakeney Williams, Louise 35, 162
Blitz, the, bombing of UK 2, 22—3, 32, 69
Bloomsbury
    Critique of nation state 52—6

Travestied in *Times* 119—20
Bowen, Elizabeth
    Bowen's Court 108
    The Last September 108
Bradbury, Malcolm 154
British Empire 27, 48, 54, 63—4, 177
    'post-imperial melancholy' 145—9
    Second World War and end of empire 1—2, 17, 48, 105—8

Calder, Angus 69
Carr, E. H. 55, 164
'Cato'
    Guilty Men 74
Chamberlain, Neville 44, 60, 64, 77—8
    see also appeasement
Chamberlain, Samuel
    This Realm, This England 25
Christianity 45—7, 66, 69, 83—4
Churchill, Randolph 121
Churchill, Winston 4, 11, 22, 57, 139, 144
    Churchillian rhetoric 11, 30, 64—5, 69, 79
civilians 6, 69—70
    see also 'people's war'
Clark, T. J. 14
Colonel Blimp, 80, 169
Connolly, Cyril 5, 12, 84, 106, 121, 135
    Enemies of Promise 47
    see also Horizon
Connor, Steven 67
Conrad, Joseph
    Heart of Darkness 40—1
    The Shadow-Line 6—7
Conservative Party
    1945 defeat 4, 136, 144—5
Cooper, John Xiros 78
Coward, Noël
    'Don't Let's be Beastly to the Germans' 57—8
Cunningham, Valentine 94—5, 120—1
Czechoslovakia 53, 59
    see also appeasement

189

Day Lewis, Cecil
  'Where are the War Poets?' 10
democracy, see propaganda and 'people's war'
Douglas, Keith 5–6
Drabble, Margaret 142
Dunkirk 2, 74, 151

Eliot, T. S. 1, 3–4, 18–19, 40, 46–7, 71–90
  Burnt Norton 71, 76–7, 78, 82
  'A Dedication to My Wife' 71
  'Defense of the Islands' 72, 86–7
  The Dry Salvages 85–8
  East Coker 3, 73–7, 81–5, 89
  Four Quartets 1, 18–19, 71–90
  'Gerontion' 73, 74
  The Idea of a Christian Society 79, 80–1
  'To the Indians Who Died in Africa' 71, 72, 87–8
  Little Gidding 1, 77–8, 88–90
  Murder in the Cathedral 78
  Notes Towards the Definition of Culture 80–1, 138
  'A Note on War Poetry' 71, 72, 74
  'Ulysses, Order and Myth' 65–6, 82
  The Waste Land, 7–8, 85
Ellis, Steve 79
Elton, Lord
  Notebook in Wartime 119
Emergency Powers (Defence) Act 118
Empire Windrush 147
Esher, Viscount 127–8
Esty, Jed 16–17, 39, 79, 80
Europe, Britain's relations with continent 2, 42–3, 44–5

Faber, Geoffrey 119–20
Fascism 160–1, 35
  see also Nazism
First World War
  and poetry 5–6, 73, 89–90
  and propaganda 3, 11, 25, 32, 113–14
Ford, Ford Madox 44
  The Good Soldier 6–7, 24, 153
Forster, E. M. 34–7
  'The Challenge of Our Time' 35
  A Diary For Timothy 35
  'Does Culture Matter?' 34
  England's Pleasant Land 34–5
  'George Orwell' 10
  Howards End 24, 37, 142
  'The New Disorder' 115–16
  'What I Believe' 53
France
  falls to Germany 66
Fussell, Paul 10, 11, 112

Gardner, Helen 78
Gąsiorek, Andrzej 101
General Strike 130
Gestapo blacklist 58, 122
Gordon, Lyndall 77
Graves, Robert 155–6
Green, Henry 19, 91–117
  Back 109–12
  'Before the Great Fire' 104
  Caught 98–103
  Concluding 136
  Doting 115
  Living 97–8
  Loving 103–9
  Nothing 116–17
  Pack my Bag 98–9, 112–13, 114–15, 119
  Party Going 93–8
Green, Martin 120

Hamilton Fyfe, Henry
  The Illusion of National Character 59
Harris, Jose 139
Harrisson, Tom 35, 110
Hendry, J. F.
  'Midnight Air Raid' 84
heritage industry 48, 145–6
Hewison, Robert 122, 146
Hodge, Alan 155–6
Horizon 5, 38, 62, 84, 106, 124–5, 142
  satirised by Evelyn Waugh 121–2
Howard, Brian 120–1
Hynes, Samuel 89

Inge, William (Dean) 59
Invasion fears 41–3
  'If the Invader Comes' 42
Ireland
  neutrality 103–8
Ishiguro, Kazuo
  The Remains of the Day 20, 151–4

Jameson, Fredric 16
Jameson, Storm 29–30
  London Calling: A Salute to America 72, 115
Jennings, Humphrey 121
  A Diary for Timothy 35
Joad, Cyril
  'The Face of England: How it is Ravaged and how it may be Preserved' 38
  For Civilization 11–12
Joyce, James
  Ulysses 40
Judt, Tony 6

Index

Keynes, John Maynard 62, 139, 176
  The Economic Consequences of Peace 54–7, 61
  How to Pay for the War 92
  'My Early Beliefs' 67–8
Knowles, Sebastian 78–9

Labour Party 115, 116, 139–40
  1945 election victory 4, 144–5
Larkin, Philip 13
  'An Arundel Tomb' 30
Latham, Sean 135
Lawrence, D. H. 48, 67
  Lady Chatterley's Lover 24, 37
League of Nations 27
Leavis, Q. D. 148
Lees-Milne, James 129
Lehmann, John 15, 103
Levenson, Michael 73
Lewis, Wyndham
  The Art of Being Ruled 94
  Blasting and Bombardiering 13, 71
  Men Without Art 94
Liberal Party 73, 138–9
Lloyd George, David 47
  The Truth about the Peace Treaty 61
Lodge, David 142
London Can Take It! 23
Low, David 105–6
  see also 'Colonel Blimp'
Lowenthal, David 145

MacDiarmid, Hugh 70
  'To Those of My Old School who fell in the Second World War' 70
MacDonald, David
  This England 39–40
Macmillan, Harold 147
Macmillan, Hugh (Lord) 38
Malinowski, Bronislaw 98
Mansfield, Katherine 7, 40
  'The Daughters of the Late Colonel' 80
Mantel, Hilary 44
Mantoux, Etienne
  The Carthaginian Peace, or The Economic Consequences of Mr. Keynes 55, 56, 67
Marcus, Laura 24
Marwick, Arthur 153
Masculinity 6–7, 30–1
Mass-Observation 35, 39, 85, 98, 115, 175
Masterman, C. F. G. 25, 38
  The Condition of England 25
McEwan, Ian
  Atonement 20, 150–1

'Men of 1914' 9
Mengham, Rod 93, 107, 109
Mepham, John 33
Miller, Kristine 111
Miller, Tyrus 15–16
Mrs Miniver 39, 162
Mitchison, Naomi 66
  Vienna Diary 52
Mitford, Nancy 129
Modernism
  and empire, 1–2, 27, 54, 55–6, 63–4, 87–8
    see also West, Rebecca
  and First World War, 6–9, 79–80
  institutionalisation of modernism 15, 16
  late modernism, end of modernism 1, 14–18, 20–1
    see also Waugh, Evelyn
  and myth 45–6, 64–70
  and nationalism 2–3, 11, 51–6, 64–5, 79, 81
    see also West, Rebecca
  and politics of form 8–10
Montefiore, Janet 33
Muggeridge, Malcolm 75
Munich Crisis, see Czechoslovakia
Munton, Alan 124
Murrow, Edward 22

national decline 154–6
  see also British Empire
Nationalism 11, 51–2, 54, 64–5, 79, 81
Nazism 50–1
  Pact with USSR 62
New Apocalypse, Neo-Romantics 84–5, 122
New Freewoman 44
New Statesman 59, 60, 62
Nicolson, Harold
  Why Britain is at War 12
  Peacemaking 1919 56–7
North, Michael 14, 103

O'Brien, Kate
  The Last of Summer 103–4
O'Faolain, Sean 134
Orwell, George 10, 40, 46, 58, 61, 80, 105, 113–14
  Homage to Catalonia 52
  The Lion and the Unicorn 74–5
Ottoman Empire 48–9

pacifism 32, 52, 59–60, 62
Panter-Downes, Mollie 26, 113
Paris Peace Conference 54–7, 152–3
pastoralism, ruralism 23–6, 35–8, 40, 80–3, 101–8, 127–8

Index

patriotism 32, 53−4
   see also nationalism
'people's war' 22−3, 32, 72, 77, 91, 96−7, 99−100, 102−3, 144−5
   see also welfare state
'phoney war' 76−7, 84
Pilgrim Trust 37−8
Ponting, Clive 69
post-war settlement 20, 117, 139−41
   see also welfare state and 'people's war'
Priestley, J. B. 62
Propaganda 11−12
   see also USA and 'People's War'
psychoanalysis 111−12
   see also shellshock

Rainey, Lawrence 9
Rawlinson, Mark 32
Read, Herbert 32
Roberts, Michael
   The Faber Book of Modern Verse 119
Rosenberg, Isaac 6

Sackville-West, Vita 134, 135
Schuchard, Ronald 88
Shaw, George Bernard 62
shellshock 7−8
Sherry, Vincent 13−14, 73
Sinfield, Alan 124, 140
Smith, Malcolm 69
Soviet Union 12, 59
Spanish Civil War 29, 46−7, 58
   Authors Take Sides on the Spanish War 47, 78, 133−5
Spark, Muriel
   The Girls of Slender Means 144−5
Spender, Stephen 80, 119
Stevenson, Randall 6
Stonebridge, Lyndsey 100
Suez Crisis 143, 151

Taylor, A. J. P. 55, 56, 152
Thatcher, Margaret, and Thatcherism 146, 153, 154−5
Thirkell, Angela 25, 72−3
   Cheerfulness Breaks In 25
The Times 3, 19, 34, 106, 118, 119−20
Time and Tide 40, 44, 66
Torgovnick, Marianna 17
travel writing 45
Treaty of Versailles, see Paris Peace Conference
Treece, Henry 84−5

'Towards a Personal Armageddon' 85
Treglown, Jeremy 92
Trevelyan, G. M. 72
Trollope, Anthony 25

USA
   propaganda addressed to 23, 25, 86−8

Vansittart, Robert 58, 60−2, 77
Vansittartism 58, 165
   Black Record: Germans Past and Present 58, 60, 61−2

Wasserstein, Bernard 113
Waugh, Evelyn 2−3, 19, 47, 75, 118−41
   Brideshead Revisited 3, 126−36, 146−7
   Men at Arms 40−1, 125−6
   Put Out More Flags 120−6, 129−31, 132−3
   welfare state 3−4, 34−6, 135−41
West, Rebecca 2, 18, 44−70, 86, 131
   Black Lamb and Grey Falcon: A Journey Through Yugoslavia 18, 44−70
   The Return of the Soldier 7
'Where are the war poets?' 5−6
   see also Day Lewis, Cecil
Williams, Raymond 20, 24, 36
Wilson, Angus 115
   'Evil in the English Novel' 149
   'The Future of the English Novel' 137−8
   The Old Men at the Zoo 75
   Setting the World on Fire 20, 142−3, 147−8, 149
Women's Institute 26
Woolf, Leonard 32, 93
Woolf, Virginia 8, 11, 18, 22−43, 53−4, 105, 114−5, 120
   'Anon' 81
   Between the Acts 23, 26−43, 81, 127
   Mrs Dalloway 7−8
   'The Death of the Moth' 41
   'The Duchess and the Jeweller' 29, 160
   Jacob's Room 28, 31, 130−1
   'The Leaning Tower' 33, 91−3, 115
   To the Lighthouse 24, 33−4, 41
   'Modern Fiction' 68
   'On Not Knowing Greek' 148
   Orlando 135
   'A Sketch of the Past' 137
   'Thoughts on Peace in an Air Raid' 26
   Three Guineas 28, 29, 30, 31, 79, 124
   The Voyage Out 80
Wright, Patrick 140